Tax Policy and the Economy 37

Tax Policy and the Economy 37

Edited by
Robert A. Moffitt

The University of Chicago Press
Chicago and London

NBER Tax Policy and the Economy, Number 37, 2023

Published annually by The University of Chicago Press.
www.journals.uchicago.edu/TPE/

Subscriptions: For individual and institutional subscription rates, visit www.journals .uchicago.edu, email subscriptions@press.uchicago.edu, or call (877) 705-1878 (US) or (773) 753-3347 (international). Free or deeply discounted institutional access is available in most developing nations through the Chicago Emerging Nations Initiative (www .journals.uchicago.edu/inst/ceni).

Please direct subscription inquiries to Subscription Fulfillment, 1427 E. 60th Street, Chicago, IL 60637-2902. Telephone: (773) 753-3347 or toll free in the United States and Canada (877) 705-1878. Fax: (773) 753-0811 or toll-free (877) 705-1879. E-mail: subscriptions @press.uchicago.edu.

Standing orders: To place a standing order for this book series, please address your request to The University of Chicago Press, Chicago Distribution Center, Attn. Standing Orders/Customer Service, 11030 S. Langley Avenue, Chicago, IL 60628. Telephone toll free in the U.S. and Canada: 1-800-621-2736; or 1-773-702-7000. Fax toll free in the U.S. and Canada: 1-800-621-8476; or 1-773-702-7212.

Single-copy orders: In the U.S., Canada, and the rest of the world, order from your local bookseller or direct from The University of Chicago Press, Chicago Distribution Center, 11030 S. Langley Avenue, Chicago, IL 60628. Telephone toll free in the U.S. and Canada: 1-800-621-2736; or 1-773-702-7000. Fax toll free in the U.S. and Canada: 1-800-621-8476; or 1-773-702-7212. In the U.K. and Europe, order from your local bookseller or direct from The University of Chicago Press, c/o John Wiley Ltd. Distribution Center, 1 Oldlands Way, Bognor Regis, West Sussex PO22 9SA, UK. Telephone 01243 779777 or Fax 01243 820250. E-mail: cs-books@wiley.co.uk.

The University of Chicago Press offers bulk discounts on individual titles to Corporate, Premium and Gift accounts. For information, please write to Sales Department—Special Sales, The University of Chicago Press, 1427 E. 60th Street, Chicago, IL 60637 USA or telephone 1-773-702-7723.

This book was printed and bound in the United States of America.

ISSN: 0892-8649
E-ISSN: 1537-2650
ISBN-13: 978-0-226-82825-1 (pb.:alk.paper)
ISBN-13: 978-0-226-82826-8 (e-book)

Relation of the Directors to the Work and Publications of the NBER

1. The object of the NBER is to ascertain and present to the economics profession, and to the public more generally, important economic facts and their interpretation in a scientific manner without policy recommendations. The Board of Directors is charged with the responsibility of ensuring that the work of the NBER is carried on in strict conformity with this object.

2. The President shall establish an internal review process to ensure that book manuscripts proposed for publication DO NOT contain policy recommendations. This shall apply both to the proceedings of conferences and to manuscripts by a single author or by one or more coauthors but shall not apply to authors of comments at NBER conferences who are not NBER affiliates.

3. No book manuscript reporting research shall be published by the NBER until the President has sent to each member of the Board a notice that a manuscript is recommended for publication and that in the President's opinion it is suitable for publication in accordance with the above principles of the NBER. Such notification will include a table of contents and an abstract or summary of the manuscript's content, a list of contributors if applicable, and a response form for use by Directors who desire a copy of the manuscript for review. Each manuscript shall contain a summary drawing attention to the nature and treatment of the problem studied and the main conclusions reached.

4. No volume shall be published until forty-five days have elapsed from the above notification of intention to publish it. During this period a copy shall be sent to any Director requesting it, and if any Director objects to publication on the grounds that the manuscript contains policy recommendations, the objection will be presented to the author(s) or editor(s). In case of dispute, all members of the Board shall be notified,

and the President shall appoint an ad hoc committee of the Board to decide the matter; thirty days additional shall be granted for this purpose.

5. The President shall present annually to the Board a report describing the internal manuscript review process, any objections made by Directors before publication or by anyone after publication, any disputes about such matters, and how they were handled.

6. Publications of the NBER issued for informational purposes concerning the work of the Bureau, or issued to inform the public of the activities at the Bureau, including but not limited to the NBER Digest and Reporter, shall be consistent with the object stated in paragraph 1. They shall contain a specific disclaimer noting that they have not passed through the review procedures required in this resolution. The Executive Committee of the Board is charged with the review of all such publications from time to time.

7. NBER working papers and manuscripts distributed on the Bureau's web site are not deemed to be publications for the purpose of this resolution, but they shall be consistent with the object stated in paragraph 1. Working papers shall contain a specific disclaimer noting that they have not passed through the review procedures required in this resolution. The NBER's web site shall contain a similar disclaimer. The President shall establish an internal review process to ensure that the working papers and the web site do not contain policy recommendations, and shall report annually to the Board on this process and any concerns raised in connection with it.

8. Unless otherwise determined by the Board or exempted by the terms of paragraphs 6 and 7, a copy of this resolution shall be printed in each NBER publication as described in paragraph 2 above.

Contents

Acknowledgments

Robert A. Moffitt, *Johns Hopkins University and NBER,* United States of America

This issue of the NBER's *Tax Policy and the Economy* journal series contains revised versions of papers presented at a conference on September 22, 2022. The papers continue the journal's tradition of bringing high-quality, policy-relevant research by NBER researchers to an audience of economists in government and in policy positions in Washington and to economists around the country with interests in policy-oriented economic research. The topics in this issue are wide-ranging and diverse, from the distributional consequences of gasoline and other mobility-related taxes to the use by multinational corporations of intellectual property for tax-avoidance purposes, to whether experience rating in the unemployment insurance system stabilizes employment, to whether older individuals are losing Social Security retirement benefits by retiring too early, and to whether the Earned Income Tax Credit for childless individuals affects their labor-force decisions.

I would like to thank Rob Shannon of NBER for his usual expertise and organizational acumen in overseeing the logistical details, invitations, and operational aspects of the conference, and I thank Jim Poterba for his continued assistance with the organization of the meeting. I thank Helena Fitz-Patrick for assistance in many other aspects of the conference, especially the shepherding of the papers toward final publication. Also, I would like to acknowledge the continued financial support of the Lynde and Harry Bradley Foundation. Finally, let me express my thanks to the authors themselves for the hard work they devoted to producing high-quality papers living up to the *Tax Policy and the Economy* standard.

Tax Policy and the Economy, volume 37, 2023.

Introduction

Robert A. Moffitt, *Johns Hopkins University and NBER,* United States of America

The five papers in this issue of *Tax Policy and the Economy* are directly related to important issues concerning US taxation and transfers.

In the first paper, Edward L. Glaeser, Caitlin S. Gorback, and James M. Poterba examine the distributional implications of taxes on transportation such as gasoline taxes, highway tolls, charges for buses and light-rail usage, and a vehicle-miles-traveled (VMT) tax, all of which address long-recognized problems of externalities from those forms of transportation. The authors note that gasoline taxes and highway tolls are regressive because their expenditures decline as a share of both total household expenditures and income as those quantities rise, which is part of the reason for their political unpopularity. They also note that the regressivity of the gasoline tax will rise over time as higher-income and higher-expenditure households shift to hybrid and electric vehicles, and hence reduce their gasoline usage per mile driven. Comparing a gasoline tax to a VMT tax, including a calculation of how a VMT tax will shift miles driven, the authors find the VMT tax to be relatively more progressive because it shifts some tax burdens to higher-income households that drive very fuel-efficient vehicles. Although the magnitude of the difference is currently small, they estimate it will rise as hybrid and electric vehicles become more widespread. But a VMT tax imposed on commercial vehicles, such as trucks, would be more regressive because lower-expenditure households disproportionately consume the goods moved by that form of transport. The authors also provide new information on the distributional burden of taxes on public transportation, again finding the burden to vary with

Tax Policy and the Economy, volume 37, 2023.

income and expenditure class: lower-income households disproportionately use buses, but higher-income households disproportionately use rail and air transportation.

In the second paper, Katarzyna Bilicka, Michael Devereux, and Irem Güçeri address the long-standing problem of multinational companies (MNCs) who are able to shift taxable income to low-tax countries. Recent international discussions of a Global Minimum Tax (GMT) have shown the policy salience of this issue. The authors use a new data set on global patent applications by country that they are able to link to company ownership as well as the location of MNC subsidiaries. The authors find striking evidence of the shifting of such intellectual property (IP) to tax havens, in some cases by shifting ownership of IP to a low-tax jurisdiction and, in other cases, by cost-sharing agreements between the parent company and tax-haven affiliates that facilitates profit shifting. A large share of patenting and patent ownership in the world is in large, innovating countries. However, a disproportionately large share of patenting activity takes place in tax havens where little or no research and development takes place. Many IP transfers go from high-tax to low-tax jurisdictions early in the life of a patent. Further findings show that affiliates located in Europe have a high proportion of patent applications that end in tax havens, that tax havens play a particular role in patents with high predicted value, and that tax havens play a large role in MNCs with large subsidiary networks. These firms have subsidiaries that are likely to be subject to a GMT.

In the third paper, Mark Duggan, Audrey Guo, and Andrew C. Johnston conduct a new investigation of the role of experience rating in the unemployment insurance (UI) system. Although past work has focused on imperfections in that rating system, Duggan and coauthors focus on the possible role of the current UI system in stabilizing the labor market through penalties on firms with high rates of UI-eligible layoffs. Using a newly constructed data set, the authors construct a new variable for the marginal tax cost (MTC) of layoffs, equal to the average 1-year increase in UI taxes a firm could be expected to pay. This depends on the tax schedule in each state's experience-rating system and on potential UI claims, and hence benefits, that the layoffs are expected to generate. The MTC varies across states, industries, and over time, and the authors exploit that variation to determine how variation in that cost affects the employment response by firms to exogenous firm demand shocks. The results show a strong and significant stabilizing response of the UI experience-rating system, with, on average, the tax penalty reducing the firm adjustment to negative shocks by 11%. A rough calculation of the impact of experience rating in the Great Recession based on the results suggests that experience rating saved nearly a million jobs in that downturn.

In the fourth paper, David Altig, Laurence J. Kotlikoff, and Victor Yifan Ye examine how decisions about when to retire affect the amount of Social Security retirement benefits that will be received over the years after retirement. The authors note the widely acknowledged problem that many individuals reach retirement age with little or no liquid assets to finance consumption during retirement and rely almost wholly on Social Security. However, the amount of Social Security retirement benefits an individual will receive for the rest of their life depends in critical ways on the actual date of retirement, because benefits increase the later the individual retires (and increase in present value terms as well, up to a point). The authors study whether individuals could receive much more in retirement benefits were they to start their Social Security retirement benefits at later ages or suspend them at full retirement age and restart them at 70. Estimating not only retirement ages for existing retirees but also retirement ages for future cohorts, the authors do a sophisticated calculation of how retiring at different ages will affect consumption and well-being over the rest of the lifetime, taking into account taxation, other benefits, and a number of other key factors. Their results show that most retirees are retiring far too early to maximize their benefits from the program. Virtually all individuals 45–62 should wait until age 65 or later to retire. Indeed, 90% should wait until age 70, but only 10% do so. The amount of dollars in consumption spending lost by early collecting is large, about 17% for four-fifths of the population. The median loss in lifetime benefits for those 45–62 exceeds $182,000.

In the final paper, Jonathan Meer and Joshua Witter examine the potential impact of the Earned Income Tax Credit (EITC) on the labor-force decisions of childless adults. The EITC, a program that provides a tax credit for workers, is one of the most important programs in the country for individuals with children. It has been shown to encourage additional labor-force activity for many parents, especially single mothers. But there is also a small credit for childless individuals, and extending and expanding that credit has been widely discussed by policy makers in recent years. Childless workers constitute about 25% of taxpayers receiving an EITC, but the amount of the credit is quite small for those without children. The authors provide new evidence on whether childless workers increase their labor-force attachment as a result of the credit, leveraging the feature that the credit becomes available to them at age 25. Conducting a careful study of how labor-force attachment changes from just before to just after age 25,

Meer and Witter find no evidence of any change in labor-force participation or employment. The authors speculate that this low responsiveness could be a result of lack of information and understanding of the credit, or it could be a result of the small credit amounts. They also suggest that childless individuals typically already have high levels of labor-force attachment, much greater than those of low-income parents who appear to increase their levels of attachment because of the EITC, suggesting that further increases for the childless group may be less likely for this reason as well.

Endnote

For acknowledgments, sources of research support, and disclosure of the author's material financial relationships, if any, please see https://www.nber.org/books-and-chapters/tax-policy-and-economy-volume-37/introduction-tax-policy-and-economy-volume-37.

How Regressive Are Mobility-Related User Fees and Gasoline Taxes?

Edward L. Glaeser, *Harvard University and NBER,* United States of America

Caitlin S. Gorback, *University of Texas at Austin,* United States of America

James M. Poterba, *Massachusetts Institute of Technology and NBER,* United States of America

Executive Summary

Pigouvian taxes and user fees can address environmental externalities and efficiently fund transportation infrastructure, but these policies may place burdens on poorer households. This paper presents new evidence on the distributional consequences of the gasoline tax, bus and light-rail charges, and a vehicle miles traveled (VMT) tax. Gas taxes have become more regressive over time, partially because of environmentally oriented technological change, although the share of expenditures on gas taxes declines with expenditures much less than the share of income spent on gas taxes declines with income. Replacing the gasoline tax with a household-level VMT tax would increase the average tax burden on households in the top income and expenditure deciles, because of their greater use of hybrid-electric and battery-electric vehicles. This progressive shift would be small given current levels of hybrid and electric vehicle ownership, but will be larger in the future if such vehicles continue to be more common among higher- than lower-income households. An expanded commercial VMT would place a larger burden, as a share of expenditures, on lower-income or lower-expenditure households, because better-off households consume more nontradable goods that do not require transportation. User charges for airports, subways, and commuter rail are progressive, and bus fees loom much larger for lower-income households.

Tax Policy and the Economy, volume 37, 2023.

I. Introduction

Consumption of transportation services is replete with externalities such as carbon emissions, traffic congestion, and motor vehicle fatalities. Economists have long embraced user fees to address these externalities. In *The Wealth of Nations*, Adam Smith wrote that user-fee financing would promote efficient investment decisions, because if transportation infrastructure is "made and supported by the commerce which is carried on by means of them, they can be made only where that commerce requires them, and consequently where it is proper to make them." William Vickrey (1952) called for taxes and time-varying charges for subways to address congestion externalities, and Small, Winston, and Evans (1989) were early advocates of a commercial vehicle miles traveled (VMT) tax to charge truckers for the marginal damages they impose on roads. Yet Pigouvian mobility charges such as highway tolls and gas taxes remain politically unpopular because they are salient and seen as regressive. When President Biden called for a gas-tax holiday on June 22, 2022, he justified this policy by arguing that "high gas prices pose a significant challenge for working families."[1]

Transportation infrastructure in the United States is funded through a combination of user fees, such as tolls and gasoline taxes, and general government resources. User fees play a significant role in funding airports and public transportation. When purchasing an airline ticket, for example, a consumer will pay a variety of user fees to different government entities, including taxes or fees to the Federal Aviation Administration, the Environmental Protection Agency (EPA), the Department of Homeland Security, and the local airport.

But gasoline and diesel taxes at the federal level have declined in real value over time, because nominal tax rates have been fixed since 1993 and total fuel consumption has plateaued for the past 15 years. The US Energy Information Administration (EIA) reports that total US consumption of gasoline reached 3.39 billion barrels in 2007, and was at roughly the same level (3.40 billion barrels) in 2019, before a pandemic-related drop to 2.95 billion barrels in 2020.[2] As electric vehicles replace cars and light trucks powered by internal combustion engines (ICEs), the revenue from gasoline and diesel taxes, which currently fund the Highway Trust Fund, will grow more slowly and eventually decline. The gas tax will also become more regressive, because higher-income households disproportionately own hybrid-electric vehicles (HEVs) and battery-electric vehicle (BEVs), which we collectively refer to as battery and hybrid electric vehicles (BHEVs). Owners of these vehicles pay much less—nothing, in the case of BEVs—in gasoline taxes per mile than the drivers of ICE vehicles. The EIA reports, based on the 2017 National Household Travel Survey, that 42% of the households owning a plug-in hybrid or electric vehicle have household income of more than $150,000, and only 14% of all households are in this income range (Stone 2018). The gap between transportation-related revenues and expenditures and the increasingly regressive nature of the gas tax has generated interest in new funding sources, including a VMT tax, which can be levied on both households and commercial drivers. At the same time, there is new attention to expanding transportation infrastructure, which is often financed in part with user fees. The Infrastructure Investment and Jobs Act of 2021 provides grants for states and localities to build vehicle-charging infrastructure, to replace or update public buses with low- or no-emission vehicles, and to explore options for electrification of commercial trucking at US ports. This paper considers the distributional impact of mobility-related user fees, including charges for airports, subways, commuter rail, and buses, with particular attention to gasoline taxes and VMT taxes.

We begin by presenting information on the distribution of outlays on current user charges that support transportation infrastructure, such as public-transportation user fees and the federal gasoline tax. Like Chernick and Reschovsky (1997) and Poterba (1991), we compare payments relative to income, the more common test of regressivity, with payments relative to household expenditures. The logic of the permanent-income hypothesis suggests that household expenditure may provide a better measure of long-term well-being than current income. Consequently, we focus more on the expenditure-based measure, but we also report income-based measures for completeness.

The share of expenditure devoted to public transportation declines with total expenditure over much of the expenditure distribution, although it rises at high expenditure levels as a result of commuter-rail and air-travel usage. Bus trips are far more frequent for low-income individuals. Commuter-rail and air-travel usage increase with expenditure. In areas with developed subway systems, subway trips are relatively independent of total expenditures.

Households in the highest income or spending category devote a smaller share of their budget to gasoline expenditures than do less-well-off households. Gasoline spending accounts for close to 5% of total expenditures, among those spending less than $30,000, and less than 2% of spending among the highest-expenditure households. Take, for example, a household with two cars, each delivering 24 miles per gallon (MPG), that drives a total of 18,000 miles per year and purchases 750 gallons of gasoline annually. With an 18.4-cent-per-gallon federal gasoline tax, and an average state gasoline tax of 26 cents per gallon, this household would pay $333 in gasoline taxes, which could be 1% of a poorer household's total expenditure. Not only would these tax payments represent a much smaller share of a wealthy household's annual expenditure, but also such a household could avoid these taxes altogether by replacing both vehicles with BEVs. Imposing a VMT would eliminate the implicit tax benefit given to hybrid-electric and battery-electric vehicles and charge drivers for their impact on road wear and tear.

BHEVs currently account for only about 3% of the US auto fleet, so even with the skew toward higher-income owners, the distributional pattern of payments for a VMT tax would be very similar to that for an equal-revenue gasoline tax. However, the share of BHEVs in the fleet is rising, particularly among well-to-do households. In the fourth quarter of 2021, the EIA (Dwyer 2022) reports that 6.1% of new sales were hybrids, 3.4% were electrics, and 1.4% were plug-in hybrid electrics. In addition to considering the current setting, we therefore also consider the relative distribution of burdens from a gasoline and a VMT tax in a future year in which BHEVs account for one-third of the vehicle fleet. If the new BHEVs are distributed across the households in roughly the same way as current ones, the distributional burdens of the gasoline tax and VMT tax will diverge, with substantially lower burdens for gasoline taxes than for VMT taxes at high income or expenditure levels.

We also consider a commercial VMT (CVMT) tax. Four states—Kentucky, New York, Oregon, and New Mexico—have already adopted such taxes. Under the assumption that trucking costs are fully passed through to consumers of tradable goods, and that CVMT tax charges are added to trucking costs, a household's burden from a commercial VMT tax depends on the share of its budget share that is spent on tradable goods that need to be transported. Our estimates suggest that as a share of household expenditures, the current diesel tax and any expanded commercial VMT tax fall more heavily on less-well-off households than on those in the upper strata of the income or expenditure distribution. Better-off households consume more services, which do not require much transportation, and devote a smaller budget share to tradable goods.

This paper builds on a long literature on the distributional impacts of transportation-related Pigouvian taxes. Metcalf (1999) noted that environmental taxes meant to mitigate the social damage of pollution tend to be regressive, and Levinson (2019) found that regulating fuel efficiency was more regressive than imposing fuel taxes to reduce consumption. The closest antecedent to our study is Metcalf's (2022) comparison of the distributional impact of a VMT tax and a gasoline tax. It relies on data from one of the two surveys that we analyze, and reaches similar conclusions about the progressivity of the VMT-for-gas tax swap. Our study makes different assumptions in forecasting the future growth of EVs in the vehicle fleet and takes a less parametric approach to summarizing distributional burdens, so the two studies are complementary. Our study also builds on earlier studies of the VMT tax including Davis and Sallee (2020), Fox (2020), Langer, Maheshri and Winston (2017), van Dender (2019), and Weatherford (2012). Our analysis focuses exclusively on tax burdens, and does not consider the distribution of transportation-related externalities, such as pollution, that may be reduced by a gasoline tax or a VMT tax. Banzhaf, Ma, and Timmins (2019) find these externalities to disproportionately burden low-income households. Jacqz and Johnston (2022) investigate the effect of current patterns of BHEV adoption in reducing environmental and other externalities, and they observe that these effects would be larger if there were higher BHEV penetration in lower-income communities.

The remainder of this paper is divided into six sections. Section I introduces the two main data sets, the Consumer Expenditure Survey and the National Household Travel Survey, that underlie our analysis. The next presents our core findings on the distributional impacts of current public-transportation user fees. Section III summarizes current gasoline-expenditure and gasoline-tax burdens and highlights changes in the characteristics of the US vehicle fleet over time. Section IV considers the difference in the distribution burden of a VMT tax and a gasoline tax, both with the current level of HEV penetration in the vehicle fleet and a higher level designed to reflect a future year. Section V examines the impact of a CVMT tax on the prices paid by consumers for various final goods and presents estimates of the distribution of burdens associated with this tax. There is a brief conclusion in Section VI.

II. Data Sources on Consumer Transportation Outlays: NHTS and CEX

Our household travel and expenditure analysis draws on two primary data sets. One is the National Household Travel Survey (NHTS), which includes information on transportation utilization by mode, vehicle characteristics, and driving behavior. It also includes information on household income. The NHTS is conducted every 8 years to study household travel patterns and is a key input into national, state, and regional infrastructure planning. The survey recruits households and asks them about their trips in a 24-hour period, including mode, purpose, trip length, and time of day, among other characteristics. These surveys are then linked to a suite of demographic, socioeconomic, vehicle, and location characteristics. We use data from three 2017 NHTS products: the household survey, the trip-level survey, and the vehicle survey. This survey covers roughly 139,000 households that use 256,000 distinct vehicles and make nearly 925,000 trips on the survey date. The data are collected at the person level and then aggregated to households. The survey also provides weights used to aggregate households to population-level statistics. We use this data set to estimate the number of households in various income ranges that are using each mode of transportation, to calculate their driving behavior, and to examine vehicle characteristics. We focus on data from the 2017 NHTS, but in some cases, we also draw on comparative data from the 2001 survey.

We use data on trips to study outlays on infrastructure user charges of various types. We focus on private vehicle, bus, subway, commuter rail, and airplane. The NHTS also includes data on the vehicles owned by each household, including their age, fuel type, and annual miles traveled. The NHTS has information on travel mode utilization but not on travel expenditure or total expenditures.

The second data set that we use, the Consumer Expenditure Survey (CEX), is a nationwide survey conducted quarterly by the Bureau of Labor Statistics (BLS). It provides estimates of annual expenditures on a variety of consumer goods and services as well as total household expenditure and income. We convert CEX data from the 2019 survey, the primary focus of our analysis, to real 2017 dollars for comparability with the NHTS data. We verify, and report in table B1, that aggregate measures computed from the public-use microdata version of the CEX are comparable to the published tabulations from the BLS.

The CEX reports tax-inclusive expenditures on gasoline, but it does not distinguish tax payments from the retail cost of gasoline. To calculate how many gallons of gasoline households have purchased and back out total federal plus state taxes paid on them, we complement the CEX sample with annual data on state gasoline prices and taxes. State motor fuels tax-rate data come from the Brookings-Urban Tax Policy Center. Our focus is on the total federal gasoline user fee levied in each state in each year. To estimate gasoline costs per gallon, we use the "all grades all formulations" retail price average as reported by the EIA. The EIA reports annual data for nine states. For the other 41 states and Washington, DC, we use the averages that EIA reports for each of seven regions assigned by the EIA.

Most studies of household spending on gasoline and other transportation-related outlays report expenditures as a share of income. In the lowest decile of the household income distribution, reported income is substantially below household expenditure. This likely reflects the omission of some transfer program receipts in the measure of income, transitory fluctuations in income that render current income below permanent income (which is more likely to drive expenditures), and measurement error. At the highest income levels, the transitory income fluctuations may also be important, leading reported income to overstate permanent income; for example, if a household realizes substantial capital gains in a particular year. These issues with reported income suggest that scaling outlays on transportation by total expenditure, rather than total income, as in Poterba's (1991) study of excise tax incidence, may provide a more informative measure of relative burdens than scaling by income.

Panel *a* of figure 1 shows the ratio of expenditures to income for households in the 2017 CEX, with households grouped into deciles based on total household income. This ratio is nearly 3 in the lowest income decile, dropping to 1.5 in the second decile and declining smoothly to less than 0.6 in the top decile. To provide some context for the distribution, households in the lowest income decile have annual incomes below $12,158 (in $2017), those in the fifth decile have incomes up to $52,147, and those in the top decile have incomes of at least $160,044.

Panel *b* shows the expenditure-to-income ratio when households are ranked by total expenditures. It is much more stable, ranging from between 1.25 and 1.5 at the lowest 2 deciles, to values just above 1 in the middle of the distribution, and rising again at the highest expenditure decile. This may reflect the presence of infrequent outlays, such as car purchases, at the top of the expenditure distribution. Households in the lowest expenditure decile report total spending of less than $16,620. Those at the median (just above the fifth decile) report expenditures of up to $39,774, and those in the top decile have expenditures of at least $107,256. These break points for the deciles make clear that the gradient in expenditure is not as steep as the gradient in income.

Table 1 shows the distribution of CEX households across income and expenditure deciles. Nearly half of the households in the bottom income

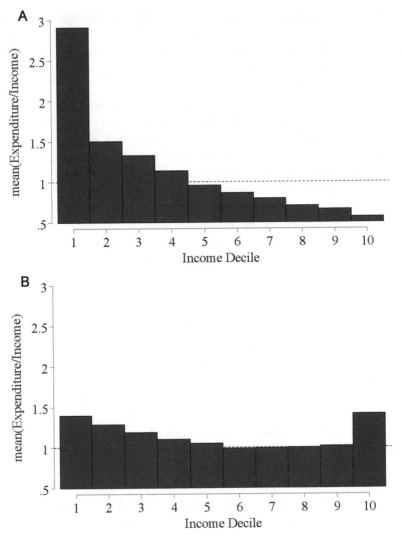

Fig. 1. Expenditure/income by income and expenditure decile, 2017 CEX. Data are from the Consumer Expenditures Survey (CEX) 2017. Panel *a* shows the average expenditure/ income ratio within income deciles. Panel *b* shows the same ratio, averaged within expenditure deciles. All ratios winsorized at the 5th and 95th percentiles for ease of inspection. A color version of this figure is available online.

decile are in the bottom expenditure decile, and vice versa. The same is true for the top decile of each distribution. However, one-third of those in the bottom income decile are in the third or higher expenditure decile, and almost one fifth of those in the highest income decile are in the eighth or lower decile of expenditures. In the middle of both the income

Table 1
Joint Distribution of Expenditure and Income Deciles

	Expenditure Decile									
Income Decile	1	2	3	4	5	6	7	8	9	10
1	49	18	11	7	5	3	3	2	1	2
2	32	28	15	9	5	4	3	2	1	1
3	12	25	20	15	11	6	4	3	2	3
4	4	14	22	18	15	9	6	4	3	3
5	2	8	16	20	18	15	9	5	4	3
6	1	4	10	15	18	18	14	9	6	5
7	0	1	4	9	15	20	20	15	8	7
8	0	1	2	5	8	15	22	23	17	8
9	0	0	1	2	4	9	16	23	29	18
10	0	0	0	0	1	2	5	11	28	51

	Income Decile									
Expenditure Decile	1	2	3	4	5	6	7	8	9	10
1	50	31	11	4	2	1	0	0	0	0
2	19	28	25	14	8	4	1	1	0	0
3	12	15	19	22	16	10	4	2	1	0
4	7	9	15	19	20	15	9	5	2	0
5	5	4	11	15	18	18	16	8	4	1
6	3	3	5	9	14	18	20	15	9	2
7	3	3	4	6	9	13	20	23	15	5
8	2	2	3	5	5	9	16	24	23	12
9	1	1	2	3	4	6	8	17	29	28
10	2	1	2	3	3	5	7	8	17	51

Note: Entries in each panel denote the percentage of customer units in the income or expenditure decile listed in the row that are found in the income or expenditure decile in the column, as in Poterba (1991). Calculations are based on the 2017 Consumer Expenditure Survey.

and expenditure distribution, the share of households in the same decile of both distributions is lower, in part reflecting the narrower band of incomes or expenditures that correspond to each decile.

We compare expenditures for various transportation services to total household expenditures rather than reported income. We group households into deciles based on their total expenditure levels; we do not make any adjustment for household size. For transportation outlays reported in the CEX, we can compute the expenditure share directly. For transportation outlays or utilization measures drawn from the NHTS, we need to impute total expenditures; the NHTS records household income in intervals, but it does not report expenditures. We use variables other than expenditure that are observed in both the CEX and NHTS, as well as the full range of expenditure data in the CEX, to predict total expenditures in the CEX, and we then use the resulting model to impute total expenditures to NHTS households.

We impute total expenditures as a function of reported household characteristics using data from all CEX surveys for 2000 through 2019. We estimate Engel curves for total expenditure using weighted regression, with population weights in the CEX, of total expenditure on state and year fixed effects, a fourth order polynomial in household income, and indicators for the household head's race, Hispanic status, employment, retirement, student status, gender, and homeowner status. We include information on education level and age by grouping households into 5-year age bins, and interact the education categories with each of the age bins. We include indicator variables for families with each number of household members, along with indicators for number of children, the head of household's marital status, and the interactions between marital status and number of children. The R^2 for total expenditure in our estimating equation is 0.41, so the correlation between actual and fitted outlays is about 0.64. Figure 2 shows the scatterplot of actual and fitted total expenditure in the CEX.[3]

We predict total expenditures for NHTS households using the estimated Engel curves by harmonizing variables between the NHTS and

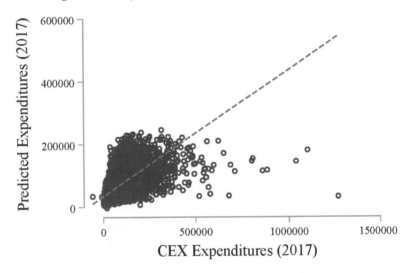

Fig. 2. Model fit: actual and predicted expenditures in CEX 2017. This figure shows the model fit for predicting total expenditures in the Consumer Expenditures Survey (CEX). The horizontal axis measures observed expenditures for 1 year in our data, 2017. The vertical axis shows the expenditures predicted from our model. The dots each map to one household, and the dashed line shows the linear fit, weighted by each household's respective population weight. A color version of this figure is available online.

CEX. For example, we define the income for each NHTS household as the income value at the midpoint of the income ranges in that survey. As one way of judging the similarities between the imputation of total expenditures across income classes in both the CEX and the NHTS, we regressed predictive expenditures on reported income in the CEX and on our measure of income (midpoint of intervals) in the NHTS. The coefficient on reported income in the CEX is 0.41, and in the NHTS it is 0.41, suggesting some broad similarity between the two fits. The expenditure shares on gasoline from actual expenditure in the CEX and imputed expenditure in the NHTS exhibit a similar pattern, shown in figure C1; this provides some validation for our exercise.

III. Heterogeneity in the Use of Public Transit and Airports

We report utilization and outlays for a number of public-transportation modes. Information on utilization is essential to assessing the potential distributional impacts of levying increased fees on the use of these transport modes. Although the CEX documents expenditure on public transportation, it does not differentiate modes. Detailed utilization information by mode is reported in the NHTS. As such, our baseline results focus on NHTS households classified by predicted total expenditures. The NHTS reports the number of trips taken on different modes of transportation, not the charges associated with these trips. Trip counts are, however, a key determinant of the distribution of potential burdens from user fees.

Figure 3 panels *a*, *b*, and *c* report the average number of trips taken each day per household for three types of public transit—bus, subway, and commuter rail—as reported in the NHTS. We plot two bars in each case. The lighter corresponds to cities with at least 10% of the population commuting by public transit (New York, Chicago, Washington, DC, Boston, Philadelphia, and San Francisco), and the darker bars correspond to all the other major metro areas and submetro areas in the NHTS.

Bus utilization declines as total household expenditure rises, reflecting a substitution of private for public transit. Households in the lowest expenditure decile use the bus approximately 0.7 times each day in high-public-transit cities, and about 0.2 times per day in other locations. In contrast, households in the highest expenditure decile use the bus only about 0.1 times each day in the high-public-transit cities, and about half that often elsewhere.

In contrast to riding the bus, using the subway is very popular for households in all expenditure deciles in high-public-transit cities, and

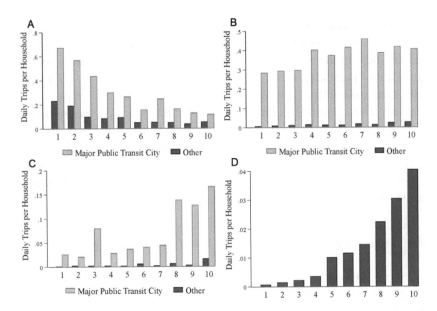

Fig. 3. Public-transit utilization in the NHTS by expenditure decile. Data are from the National Household Travel Survey (NHTS) 2017, trip-level data set aggregated to households. Figures do not include households with negative expenditure. Panel *a* shows the distribution of daily household trips by bus, panel *b* by subway, panel *c* by commuter rail, and panel *d* by air. Figures do not include households with negative expenditure. Panels *a*, *b*, and *c* split by a city's status as a major public transit city: New York City, Chicago, Boston, Washington, DC, Philadelphia, and San Francisco.

subway use increases with expenditure. This reflects the combination of reliance of low-income inner-city neighborhoods on public transit and the use of subways in many high-income neighborhoods; an example is Manhattan, where proximity to a subway is highly valued.

Commuter-rail use is the most progressive of the various forms of land-based public transit. In high-public-transit cities, utilization is sharply higher, averaging about 0.15 trips per day, for households in the top three deciles of the expenditure distribution than for other households, for whom the average is less than one-third this level. Commuter rail tends to be colocated with wealthy suburbs surrounding dense cities, and fare costs are higher than public bus or subways.

The National Transit Database (2021) reports that for the 50 largest transit authorities in the United States, passenger fares cover only about 40% of operating costs in 2019. Thus, even before considering capital costs, which are critical in public transportation, these systems are not covering costs. Increased user fees offer one potential means of closing the funding gap, and at least for commuter rail, it may be possible to raise revenues without placing disproportionate burdens on households lower in the economic distribution.

In addition to bus, subway, and commuter rail, where many of the service providers are public authorities, we also consider the distribution of airline trips across households, in figure 3d. Air travel involves substantial use of public infrastructure in the form of airports and air traffic control, even though airlines in the United States are private firms. The infrastructure services are partially funded by various taxes on airline tickets and airport utilization. The consumption of air travel is even more progressive than commuter-rail use. Households in the highest expenditure decile report roughly 22 times as many trips as those in the lowest deciles, where utilization is negligible. Households in the top decile report roughly one airline trip each month. Households in the top two expenditure deciles are about twice as likely to use air travel as those in the next two deciles. These four deciles account for most airline trips. This provides guidance on the potential incidence of higher user fees for airlines, or ticket taxes for airline travel.

IV.   Gasoline-Tax Burdens by Expenditure and Income Groups

The transportation-related user charge that attracts the most attention is the gasoline tax, and it is the focus of the balance of this study. The CEX has information on household outlays on gasoline. We impute gasoline taxes based on gasoline expenditure by converting expenditures to gallons based on average per-gallon prices, and then applying the average federal or federal plus state gasoline-tax rate.

A.   The Distribution of Gasoline and Gasoline-Tax Outlays

Figure 4a shows outlay shares on gasoline for households across expenditure deciles. For households in the lowest expenditure decile in 2017, gasoline accounts for about 4% of total expenditures, and for those in the highest expenditure decile, it accounts for about 2%. The expenditure share for gasoline is highest in the middle of the expenditure distribution, where it rises to 5%, more than twice the level of the highest decile.

The figure shows the expenditure shares for 2001 and 2017.[4] The 2 years are similar in the real ($2017) price of a gallon of gasoline: $2.27 and $2.14, respectively. Higher gasoline prices reduce gasoline demand. Levin, Lewis, and Wolak (2017) suggest a price elasticity of about −0.30 as a middle-range value, based on many studies. The expenditure share does not rise

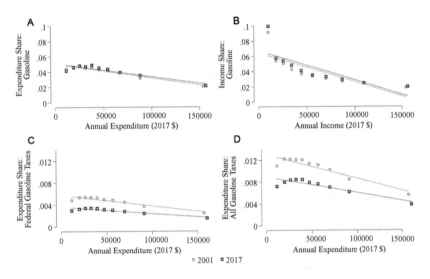

Fig. 4. Gasoline and tax expenditures in the CEX. Data are from the 2001 and 2017 Consumer Expenditures Survey (CEX) waves. The figure plots binned scatters and their associated linear fits. Panel *a* shows the average expenditure share devoted to gasoline by expenditure decile. Panel *b* shows the average income share devoted to gasoline expenditures by income decile. Panels *c* and *d* plot expenditure share on federal gasoline taxes, or on total taxes (state and federal), by expenditure decile. Expenditure is winsorized at the 1st and 99th percentiles prior to binning, for positive values of expenditure. Income is trimmed at the 5th and 95th percentiles prior to binning, for positive values of income. Data on annual fuel prices by state or region are from the Energy Information Administration's "all grades all formulations" retail price average. State motor fuels tax rates data come from the Brookings-Urban Tax Policy Center. A color version of this figure is available online.

or fall in exact proportion to movements in gasoline prices, but higher gasoline prices are associated with higher expenditure shares.

One factor that has limited the increase in the expenditure share of gasoline, despite rising miles driven, is the rising fuel efficiency of vehicles. The average fuel economy of the light-duty vehicle fleet was 22.3 MPG in 2017, up from 20.2 in 2001 and 19.2 in 1994, when the current federal gasoline tax rate was set.[5] Thus, the amount of gasoline needed, on average, to drive a mile declined by about 14% between 1994 and 2017. The average fuel economy for new vehicles is currently much higher than for the existing stock. Hula et al. (2021) report that for 2021, the EPA estimates that the realized MPG—the fuel efficiency achieved in actual driving—was 28–32 for cars and 19–24 for trucks. This suggests that the average fuel economy of the light-duty fleet is likely to continue to rise in future years as newer vehicles continue to replace older ones. Data from the 2017

NHTS show that the average household drives about 12,000 miles per year or about 33 miles per day. There is substantial heterogeneity, with the 25th percentile driving 15 miles per day and the 75th nearly triple that at 42 miles per day. Higher-expenditure households tend to drive more per annum than their low-expenditure counterparts; this is a factor pushing toward progressivity in the distribution of gasoline tax burdens. However, the expenditure share on gasoline depends not only on how many miles households drive, but also on how many gallons are needed per mile. On average, lower-expenditure households drive older and less fuel-efficient vehicles. This counterbalances the pattern of miles driven per household, and in extreme cases—when the high-expenditure household owns an electric vehicle—can result in no gasoline tax burden at all. We revisit the ownership of electric vehicles when we consider VMT taxes below.

Figure 4a shows annual expenditure on gasoline, not gasoline taxes, as a share of total expenditure. To place the tax burden in perspective, in 2017 the federal gasoline tax was 18.4 cents per gallon, when average gasoline prices were $2.53, so federal taxes were approximately 7% of the total cost of gasoline. The average state gasoline tax in 2017 was $0.28. The total tax burden therefore represents about 18% of the retail, tax-inclusive price of gasoline. Figures 4c and 4d present our estimates of expenditures on gasoline taxes by expenditure decile. These are estimates, because we calculate gallons of gasoline purchased from the amount spent on gasoline, divided by the mean state gasoline price provided by the EIA, and then multiply by the federal and state tax rates to compute expenditure on gasoline taxes.

If the federal gasoline tax had been indexed for inflation when it was set in 1993, today it would be more than 34 cents per gallon. Brooks and Liscow (2019) and Mehrotra, Turner, and Uribe (2023) find that inflation in the cost of building new highways has outpaced general inflation, so even had the tax kept up with overall inflation, its buying power would have diminished. There is a growing gap between federal gasoline tax revenues, which are dedicated to the Federal Highway Trust, and federal highway outlays. In 2021, the former was $43.4 billion, and the average expected outlay for the FY2021–25 period was $60.4 billion (Kirk and Mallett 2020). If the federal gasoline tax rate were increased to a level that would cover average expected federal highway revenues, it would be approximately 26 cents per gallon, and the expenditure shares for federal taxes would be about one-third greater than those shown in figure 4c.

To illustrate the importance of focusing on annual expenditure rather than annual income as the denominator when measuring gasoline expenditure burdens, figure 4b presents the share of gasoline expenditures relative to reported income in the CEX for 2001 and 2017. Gasoline expenditures account for almost 10% of income in the lowest decile, compared with only 2% in the highest groups. For those in the second lowest decile, however, gasoline expenditure as a share of income falls to about 6%. Gasoline tax burdens appear regressive in both figures 4a and 4b, but the relative burden on less-well-off relative to better-off households is greater in figure 4b, in part because the income measure for those in the lowest income decile may not be a complete measure of economic well-being.

Rural households travel longer distances than their urban and suburban counterparts, and are more likely to drive larger vehicles, so they can face heavier burdens from gasoline taxes. Figures 5a and 5b compare the expenditure share and income share distributions for households by local area population. In the 2017 CEX, 25% of sample households live in cities with populations higher than 5 million, 28% in cities with between 1 million and 5 million, and 48% in communities with fewer than 1 million residents, including rural areas.[6] In both the income and expenditure share distributions, those living in smaller cities spend higher shares on gasoline. Metcalf (2022) presents complementary findings on urban/rural differences in gasoline expenditures as a share of income using 2017 NHTS data; his findings also suggest greater expenditure by rural households.

In the bottom half of the expenditure or income distribution, and especially in the bottom decile, gasoline expenditures are significantly greater—close to 3% of either income or expenditure in the bottom decile—for rural households than for those in large cities. At the top of both distributions, there are almost no urban-rural differences. When households are ranked by total expenditure, the disparity between urban and rural households at the bottom of the distribution is larger than when households are ranked by income, in part reflecting that the denominator in the share calculations—expenditure—is smaller than income. Prospectively, rural households may have some advantages in BHEV adoption, notably because they are more likely to live in stand-alone dwellings that can be configured to support at-home charging.

B.   *Technological Change, Vehicle Ownership Patterns,*
     and Distributional Burdens

Technological change will respond to Pigouvian taxes in any setting, and if new technologies are used disproportionately by the rich, then

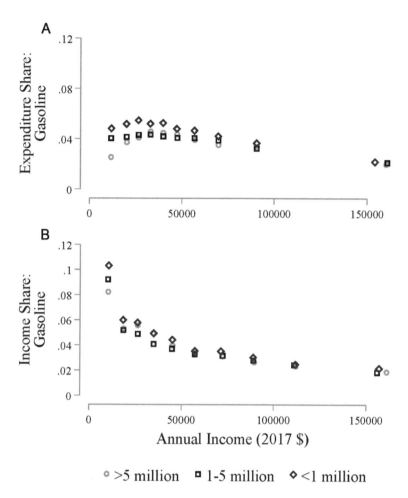

Fig. 5. Gasoline expenditure and income shares by city size. Data are from the 2017 Consumer Expenditures Survey (CEX). All panels plot binned scatters and their associated linear fits. Panel *a* shows the gasoline expenditure share by expenditure decile and city size. Panel *b* shows gasoline income share by income decile and city size. Expenditure is winsorized at the 1st and 99th percentiles prior to binning, for positive values of expenditure. Income is trimmed at the 5th and 95th percentiles prior to binning, for positive values of income. A color version of this figure is available online.

Pigouvian taxes will become more regressive over time. When all vehicles were powered by ICEs, the central question was how average fuel economy varied across deciles. More recently, as BHEVs have entered the market, some better-off households have reduced their gasoline expenditures to zero while still driving. Technological change—the advent of BHEVs—has made a Pigouvian tax less progressive over time.

The first reason why technological change may lead Pigouvian taxes to become more regressive over time is that most durable goods, including cars, refrigerators, and houses, depreciate in quality over time. Higher-income households tend to own newer durable goods than their lower-income counterparts, who either keep their durable goods longer or purchase used durable goods. Lowry (1960) labeled this "filtering" in the housing context.

Table 2 shows that in 1977, the average household earning more than $50,000 owned a car that was 4.5 years old, and the average household earning less than $10,000 owned a car that was more than 8 years old. Introducing a Pigouvian tax induces innovation that creates products that generate less of the taxed externality. Because better-off households

Table 2
Vehicle Characteristics by Income

	1977 Nationwide Personal Transportation Survey		
Income (1977$)	Average Vehicle Age	Average MPG	Average Curb Weight
<$5,000	8.38	19.7	3,469
$5,000–$9,999	7.23	19.1	3,572
$10,000–$14,999	6.54	18.9	3,630
$15,000–$24,999	6.04	19.0	3,639
$25,000–$34,999	5.56	19.1	3,728
$35,000–$50,000	5.32	18.4	3,796
>$50,000	4.56	16.8	3,835
Average	6.4	19.0	3,640
	2017 National Household Travel Survey		
Income (2017$)	Average Vehicle Age	Average MPG	
<$10,000	12.99	21.38	
$10,000–$14,999	12.96	20.97	
$15,000–$24,999	12.19	21.49	
$25,000–$34,999	11.38	21.41	
$35,000–$49,999	11.07	21.49	
$50,000–$74,999	10.34	21.55	
$75,000–$99,999	9.48	21.73	
$100,000–$24,999	9.28	21.89	
$125,000–$149,999	8.57	22.18	
$150,000–$199,999	8.38	22.17	
>$200,000	7.82	22.52	
Average	10.11	21.73	

Note: Data in the top panel are from the 1977 Nationwide Personal Transportation Survey "Household Vehicle Ownership: Report 2," 1980. Data in the lower panel are based on author's calculations using the 2017 NHTS vehicle survey, for vehicles with positive miles driven. MPG = miles per gallon.

buy more new products than the poor, externality-reducing innovation will mean that they pay less of the Pigouvian tax.

A second reason Pigouvian taxes may become less progressive over time is that the interest groups that supported the adoption of the tax may also try to create a sense of moral obligation to avoid generating the externality in question. For decades, environmentalists have tried to both tax and regulate environmental harms and to spread environmental consciousness through books, such as Carson's (1962) *Silent Spring*, advertisements, and environmental education in school curricula (Carleton-Hug and Hug 2010; Glaeser 2014). Persuasion in the classroom and through the written word may be more effective with more educated individuals, who also tend to have higher incomes. In a March 2021 Gallup poll, 46% of American college graduates identified themselves as environmentalists, compared with only 37% of those who had not completed high school. Wang et al. (2022) find that arguably exogenous shifts in education due to compulsory-schooling law changes in China lead to increases in pro-environmental attitudes and behavior. Even if persuasion generates an equal taste for environmentalism in all income strata, if that taste is a normal good, then it will tend to have a larger impact on the behavior of higher-income households.

Finally, innovation related to the Pigouvian tax may be directed toward more luxurious consumer products that are disproportionately demanded by higher-income households. If richer customers generate higher profit margins, then technological change, green or otherwise, will be targeted toward products consumed by the rich. This effect suggests that even within the set of new products, those targeted to the top income strata may benefit from faster innovation and greater externality avoidance.

Figure *6a* shows the vehicle age distribution, based on data from the NHTS, in 2017 for households ranked by expenditure class. Panel *b* plots the average MPG for the vehicles owned by households in each part of the expenditure distribution. Improvements in production technologies have extended vehicle lives, and today, vehicles last longer than they did in the past. In 2017, the average vehicle had been owned by its current owner for 2 years longer than the average vehicle in 2001. In addition, fuel efficiency rose at every point in the expenditure distribution, especially so at higher expenditure deciles. In 2001, the MPG-expenditure profile was nearly flat, with both the highest and lowest deciles owning cars that ran around 20 MPG. By 2017, the highest-expenditure households drove cars that were 1.5 MPG more efficient than the lowest-decile households. Figure *6a*

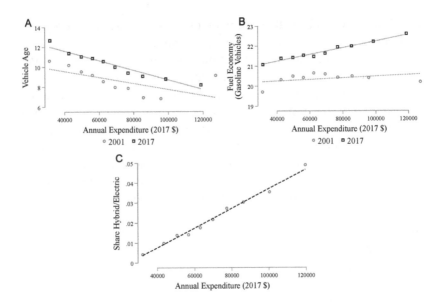

Fig. 6. Vehicle characteristics in the NHTS by expenditure level. Data are from the National Household Transportation Survey (NHTS) waves from 2001 and 2017. Only vehicles that run on gasoline are considered, including hybrid vehicles. All panels plot binned scatters and their associated linear fits. Panel *a* shows vehicle age by expenditure decile. Panel *b* shows mean fuel economy, calculated as observed miles driven divided by gallons purchased, by expenditure decile. Panel *c* shows the binned scatter and associated linear fit for the share of hybrid and electric vehicles. Expenditure is winsorized at the 1st and 99th percentiles prior to binning, for positive values of expenditure. A color version of this figure is available online.

shows one puzzling finding: the jump of more than 2 years in average vehicle age between the second-highest and highest expenditure deciles. This may reflect purchases of more durable luxury models by those at the top of the distribution; the pattern is present in 2001 but not 2017.

In the 1977 National Personal Travel Survey (NPTS), higher-income households owned less-fuel-efficient vehicles.[7] On average, households in the top income bracket—more than $50,000, about $250,000 with Consumer Price Index adjustment to 2022—owned cars that averaged 2.9 fewer MPG than those in the lowest-income group, which was less than $5,000 in 1977 or about $25,000 today. The lowest-income group owned cars on average that were 4 years older than those in the highest-income group.

The relationship between vehicle age and income is similar in the 2017 and the 1977 data. In 2017, the average age of a vehicle owned by a household with income of less than $25,000 was 13.0 years. It was 11.5

for income \$25,000–\$49,999, 10.7 for \$50,000–\$74,999, 9.9 for \$75,000–\$99,999, and 8.9 for households with incomes above \$100,000.[8] But the pattern of fuel economy was very different in the 2 years.[9] The 2017 NHTS data show that the highest-income households own vehicles that run, on average, 1.5 more MPG than those in the lowest income categories (consistent with the expenditure results in fig. 9). This pattern offsets the tendency of better-off households to drive more miles than their less-well-off counterparts.

The rise of hybrid-electric and battery-electric vehicles accentuates the declining fuel use of better-off households. Figure 6c shows the BHEV fraction of the light-duty vehicle fleet by household expenditure category in 2017. The emergence of BHEVs, which allow the driver to avoid paying gasoline taxes, is an example of a setting in which, in the presence of two technologies, the distributional burden of a tax on an input to one of them will depend both on the nature of the two technologies and the resulting pattern of use across income classes. When better gas mileage meant reducing car weight and power, low-income households were more likely to take advantage of that possibility, so in the 1970s, gas taxes were paid disproportionately by high-income households driving heavy, low-MPG cars. When better mileage means buying a relatively expensive electric vehicle with higher up-front capital costs than an ICE-powered car, then gas taxes become a disproportionate burden on the poor, who may not be able to afford—even with access to credit markets—the greater up-front cost of the cleaner technology. Appendix A presents a simple model illuminating the interplay between household income and the adoption of an energy-saving technology. When well-to-do households demand more transportation services that use energy than less-well-off households, a tax on energy inputs will place greater burdens on them, but that can be reversed if the well-do-to are more likely to adopt the greener, and less heavily taxed, alternative technology.

V. The Distributional Impact of a Gasoline Tax versus a Household VMT Tax

All-electric vehicle sales alone have grown from 0.1% of all sales in 2011 to 1.7% in 2020, according to Davis and Boundy (2019). As the BHEV market has grown, it has sparked discussion of a VMT tax, which would tax drivers based on their road usage rather than their gasoline consumption. With a VMT tax, both BHEV drivers and those driving ICE vehicles would contribute to the costs of infrastructure maintenance.

Because BHEVs are typically between 10% and 40% heavier than ICE vehicles, there is a case for charging them even more per mile driven. In this section, we compare the distribution of the 2017 federal gasoline tax with an equal-revenue VMT tax applied to households. We also consider the distribution of both taxes at a hypothetical future date when BHEVs represent one-third of the stock of light-duty vehicles. In the next section, we consider a commercial VMT tax levied on vehicles that burn diesel fuel.

A. Modeling the Driving Response to a VMT Tax

Shifting from a gasoline tax to an equal-revenue VMT tax would change the pricing of driving services. Households with BHEVs would experience an increase in their cost per mile, and those driving ICE-powered cars would experience a decrease because some taxes would now be collected from BHEV drivers. To estimate the distribution of taxes paid with a VMT tax, we must model how the miles driven by different households would change if such a tax were adopted.

We assume that each household i has a quasi-linear separable utility with the utility from travel in miles, T_i, generated through a power function:

$$U_i(T_i) = Y_i - pT_i + AT_i^\sigma. \tag{1}$$

Households earn income Y_i and purchase T_i at price per mile p. The first-order condition $(\partial U_i/\partial T_i) = 0$ can be rewritten as

$$ln(T_i) = \frac{1}{1-\sigma}ln(A\sigma) - \frac{1}{1-\sigma}ln(p). \tag{2}$$

The price elasticity of demand for travel miles is $\varepsilon_g = -[1/(1-\sigma)]$. We assume a value for this parameter of $\varepsilon_g = -0.31$ based on Levin et al. (2017). The authors use high-frequency data on credit-card swipes at gas stations to measure how gasoline demand responds to price changes; importantly, their model can accommodate drivers substituting expenditure across days, allowing current price changes to affect expenditure more flexibly across time.

The −0.31 value is an elasticity of gasoline consumption with respect to the price of gasoline, but the elasticity that is relevant for our analysis is that of miles traveled with respect to the cost per mile of travel. Using data from the 1997–2001 period, a period when there were no BHEVs, Small and van Dender (2007) estimate a long-run elasticity of vehicle

A critical question for the comparative distribution of future gasoline and VMT taxes is where, in the income or expenditure distribution, new BHEV purchases will take place. Different assumptions in this regard will result in different outcomes. Metcalf (2022), for example, reports some counterfactuals in which he adjusts vehicle ownership in the 2017 NHTS by assuming that the most recent ICE-vehicle purchases were replaced by BHEVs. In our projection, we assume that the greater propensity for high- than for low-income households to purchase BHEVs, which has been observed in the past 2 decades, will continue. This reflects both the tendency for new cars to be purchased by higher- rather than lower-income households, and the relatively expensive pricing, particularly of EVs, to date. In light of recent changes in eligibility for BHEV tax credits at high incomes, the strong tilt toward BHEV purchases at higher incomes may attenuate over the next 15 years. Our results may therefore be seen as an upper bound for the disparity in future distributional differences between the gasoline and the VMT tax.

Table B3 reports the 2017 NHTS vehicle composition by expenditure decile. The share of vehicles owned by households in an expenditure decile that are BHEVs rises monotonically with expenditure level. In 2017, about 27% of all BHEVs were owned by households in the highest expenditure decile, and only 1% of these vehicles were owned by those in the lowest decile. We apply these shares to the number of BHEVs that we project in the 2037 vehicle fleet, thereby predicting BHEV^{2037} by decile, and then we compute the number of ICE-powered vehicles by decile as $\text{ICE}^{2037} = \text{Vehicles}^{2037} - \text{BHEV}^{2037}$.

To determine which households within a decile are net purchasers of additional vehicles between 2017 and 2037, we proceed in three steps. First, for every vehicle that is owned in the 2017 NHTS, we assign a 15% probability that the owner will have one more vehicle in 2037. This randomly assigns an increase in the vehicle fleet of 15% across households that currently own vehicles. We do not assign any of the net increase in vehicle ownership to households that did not own cars in 2017. Second, when we assign a net new vehicle to a household, if the 2017 vehicle being "cloned" was a BHEV, we assume the new vehicle will also be a BHEV. If the 2017 vehicle was ICE-powered, we assign the new vehicle either BHEV or ICE status based on the fraction of net new vehicles that need to be HEV to achieve the overall share of BHEVs in the expenditure decile. This means that the probability that a new vehicle is assumed to be a BHEV varies across expenditure deciles. Finally, after we have allocated all net new vehicles, if the share of BHEVs in the vehicle fleet for a decile is still below the share of BHEVs that result from our aggregate projections, we randomly reassign a fraction of the ICE-powered vehicles in the 2037 fleet to HEV status. Some such "swapping" of ICE-powered cars for BHEVs is required in each of the top seven expenditure deciles, but it is particularly prevalent in top two.

C. Comparing Gasoline-Tax and VMT-Tax Burdens

We compare the distributional burden of the current gasoline tax with a gasoline tax that would raise the same revenue per vehicle in our future scenario, allowing for the change in fleet composition between 2017 and that date. In 2017, we estimate that the federal gasoline tax raised about $20 billion. With the 15% increase in the vehicle fleet, we adjust this target to a tax that can raise $23 billion in revenues. This involves setting the future gasoline tax to 25.8 cents per gallon, roughly 40% higher than the current federal tax. This tax rate corresponds to an average tax of 1.15 cents per mile. We also consider the effect of using the VMT tax to raise $23 billion and calculate that the required VMT tax rate is 0.93 cents per mile.

Figure 9 shows the distributional results of adopting a VMT tax versus adjusting the gasoline tax. Panel a shows drops in mileage in the top six deciles of the expenditure distribution under a VMT tax relative to a gasoline tax. The average decline is about 1.2%. Panel b shows the average taxes paid by household, by tax scheme. The first through sixth deciles pay significantly less under the VMT tax than under the fuel tax. Taxes even out in the seventh expenditure decile, and increase through the rest of the distribution. At the lowest decile, households save on average of $32 per year in federal fuel taxes with the VMT tax, and the average tax burden on households in the highest expenditure decile rises from $191 to $305. Again, we show in figure C3 that these results are driven primarily by changes in the vehicle-fleet composition rather than the specific elasticity governing households' driving responses to increases in travel costs.

We also explore average taxes paid by drivers of each type of vehicle—gasoline, hybrid, and electric—under the VMT tax with the future fleet. Table 4 shows the annual average taxes paid per household, by expenditure decile and vehicle type. The first column presents payments under the 2017 composition and baseline taxes. The second column shows payments using the future-fleet VMT proposal without allowing for the behavioral response described in equation (3); that is, this calculation sets the price

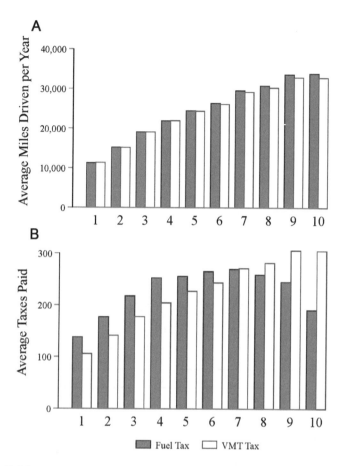

Fig. 9. Raising constant revenues with gas tax versus VMT (future fleet). Data are from the 2017 National Household Transportation Survey (NHTS). Panels show the mean miles traveled and mean federal taxes paid, comparing a gasoline tax and a vehicle miles traveled (VMT) tax calibrated to match current revenues inflated by 15% in line with the vehicle fleet expansion. The figures use the forecast vehicle fleet, assuming a 60%/40% split of new nongasoline vehicles by electric and hybrid. All results conditional on having positive predicted expenditures. A color version of this figure is available online.

elasticity of travel demand to 0. The third column shows payments using the full behavioral model under the future VMT-tax proposal.

Under the current tax policy, hybrid and electric vehicles pay significantly less or even no gasoline tax relative to households with gasoline vehicles. Comparing the second and third columns, for gasoline vehicles, the increase in per-mile costs under the future VMT tax induce an increase in taxes paid, with little adjustment due to behavioral response, on account

Table 4
Mean Taxes Paid by Expenditure Decile: Future Fleet with VMT

	Baseline ($)	Paid (No ΔMiles) ($)	Paid (ΔMiles) ($)
	Gasoline Vehicles		
1	91	103	103
2	121	129	129
3	151	158	158
4	177	181	181
5	192	193	192
6	207	194	193
7	231	197	197
8	235	193	192
9	255	184	183
10	256	158	157
	Hybrid Vehicles		
1	29	88	82
2	67	99	92
3	57	106	98
4	71	119	110
5	54	143	133
6	59	153	142
7	59	161	149
8	58	157	146
9	66	165	154
10	70	178	165
	Electric Vehicles		
1	0	88	82
2	0	99	92
3	0	106	98
4	0	119	110
5	0	143	133
6	0	153	142
7	0	160	149
8	0	157	146
9	0	165	154
10	0	178	165

Note: This table shows the mean amount of federal taxes paid per household, by vehicle type and expenditure decile, for three scenarios. In the first column, we present annual federal fuel taxes paid by vehicle type under the current federal gasoline tax. In the second column, we present annual taxes paid under our vehicle miles traveled (VMT) tax proposal, assuming no change in driving behavior after the policy change. In the final column, we present annual user fees paid under our VMT proposal, allowing for driving behavior to respond to changes in per-mile driving costs induced by the tax change. We calibrate the VMT tax to match current revenues inflated by 15%, use the 2037 forecast vehicle fleet, with a 60%/40% battery electric vehicle/hybrid electric vehicle breakdown of new vehicles. For households with multiple types of vehicles (e.g., a gasoline vehicle and a hybrid vehicle), total payment is split across the categories.

of the low relative change in the price paid before and after policy adoption. In contrast, we estimate that the group with the largest increase in per-mile costs, electric vehicle owners, would pay about 8% more in driving-related taxes if they did not adjust their driving behavior in response to the per-mile price increase.

None of these calculations include the potential benefits of reducing other taxes that are currently levied to fund highway maintenance, or the lower driving externalities, such as reduced congestion and emissions, that might be associated with higher taxes. We note that a VMT tax would not be levied at the gas pump, but rather might be paid in a few installments each year. This could affect price salience and might change the price elasticity of demand for miles traveled.

VI. Distributional Effects of a Commercial VMT Tax

Section V focused on a VMT tax levied on household vehicle use, but we can also consider a CVMT tax as a replacement for or addition to the current federal excise tax of $0.24 per gallon on diesel fuel. In addition to diesel-fuel charges, commercial truckers also pay some per-truck fees for interstate highway use. This results in trucks often maximizing their loads, which can increase road damage because the marginal damage function rises sharply in weight per axle. In most states, the majority of trucking taxes paid are fuel taxes, registration fees, and tire taxes. Small et al. (1989) note that in a handful of states, taxes have varied by miles traveled or by vehicle weight. New Mexico, New York, and Oregon have adopted VMT taxes for commercial trucks that varies with the trucks' maximum load capacity.[15] These state taxes vary from 1 cent to 29 cents per mile, as a function of the weight of the truck. Kentucky has a flat-rate CVMT of 3 cents per mile, regardless of truck weight.

Our analysis of the CVMT tax differs from that of the personal driver VMT tax in two ways. First, we consider the CVMT tax as an addition to, not a replacement for, the existing diesel tax. This allows us to start from the status quo costs per miles driven and add the new tax per mile. Second, because the CVMT tax is levied on intermediate goods (transport services), to describe the incidence on households, we need to determine how it would affect the end-user price of traded goods. This unifies our analysis of the commercial and personal VMT tax policies. For the CVMT tax, we first estimate the share of trucking service costs and indirect diesel taxes in household expenditures, and then explore how an add-on CVMT tax would affect household expenditures. We incorporate data from the

Bureau of Economic Analysis (BEA) Total Requirements tables, specifically the "Industry by Commodity/After Redefinitions/Producer Value" table for 2012, the most recent data available. These tables provide estimates of the inputs required, measured in dollars, to produce one dollar's worth of a given output. We focus on the trucking transportation inputs needed to produce various consumer products listed in the CEX Table 1203.[16]

A. Current Distributional Burdens of the Federal Diesel Excise Tax

Before considering a CVMT tax, we examine the distribution of burdens associated with the current diesel-fuel tax. This analysis proceeds in the spirit of several earlier studies of both current diesel taxes and prospective CVMT taxes, including Austin (2015), Bieder and Austin (2019), and Carloni and Dinan (2021). The total requirements tables list inputs and outputs by industry code, North American Industry Classification System code, or commodity code. We link these to CEX expenditure categories. When necessary, we average the trucking costs of various products in the BEA table that are aggregated within a given CEX category. This linkage matches between 70% and 88% of the expenditures of households in the bottom eight deciles of the spending distribution. The match rate in the highest spending decile is only 59% of spending, reflecting higher expenditure shares on nontradable goods and services we were unable to crosswalk. If we exclude outlays on retirement saving and pensions—items that are included as expenditures in the CEX—our match rate rises to more than 90% for the bottom eight expenditure deciles and at least 78% in the top two deciles. For consistency with our household VMT tax analysis, however, we continue to calculate tax burdens as a fraction of total CEX expenditure.

Across all CEX categories, truck transportation services account for about 0.72 cents of each dollar of household expenditure. There is substantial variation in the trucking share across commodities. For example, rental dwellings have a low share, at 0.04 cents per dollar of expenditure, and gasoline and petroleum products are high-share goods, at 1.7 cents per dollar of household expenditure. To place the CEX values in context, we note that trucking contributes to 0.8% of gross domestic product (GDP) (Bureau of Transportation Statistics 2018). Because our estimates from the Total Requirements analysis fall a bit below this, we inflate all our trucking shares upward by about 10% to match this GDP metric.

To calculate a household's indirect diesel-tax burden, we combine the micro expenditures on trucking with macro data on revenue collected by diesel taxes. The Congressional Budget Office (2020) reports that in 2020, the federal government collected $10.5 billion in diesel-tax revenues. Beider and Austin (2019) estimate that households spend, indirectly, between 0.02% and 0.06% of their income on diesel taxes. Our earlier estimates from the CEX suggest spending of about 0.3% of income on the federal gasoline tax. These statistics would place the indirect diesel-tax burden on households at about 15% of the gasoline-tax burden, even though federal diesel revenues are about 40% of gasoline-tax revenues. Our estimates thus suggest that households indirectly bear about one-third of the diesel-tax burden; this indicates that there are likely additional goods that indirectly use diesel fuel in their production chain but are not well captured in our analysis.

To determine the burden of diesel taxes across the distribution of households, we allocate the diesel-tax revenue to households based on our estimate of the trucking expenditures they indirectly consume. This reflects in all cases indirect consumption. The diesel expenditure for household i is

$$DieselExp_i = \frac{TruckExp_i}{\sum_i TruckExp_i} \times \frac{10.5 \times \frac{1}{3}}{w_i}, \tag{5}$$

where w_i denotes the household's sample weight. We also calculate indirect diesel share of expenditures as $DieselShare_i = (DieselExp_i)/(\sum_c Exp_{ic})$, where we sum across all spending categories, c, within a household.

The two panels in figure 10 provide information on average indirect diesel-tax expenditure shares and diesel taxes paid by expenditure decile. Panel a shows that the total share of diesel taxes in the average household's expenditures ranges from 0.020% of total expenditure at the highest decile to 0.027% in the lowest decile. The share of imputed diesel taxes in total expenditures generally declines with total expenditures. Panel b shows that households in the lowest expenditure decile can expect to purchase goods each year that embody about $3 of federal diesel taxes. These households account for less than 3% of indirect diesel-fuel consumption. The highest-expenditure households consume goods, on average, that include $31 per year in embodied diesel taxes. These households collectively consume about one-quarter of the indirect household-sector use of diesel fuel.

B.   Distributional Burdens of a Commercial VMT Tax

We consider a 3-cent-per-mile flat-rate CVMT tax similar to that currently in place in Kentucky. To place this in context, assuming that the average

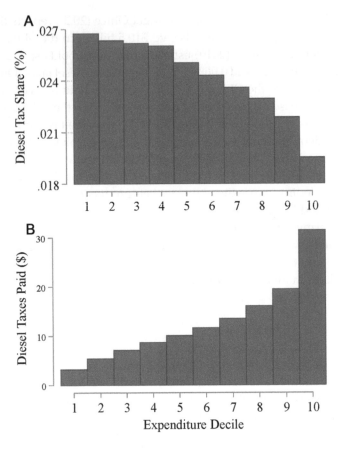

Fig. 10. Diesel tax shares and amount paid annually, by expenditure decile. Data are from the Bureau of Economic Analysis 2012 input-output tables, crosswalked to the Consumer Expenditures Survey (CEX) 2017 household expenditure categories. Panel *a* plots the diesel taxes paid indirectly as a share of household expenditure, by expenditure decile. Panel *b* shows the average annual indirect expenditures, in dollars, for households by expenditure decile. A color version of this figure is available online.

diesel truck delivers a fuel efficiency of about 6.65 MPG, the federal diesel excise tax of 24.4 cents per gallon translates to a per-mile charge of about 3.8 cents. Adding a 3-cent-per-mile CVMT tax would raise the total tax burden by about 81%.

To analyze the impact of adopting a commercial VMT, we calculate the change in expenditures needed to purchase a household's original consumption bundle under the assumption that the CVMT tax is fully passed forward in the prices of consumer goods. Final expenditure on any item c, e_{ic}^t, can be decomposed into expenditure on the good, and

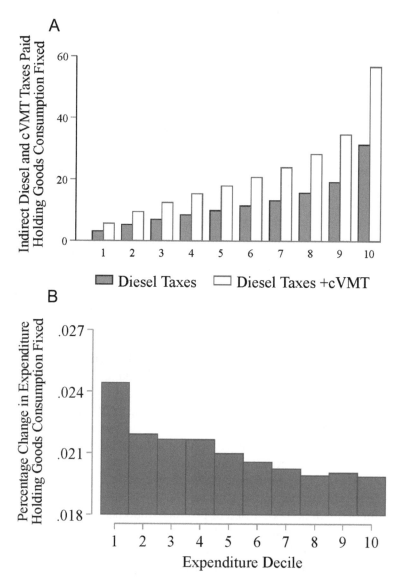

Fig. 11. Change in expenditure needed to maintain original consumption basket, by expenditure decile. Data are from the Bureau of Economic Analysis 2012 input-output tables, crosswalked to the Consumer Expenditures Survey (CEX) 2017 household expenditure categories. The figure presents the amounts of additional expenditure needed to purchase the original consumption bundle observed in the CEX, under the adoption of a new federal vehicle miles traveled (VMT) tax of $0.03/mile. Panel *a* presents the results in dollars, comparing the baseline scenario (analogous to fig. 10*b*) to the tax scheme with both diesel taxes and commercial VMT (cVMT) taxes. Panel *b* presents the percentage change in expenditure needed to accommodate this change in indirect diesel tax exposure, to keep consumption bundles constant. A color version of this figure is available online.

the expenditure on the diesel-tax component necessary to ship the good to the purchaser: $e_{ic}^t = \text{good}_{ic}^t + \text{tax}_{ic}^t$. If each household, indexed by i, spends a portion of its consumption basket α_c^t on trucking-related diesel taxes, then the burden of the new CVMT tax can be computed from the difference between α_c^0 (no CVMT tax) and α_c^1 (CVMT tax in place). We can distribute the CVMT burden based on these patterns across households. To calculate how required expenditure changes, we need to estimate the impact of the CVMT tax on α_c^t.

We assume that the distribution of the CVMT tax across trucking service providers is the same as the distribution of the current diesel tax. Our estimates suggest that consumers spend $12, on average, per year on indirect diesel taxes, and they spend $312 on average on embodied trucking services. Diesel taxes therefore comprise about 4% of trucking costs. Assuming all other costs are constant, the increment to trucking costs from a CVMT tax that raises the tax burden on trucking by about 81% must be $\Delta \text{Trucking Cost}_c^0 = (0.81) \times (0.04) \times \text{Trucking Cost}_c^0$. This expression implies that adoption of a 3-cent-per-mile CVMT tax would raise the total cost of trucking services by about 3.2%, with the sum of diesel and CVMT taxes accounting for a little more than 7% of the trucking costs. In the language used above, this implies that $\alpha_c^0 = 0.04 \times \text{Trucking Cost}_c^0$ and $\alpha_c^1 = 0.07 \times 1.0324 \times \text{Trucking Cost}_c^0$, where Trucking Cost_c^0 refers to the dollars of trucking required to produce final good c.

Figure 11 displays the results of implementing a CVMT tax on the required expenditures of households in different expenditure deciles. For those in the lowest expenditure decile, total expenditure needs to increase by 0.0245% to accommodate the near doubling of per-mile federal trucking taxes. This declines to 0.02% for the middle expenditure deciles, and falls further to 0.0195% for the top deciles. In dollar terms, the implied federal tax burden of product-embodied federal diesel-tax and CVMT-tax increases associated with taxes on trucking rises, for those in the lowest decile, from $3.12 to $5.65 per year. Those in the highest expenditure decile see their indirect payments rise from $31.40 to $56.75.

VII. Conclusion

This paper studies the impact of imposing a VMT tax on personal transportation services associated with the light-duty vehicle fleet or on commercial trucking services that are intermediate inputs to household consumption. The analysis draws on data from the 2017 NHTS and CEX to examine the burden these taxes would place on households in different strata of the income or expenditure distribution. Several findings emerge from this analysis.

First, with the current light-duty vehicle fleet, the distributional burden of a VMT tax is similar to that of a gasoline excise tax. Only 2% of the vehicle stock was hybrid or electric in 2017. Even though these vehicles are skewed toward the highest income and expenditure households, and households that own these vehicles pay less in gasoline excise taxes, the overall difference in the impact of a VMT tax-for-gasoline tax swap across income or expenditure deciles is small.

Second, in about 15 years, when current projections suggest that about one-third of the vehicle fleet will be made up of battery-electric and hybrid-electric vehicles, the choice between a gasoline tax and a VMT tax is more important from the standpoint of tax-burden distribution. If households at the top of the income and expenditure distribution continue to be the primary buyers of BHEVs, then the gasoline tax will become more regressive over time, and the VMT tax, by expanding the tax base to all vehicles, could preserve the revenue stream associated with the current gasoline tax and distribute the burden of the tax in a less regressive fashion. Whether the future distribution of BHEVs will skew as strongly toward high-income households as the current distribution is an important source of uncertainty in our analysis, however, especially in light of limitations in the availability of tax credits for EV purchases that were enacted in the 2022 IRA.

The third finding regards a commercial VMT tax levied on the trucking sector, which currently pays the diesel-fuel excise tax at a rate of 3 cents per mile for commercial trucking, raising about $3 billion per year. If such a tax were fully passed through to consumers in the form of higher goods prices for products that required truck transportation, it would place burdens on households that vary with their total expenditures. The burden of the price increases associated with such a tax would vary from roughly $2.50 per year for households in the lowest expenditure decile to about $26 per year in the highest decile. The burden as a share of total expenditures is modestly higher in the bottom half than the top half of the expenditure distribution, reflecting the larger budget share of tradable goods (which are transported) relative to services in the budgets of low-income households.

There are many open questions on the distributional impact, and other economic effects, of VMTs that warrant future study. We have not considered potential differences in the average number of miles driven per year by BHEVs and gasoline-powered vehicles, although research on the current BHEV fleet suggests that they may be used less intensively than their ICE-powered counterparts. This may be due, in part, to the limited range of many first-generation battery-electric vehicles; driving patterns may change as new BEVs with longer range are introduced. We have not considered the economic determinants of vehicle scrappage decisions or the potential trickle-down of BHEVs from high-income initial buyers to middle- and lower-income households, a prospect that may be accelerated by credits for used BHEV purchases by modest-income households that were adopted in the 2022 IRA. With regard to the CVMT, we have assumed complete pass-through of taxes to consumers, and we have not allowed for any product substitution at the household level in response to higher embodied transportation costs.

Although the paper focuses on gasoline and VMT taxes, it also presents information on the distribution of various user fees that fund public-transportation infrastructure. We find that different user charges have different distributional burdens. Although buses are disproportionately used by low-income households, commuter-rail ridership tilts toward higher-income groups. Our analysis has not considered a number of special programs that may affect the progressivity of user fees. For example, many public-transit authorities offer discounts for students or senior citizens, in line with reduced fare requirements that are a precondition for federal funding (CFR Title 49, Section 609). Some also offer low-income fare adjustments. These provisions have important effects in improving the progressivity of user fees for financing these transportation modes. The Infrastructure Investment and Jobs Act of 2021 includes more than $100 billion for public transportation, with equity and modernization highlighted as key policy goals. User-fee financing could provide a way of expanding the revenue base for new public-transit projects. We hope to consider in future work how various public-transportation policies that create differentials in user fees across households in different income strata affect the distributional burdens of these fees.

Appendix A

Technological Adoption and the Progressivity of the Gas Tax

This appendix presents a stylized model that focuses on informing the interplay between household income and adoption of an energy-saving technology such as BHEVs. The model assumes that individuals choose one of two technologies and the number of miles they drive. The choice of technology determines the energy use per mile (denoted g_i), the fixed cost of purchase (denoted k_i), and the pleasure of driving (denoted α_i). Utility from using technology i is defined as

$$U = (Y - p_g g_i d - k_i)^{(1-\rho)} + \alpha_i d^{(1-\rho)}, \tag{A1}$$

where Y is income, p_g represents the price of gas, d is the endogenous distance traveled, and $\rho > 0$. We assume a benchmark technology "0" and an energy-saving technology "1," where $g_0 > g_1$. Conditional upon the choice of technology i, the total spending on energy equals $(Y - k_i)/(1 + (p_g^{\rho-1} g_i^{\rho-1} \alpha_i)^{-1/\rho})$. It increases with income and the composite term $\alpha_i g_i^{\rho-1}$, which captures the combined impact on the technology's marginal parameter on driving. Energy use can decline with income if high-income households are more likely to adopt the energy-saving technology. The following proposition describes the link between energy-saving technology adoption and income.

Proposition.

(a) If $k_0 > k_1$ and $\alpha_1/\alpha_0 > (g_1/g_0)^{1-\rho}$, then all individuals adopt the energy-saving technology, and energy consumption rises with income. If $k_0 < k_1$ and $\alpha_1/\alpha_0 < (g_1/g_0)^{1-\rho}$, then no one adopts the energy-saving technology, and energy consumption rises with income.

(b) If $k_0 > k_1$ and $(g_1/g_0)^{1-\rho} > \alpha_1/\alpha_0$, then individuals adopt the energy-saving technology if and only if $Y > Y^*$, where Y^* is a finite value of $Y > k_0$. Energy consumption rises continuously everywhere with Y, except at the point Y^*. At $Y = Y^*$, energy consumption increases discontinuously with Y if and only if $1 > (Y^* - k_0)/(Y^* - k_1) > (\alpha_1 g_1^{\rho-1})/(\alpha_0 g_0^{\rho-1})$.

(c) If $k_0 < k_1$ and $(g_1/g_0)^{1-\rho} < \alpha_1/\alpha_0$, then individuals adopt the clean technology if and only if $Y > Y^{**}$, where Y^{**} is a finite value of $Y > k_1$. Energy consumption rises everywhere with Y, except at the point Y^{**}. At $Y = Y^{**}$, energy consumption decreases discontinuously with Y if and only if $(Y^{**} - k_0)/(Y^{**} - k_1) > (\alpha_1 g_1^{\rho-1})/(\alpha_0 g_0^{\rho-1}) > 1$.

The conditions $(Y^{**} - k_0)/(Y^{**} - k_1) > (\alpha_1 g_1^{\rho-1})/(\alpha_0 g_0^{\rho-1})$ and $(Y^* - k_0)/(Y^* - k_1) > (\alpha_1 g_1^{\rho-1})/(\alpha_0 g_0^{\rho-1})$ are equivalent to the condition $(1 + (p_g g_1)^{(\rho-1)/\rho} \alpha_1^{1/\rho}) / (1 + (p_g g_0)^{(\rho-1)/\rho} \alpha_0^{1/\rho}) > (((p_g g_1)^{(\rho-1)/\rho} \alpha_1^{1/\rho}) / ((p_g g_0)^{(\rho-1)/\rho} \alpha_0^{1/\rho}))^{(1-\rho)}$, which is written only in terms of exogenous variables.

This proposition details three possible scenarios for energy-saving technologies and the relationship between income and energy use. In the parameter ranges covered in part (a) of the proposition, the green technology is either adopted for all values of Y or not adopted for all values of Y. As all individuals use the same technology, richer people use more energy.

The parameters discussed in part (b) seem relevant for the 1970s and 1980s. Energy-saving cars, such as the Honda Civic, were typically much smaller and less expensive than gas-intensive cars such as Cadillacs. Energy savings arose primarily from having less weight and less power. Consequently, the green technology was adopted by lower- rather than higher-income households. Energy use rises with income almost everywhere, and it may jump up with income at the point of technology adoption, as long as the price gap between the two cars is not too large. If the up-front cost of two technologies is similar, which is guaranteed by $(Y^* - k_0)/(Y^* - k_1) > (\alpha_1 g_1^{\rho-1})/(\alpha_0 g_0^{\rho-1})$, then the post-purchase parameter aggregate $\alpha_i g_i^{\rho-1}$ determine the change in energy use, and we have assumed $\alpha_0 g_0^{\rho-1} > \alpha_1 g_1^{\rho-1}$ in part (b).

If the up-front cost difference is larger, then this cost will have effectively an "income effect," which means that the Cadillac buyer is pushed to drive less. The condition that $(Y^* - k_0)/(Y^* - k_1) > \alpha_1 g_1^{\rho-1} \alpha_0 g_0^{\rho-1}$ ensures that the "substitution effects" associated with the Cadillac (more fun to drive and more gas per mile) overwhelm that income effect.

The parameters discussed in part (c) are oriented toward new, expensive technologies that reduce energy use but cost more. Expensive EVs such as Teslas reduce energy use, but they are also typically more powerful and quieter. The proposition predicts that if $k_0 < k_1$ and $(g_1/g_0)^{1-\rho} < \alpha_1/\alpha_0$, then the green technology is adopted by the rich. Again, energy use is rising almost everywhere with income, but in this case, energy use jumps downward with income at the point of adoption if k_0 is low relative to k_1, that $(Y^{**} - k_0)/(Y^{**} - k_1) > (\alpha_1 g_1^{\rho-1})/(\alpha_0 g_0^{\rho-1}) > 1$ holds. In this case, price inequality is needed to generate the added income effect that pushes driving down for the Tesla driver. It is not enough for the expensive EV Tesla just to be gas-efficient to satisfy this condition, given our functional form, because improvements in gas mileage are offset by extra driving.

Proof of Proposition.

(a) Conditional upon adopting technology i, the optimal level of driving satisfies $d_i^* = (\alpha_i^{1/\rho}(Y - k_i))/((p_g g_i)^{1/\rho} + p_g g_i \alpha_i^{1/\rho})$, which implies that welfare is $(1 + (p_g g_i)^{(\rho-1)/\rho} \alpha_i^{1/\rho})^\rho (Y - k_i)^{1-\rho}$.

Consequently the net benefit of adoption technology 1 can be written as $F(Y) = (1 + (p_g g_1)^{(\rho-1)/\rho} \alpha_1^{1/\rho})^\rho (Y - k_1)^{1-\rho} - (1 + (p_g g_0)^{(\rho-1)/\rho} \alpha_0^{1/\rho})^\rho$ $(Y - k_0)^{1-\rho}$, which is positive if and only if $(1 + (p_g g_1)^{(\rho-1)/\rho} \alpha_1^{1/\rho})/(1 + (p_g g_0)^{(\rho-1)/\rho} \alpha_0^{1/\rho} > (Y - k_0)/(Y - k_1)^{(1-\rho)/\rho}$.

If $k_0 > k_1$ and $\alpha_1/\alpha_0 > (g_1/g_0)^{1-\rho}$, then $1 + (p_g g_1)^{(\rho-1)/\rho} \alpha_1^{1/\rho} > 1 + (p_g g_0)^{(\rho-1)/\rho} \alpha_0^{1\rho}$ and $(Y - k_1)^{1-\rho} > (Y - k_0)^{1-\rho}$ for all values of Y, and consequently all income groups adopt.

If $k_0 < k_1$ and $\alpha_1/\alpha_0 < (g_1/g_0)^{1-\rho}$, then $1 + (p_g g_1)^{(\rho-1)/\rho} \alpha_1^{1/\rho} < 1 + (p_g g_0)^{(\rho-1)/\rho} \alpha_0^{1\rho}$ and $(Y - k_1)^{1-\rho} < (Y - k_0)^{1-\rho}$ for all values of Y, and consequently no income groups adopt.

(b) If $k_0 > k_1$ and $\alpha_1/\alpha_0 < (g_1/g_0)^{1-\rho}$, then $0 < (1 + (p_g g_1)^{(\rho-1)/\rho} \alpha_1^{1/\rho})/$ $(1 + (p_g g_0)^{(\rho-1)/\rho} \alpha_0^{1/\rho}) < 1$, and the inequality can be written as $Y <$ $((1 + (p_g g_0)^{(\rho-1)/\rho} \alpha_0^{1/\rho})^{\rho/(1-\rho)} k_0 - (1 + (p_g g_1)^{(\rho-1)/\rho} \alpha_1^{1/\rho})^{\rho/(1-\rho)} k_1) / ((1 +$ $(p_g g_0)^{(\rho-1)/\rho} \alpha_0^{1/\rho})^{\rho/(1-\rho)} - (1 + (p_g g_1)^{(\rho-1)/\rho} \alpha_1^{1/\rho})^{\rho/(1-\rho)}) = Y^*$.

Hence there is a value of Y, denoted Y^*, at which $(1 + (p_g g_1)^{(\rho-1)/\rho} \alpha_1^{1/\rho})/(1 + (p_g g_0)^{(\rho-1)/\rho} \alpha_0^{1/\rho}) = ((Y - k_0)/(Y - k_1))^{(1-\rho)/\rho}$. For all values of $Y > Y^*$, welfare is higher with technology 0. For all values of $Y < Y^*$, welfare is higher with technology 1. Miles traveled and hence gas consumption is increasing continuously at all levels of Y other than Y^* (because within a technology $d = (\alpha_i^{1/\rho}(Y - k_i))/((p_g g_i)^{1/\rho} + p_g g_i \alpha_i^{1/\rho}))$, but at Y^*, gas consumption jumps from $g_1 d_1^*$ to $g_0 d_0^*$, where $g_i d_i^* = ((\alpha_i g_i^{\rho-1})^{1/\rho}(Y - k_i))/(p_g^{1/\rho} + p_g (\alpha_i g_i^{\rho-1})^{1/\rho})$.

Using the fact that $(1 + (p_g g_1)^{(\rho-1)/\rho} \alpha_1^{1/\rho})/(1 + (p_g g_0)^{(\rho-1)/\rho} \alpha_0^{1/\rho}) = ((Y^* - k_0)/(Y^* - k_1))^{(1-\rho)/\rho}$, then inequality simplifies to $(Y^* - k_0)/$ $(Y^* - k_1) > (\alpha_1 g_1^{\rho-1})/(\alpha_0 g_0^{\rho-1})$, or $(1 + (p_g g_1)^{(\rho-1)/\rho} \alpha_1^{1/\rho})/(1 +$ $(p_g g_0)^{(\rho-1)/\rho} \alpha_0^{1/\rho}) > (((p_g g_1)^{(\rho-1)/\rho} \alpha_1^{1/\rho})/((p_g g_0)^{(\rho-1)/\rho} \alpha_0^{1/\rho}))^{1-\rho}$.

(c) If $k_0 < k_1$ and $(\alpha_1)/(\alpha_0) > ((g_1)/(g_0))^{1-\rho}$, then $(1 + (p_g g_1)^{(\rho-1)/\rho} \alpha_1^{1/\rho})/$ $(1 + (p_g g_0)^{(\rho-1)/\rho} \alpha_0^{1/\rho}) > 1$, and the inequality can be written $Y >$ $((1 + (p_g g_1)^{(\rho-1)/\rho} \alpha_1^{1/\rho})^{\rho/(1-\rho)} k_1 - (1 + (p_g g_0)^{(\rho-1)/\rho} \alpha_0^{1/\rho})^{\rho/(1-\rho)} k_0) / ((1 +$ $(p_g g_1)^{(\rho-1)/\rho} \alpha_1^{1/\rho})^{\rho/(1-\rho)} - (1 + (p_g g_0)^{(\rho-1)/\rho} \alpha_0^{1/\rho})^{\rho/(1-\rho)}) = Y^{**}$.

Hence there exists a value of Y, denoted Y^{**} at which $(1 + (p_g g_1)^{(\rho-1)/\rho} \alpha_1^{1/\rho}) / ((1 + (p_g g_0)^{(\rho-1)/\rho} \alpha_0^{1/\rho}) = ((Y - k_0) / (Y - k_1))^{(1-\rho)/\rho}$, and for all values of Y below Y^{**}, individuals choose technology 0, and for all values of Y above Y^{**}, individuals choose technology 1. Gas consumption will drop discontinuously down as income rises at the point if and only if $(Y^{**} - k_0)/(Y^{**} - k_1) > (\alpha_1 g_1^{\rho-1})/(\alpha_0 g_0^{\rho-1}) > 1$ or $(1 + (p_g g_1)^{(\rho-1)/\rho} \alpha_1^{1/\rho}) / (1 + (p_g g_0)^{(\rho-1)/\rho} \alpha_0^{1/\rho}) > (((p_g g_1)^{(\rho-1)/\rho} \alpha_1^{1/\rho})/$ $((p_g g_0)^{(\rho-1)/\rho} \alpha_0^{1/\rho}))^{1-\rho}$.

Appendix B

Table B1
Replication of 2019 Consumer Expenditure Survey, Table 1203

Item	All	<$15,000	$15,000–$29,999	$30,000–$39,999	$40,000–$49,999	$50,000–$69,000	$70,000–$99,999	$100,000–$149,000	$150,000–$199,999	$200,000+
					Table 1203					
Number of CUs	132,242	15,848	19,856	12,991	11,208	17,470	19,119	18,225	8,266	9,260
Pretax income ($)	82,852	7,574	22,189	34,772	44,831	59,328	83,558	121,433	171,061	343,498
Annual expenditure ($)	63,036	26,194	34,201	$40,942	47,299	54,212	66,801	84,994	109,020	160,318
Gas, other fuels, motor oil ($)	2,094	970	1,170	1,699	$1,864	2,153	2,496	2,927	3,181	3,283
					Replication of Table 1203 Using PUMD					
Number of CUs	132,242	15,742	19,720	12,910	11,145	17,432	19,044	17,885	7,477	10,815
Pretax income ($)	82,451	7,368	22,048	34,643	44,679	59,122	83,592	120,952	170,183	309,772
Annual expenditure ($)	59,280	24,716	31,944	39,308	44,086	50,980	63,647	79,859	99,337	142,784
Gas, other fuels, motor oil ($)	2,094	961	1,171	1,701	1,863	2,142	2,507	2,911	3,177	3,223

Note: This table replicates Table 1203 from the Survey of Consumer Expenditures annual release for the year 2019. Replication errors occur due to sampling and adjustments made to the public-use microdata (PUMD) to maintain consumer unit (CU) anonymity.

Table B2

Forecasting Vehicle Registrations, Sales, and Retirement (in thousands)

Year	ΔRegistrations$_{t,t-1}$	$\widehat{\text{Sales}_t}$	$\widehat{\text{share}_t^{\text{BHEV}}}$	Sales$_t^{\text{BHEV}}$	Sales$_t^{\text{ICE}}$	Retire$_t$
2017	3,249	16,827	3.3	555	16,272	13,578
2018	673	16,919	3.9	660	16,259	16,246
2019	2,931	16,630	4.2	698	15,932	13,699
2020	1,768	14,114	5.4	762	13,352	12,346
2021	1,781	15,055	6.6	995	14,060	13,275
2022	1,793	15,015	8.1	1,215	13,800	13,222
2023	1,805	14,975	9.9	1,483	13,492	13,169
2024	1,818	14,934	12.2	1,810	13,124	13,117
2025	1,830	14,894	14.8	2,210	12,685	13,064
2026	1,843	14,854	18.2	2,697	12,157	13,011
2027	1,856	14,814	22.2	3,293	11,521	12,958
2028	1,869	14,774	27.2	4,019	10,755	12,905
2029	1,882	14,734	33.3	4,906	9,828	12,851
2033	1,936	14,573	56.2	8,193	6,380	12,638
2034	1,949	14,533	62.2	9,046	5,487	12,584
2035	1,963	14,493	67.9	9,843	4,650	12,530
2036	1,976	14,453	73.1	10,566	3,887	12,476
2037	1,990	14,413	77.7	11,203	3,210	12,422
Total				92,407	205,730	260,748

Note: Data on vehicle registrations and sales by fuel type are from *Transportation Energy Data Book, Edition 39* produced by Oak Ridge National Laboratory for the Department of Energy (2021). Sales and share hybrid/electric based on data up to 2020; registration data through 2019. Additional years authors' forecast. BHEV = battery and hybrid electric vehicles; ICE = internal combustion engine.

Table B3
Creating a Forecast for 2037 NHTS Data

Decile	(1) Vehicles^{2017}	(2) BHEV^{2017}	(3) ICE^{2017}	(4) P(Decile|BHEV)	(5) Vehicles^{2037}	(6) BHEV^{2037}	(7) ICE^{2037}	(8) ΔVehicles	(9) ΔBHEV	(10) ΔICE
1	11,013	41	10,972	.72	12,665	646	12,019	1,652	605	1,047
2	15,093	113	14,980	1.99	17,357	1,784	15,573	2,264	1,671	593
3	18,100	174	17,926	3.05	20,815	2,735	18,080	2,715	2,561	154
4	20,072	251	19,821	4.42	23,083	3,963	19,120	3,011	3,712	−701
5	22,312	356	21,956	6.25	25,659	5,604	20,055	3,347	5,248	−1,901
6	25,896	491	25,405	8.63	29,780	7,738	22,042	3,884	7,247	−3,363
7	28,177	713	27,464	12.55	32,404	11,253	21,151	4,227	10,540	−6,313
8	28,658	859	27,799	15.11	32,957	13,549	19,408	4,299	12,690	−8,391
9	30,005	1,161	28,844	20.44	34,506	18,328	16,178	4,501	17,167	−12,666
10	29,998	1,526	28,472	26.85	34,498	24,075	10,423	4,500	22,549	−18,049
Total	229,324	5,685	223,639	100.01	263,723	89,665	174,056	34,399	83,990	−49,591

Note: Data in columns 1–4 are based on 2017 National Household Travel Survey (NHTS) vehicle-level survey aggregated to households, by authors' household expenditure deciles. Data in columns 5–7 are based on year 2037 stock of BHEV (battery-electric and hybrid-electric vehicles) and ICE (internal combustion engine) vehicles according to authors' forecast, assuming constant distribution of BHEVs across expenditure deciles. Columns 8–10 show the difference between 2017 and 2037 findings.

Table B4

Crosswalk from BEA's Total Requirements to CEX Expenditure Categories

BEA Input-Output Commodity	CEX Category	Truck Transportation Share
All other food and drinking places	Food away from home	.0070593
Amusement parks and arcades	Fees and admissions	.0090132
Automotive equipment rental and leasing	Vehicle rental, leases, licenses, and other charges	.0043736
Automotive repair and maintenance	Vehicle maintenance and repairs	.0077437
Book publishers	Reading	.0110228
Child day care services	Education	.0078640
Civic, social, professional, and similar organizations	Cash contributions	.0070915
Clothing and clothing accessories stores	Apparel and services	.0090630
Direct life insurance carriers	Life and other personal insurance	.0009194
Dry-cleaning and laundry services	Household operations	.0094253
Elementary and secondary schools	Education	.0054672
Food and beverage stores	Alcoholic beverages	.0108911
Food and beverage stores	Food at home	.0108911
Full-service restaurants	Food away from home	.0093778
Gasoline stations	Gasoline, other fuels, and motor oil	.0154538
General merchandise stores	Household operations	.0099524
Grantmaking, giving, and social advocacy organizations	Cash contributions	.0048319
Health and personal care stores	Personal care products and services	.0055965
Health and personal care stores	Drugs	.0055965
Health and personal care stores	Medical supplies	.0055965
Home health care services	Medical services	.0052707
Hospitals	Medical services	.0072299
Independent artists, writers, and performers	Fees and admissions	.0008481
Insurance carriers, except direct life	Vehicle insurance	.0010972
Insurance carriers, except direct life	Health insurance	.0010972
Junior colleges, colleges, universities, and professional schools	Education	.0053413
Limited-service restaurants	Food away from home	.0116851
Medical and diagnostic laboratories	Medical services	.0050679
Motor vehicle and parts dealers	Vehicle purchases	.0112025
Museums, historical sites, zoos, and parks	Fees and admissions	.0070809
Newspaper publishers	Reading	.0065464
Nonstore retailers	Household operations	.0072482
Nursing and community care facilities	Medical services	.0067906

BEA Input-Output Commodity	CEX Category	Truck Transportation Share
Offices of dentists	Medical services	.0048821
Offices of other health practitioners	Medical services	.0044240
Offices of physicians	Medical services	.0033476
Other ambulatory health care services	Medical services	.0080157
Other amusement and recreation industries	Fees and admissions	.0167363
Other educational services	Education	.0060345
Other personal services	Household operations	.0041878
Outpatient care centers	Medical services	.0050748
Owner-occupied housing	Owned dwellings	.0013106
Performing arts companies	Fees and admissions	.0044224
Periodical publishers	Reading	.0080464
Personal and household goods repair and maintenance	Household operations	.0035449
Personal care services	Personal care products and services	.0053846
Religious organizations	Cash contributions	.0084143
Residential mental health, substance abuse, and other residential care facilities	Medical services	.0084259
Services to buildings and dwellings	Natural gas	.0091427
Services to buildings and dwellings	Electricity	.0091427
Services to buildings and dwellings	Fuel oil and other fuels	.0091427
Spectator sports	Fees and admissions	.0031418
Tenant-occupied housing	Rented dwellings	.0004256
Veterinary services	Pets	.0130759
Waste management and remediation services	Water and other public services	.0307979
Wired telecommunications carriers	Telephone services	.0042030
Wireless telecommunications carriers (except satellite)	Telephone services	.0071040
Mean truck transportation cost share:		.0072095

Note: Data on total requirements are from the Bureau of Economic Analysis (BEA) total requirements table, for truck transportation industry (input) to all other commodities (output). Truck transportation share denotes the dollars of trucking industry input required, both directly and indirectly, to produce one dollar of the final BEA input-output commodity for final use. Expenditure categories from the Bureau of Labor Statistics "Table 1203, Income before taxes: Annual expenditure means, shares, standard errors, and coefficients of variation, Consumer Expenditure Survey, 2019." Crosswalked by authors. CEX = Consumer Expenditure Survey.

Appendix C

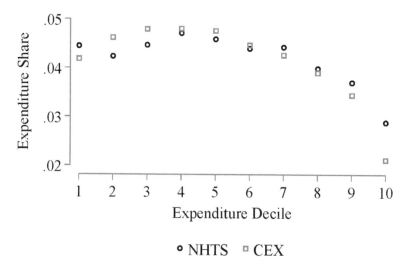

Fig. C1. Expenditure prediction validation: comparing gasoline expenditure in CEX with NHTS. This figure compares the mean gasoline expenditure shares in the National Household Transportation Survey (NHTS) and Consumer Expenditure Survey (CEX) data. We use observed expenditures on gasoline and observed total expenditures from the 2017 CEX. From the 2017 NHTS, we use imputed expenditures from our expenditure model. Gasoline expenditure in the NHTS comes from computing the gas cost per mile, based on fuel-efficiency data from the NHTS and regional gas prices from the EIA, and multiplying by the observed miles traveled in the data. We then take the average gasoline shares, weighted by each survey's respective population weights.

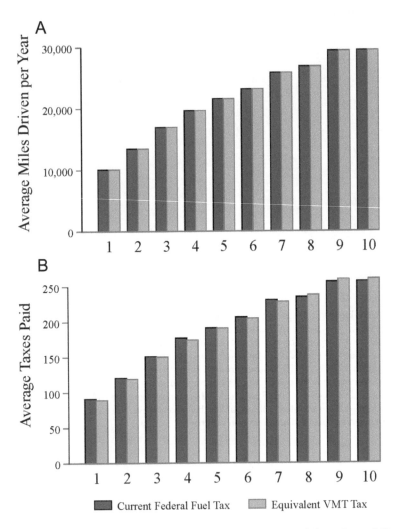

Fig. C2. Baseline versus revenue-neutral VMT (2017), no behavioral channel, $\varepsilon_g = 0$. Data are from the 2017 National Household Transportation Survey. Panels show the mean miles traveled and mean federal taxes paid, comparing the current gasoline tax and proposed revenue-neutral vehicle miles traveled (VMT) tax. All results conditional on having positive predicted expenditures.

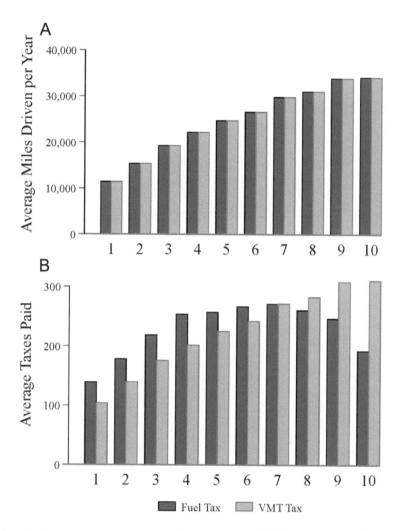

Fig. C3. Raising constant revenues with gas tax versus VMT (future fleet), no behavioral channel, $\varepsilon_g = 0$. Data are from the 2017 National Household Transportation Survey. Panels show the mean miles traveled and mean federal taxes paid, comparing a gasoline tax and a vehicle miles traveled (VMT) tax calibrated to match current revenues inflated by 15% in line with the vehicle fleet expansion. The figures use the forecasted vehicle fleet, assuming a 60%/40% split of new nongasoline vehicles by electric and hybrid. All results conditional on having positive predicted expenditures.

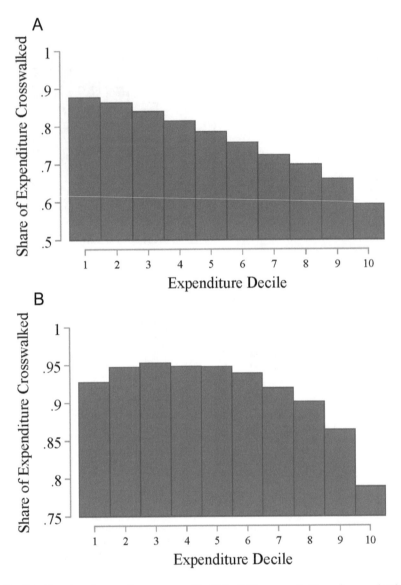

Fig. C4. Fraction of expenditures covered by BEA–CEX crosswalk. These figures plot the share of total expenditures we are able to account for with the crosswalk constructed from table 9. Services that are not traded, such as pension outlays, do not crosswalk from the Bureau of Economic Analysis (BEA) input-output tables to the Consumer Expenditure Survey (CEX) data. Panel *a* plots the share of expenditure we can link to trucking costs, by expenditure decile based on total expenditure, in line with the rest of the results in the paper. Panel *b* plots the share of expenditure we can link, by expenditure decile based on total expenditure (less outlays for retirement and pension funds, as these could be classified as "savings," are a major component of outlays in higher expenditure deciles, and

Endnotes

Author email addresses: Glaeser (eglaeser@harvard.edu), Gorback (caitlin.gorback@mccombs.utexas.edu), Poterba (poterba@mit.edu). Glaeser and Gorback acknowledge support from the US Department of Transportation under NSF grant SES1559013 to the NBER. The authors thank David Austin, Elaine Buckberg, Dorian Carloni, Gilbert Metcalf, Clifford Winston, and participants at the NBER Environmental and Energy Economics Summer Institute and Tax Policy and the Economy conference for helpful comments and guidance. For acknowledgments, sources of research support, and disclosure of the authors' material financial relationships, if any, please see https://www.nber.org/books-and-chapters/tax-policy-and-economy-volume-37/how-regressive-are-mobility-related-user-fees-and-gasoline-taxes.

1. Available at https://www.whitehouse.gov/briefing-room/statements-releases/2022/06/22/fact-sheet-president-biden-calls-for-a-three-month-federal-gas-tax-holiday.

2. See "Finished Motor Gasoline" dispositions available at the US EIA: https://www.eia.gov/dnav/pet/pet_sum_snd_d_nus_mbbl_a_cur-1.htm.

3. The estimated Engel curve appears to underpredict expenditures for high-expenditure households. In 2017, for a CEX household with income of $73,590, the sample average, our estimated Engel curve implies a marginal propensity to spend out of income of 0.33. This is substantially below the average propensity to spend.

4. In the 2001 CEX, gasoline and motor-oil spending equals 3.2% of total expenditure, and in the 2017 CEX, the comparable value is 3.3%. In 2020, the expenditure share for gasoline and motor oil was 2.6%, presumably lower than in the past because of both low gasoline prices and low driving during the pandemic.

5. See Bureau of Transportation Statistics 2022, https://www.bts.gov/content/average-fuel-efficiency-us-light-duty-vehicles.

6. Our CEX sample includes fewer rural households than the population. Although the 2017 CEX has 8% "rural" and 92% "urban" households, the 2020 Census estimates that 20% of the US population lives in rural areas.

7. Data are from table 28 in the Federal Highway Administration's 1977 NTPS on Household Vehicle Ownership (Report 2).

8. See https://www.eia.gov/todayinenergy/detail.php?id=36914.

9. The NPTS, like the NHTS, only provides reports based on income, so we are unable to compare vehicle characteristics by expenditure across the two data sets.

10. These findings are broadly consistent with Metcalf's (2022) analysis of the 2017 NHTS data. He estimates the income elasticity of fuel intensity across the income distribution and finds that a revenue-neutral VMT tax-for-gas tax swap is progressive at all but the highest income levels.

11. Ewing and Eavis (2022) describe ways in which auto manufacturers may be shifting their product lineups to target BHEVs to middle-income households in future years.

12. Other studies that describe the demand for BHEVs and the challenges of predicting future adoption patterns include Archsmith, Muehlegger, and Rapson (2022); Holland, Mansur, and Yates (2020); and Rapson and Muehlegger (2021).

13. US Internal Revenue Service (2021) data on the 157.8 million tax returns filed in 2019 can provide some guidance on the impact of these limits. Analysis of information on the adjusted gross income (AGI) of tax returns by filing type, assuming that within the $100,000–$200,000 and $200,000–$500,000 AGI brackets tax filers are uniformly distributed by income (an assumption that is likely to overstate the number of returns above the $150,000 and $300,000 income limits) indicates that as many as 3.05 million single filers, 0.76 million heads of household, 0.11 million married filing separately, and 5.55 million

---

will not be affected by a commercial vehicle miles traveled tax). Panel *b* shows that we do account for most household expenditures, especially in the bottom eight deciles, and at the top end, we continue to miss expenditure on other nontradable services unrelated to our tax policy. A color version of this figure is available online.

married joint filers—a total of 9.47 million households—could be ineligible for BHEV tax credits after 2022. Even if the actual number of ineligible households is only two-thirds this large, it represents a significant group. Most of these households would have been in the top two income or expenditure deciles.

14. The logistic curve is takes the form $SalesShare_t^{BHEV} = 1/(1 + e^{-0.25(t-2032)})$.

15. The experience of the four states that currently impose commercial VMT taxes can provide some guidance on the implementation of VMT taxes. These states rely primarily on self-reported odometer readings. Oregon also uses electronic logging devices to track miles traveled. These are onboard devices already used in more than a quarter of commercial trucks due to their requirement in interstate commerce. To extend this approach to the light-duty fleet would require vehicle owners to purchase new devices or vehicle makers to incorporate them into new production. Beider and Austin (2019) discuss enforcement costs related to VMT taxes, including the possibility of using radio-frequency identification readers placed on roads for some VMT tax implementation.

16. For a breakdown of consumers' expenditure groups, please refer to https://www.bls.gov/cex/tables/calendar-year/mean-item-share-average-standard-error/cu-income-before-taxes-2019.pdf. We outline the crosswalk from the CEX to the Total Requirements table in table B4 and show crosswalk coverage in figure C4.

References

Advanced Vehicles Testing Activity. 2011. "Comparing Energy Costs per Mile for Electric and Gasoline-Fueled Vehicles." Report INL/MIS-11-22490, Idaho National Laboratory, Idaho Falls, ID.

Archsmith, James, Erich Muehlegger, and David Rapson. 2022. "Future Paths of Electric Vehicle Adoption in the United States: Predictable Determinants, Obstacles, and Opportunities." In *Environmental and Energy Policy and the Economy*, Vol. 3, eds. Matthew Kotchen, Tatyana Deryugina, and James Stock, 71–110. Chicago: University of Chicago Press.

Austin, David. 2015. "Pricing Freight Transport to Account for External Costs." Working Paper 2015-03, Congressional Budget Office, Washington, DC.

Banzhaf, Spencer, Lala Ma, and Christopher Timmins. 2019. "Environmental Justice: The Economics of Race, Place, and Pollution." *Journal of Economic Perspectives* 33 (1): 185–208.

Beider, Perry, and David Austin. 2019. "Issues and Options for a Tax on Vehicle Miles Traveled by Commercial Trucks." Report 55688, Congressional Budget Office, Washington, DC.

Brooks, Leah, and Zachary D. Liscow. 2019. "Infrastructure Costs." *American Economic Journal: Applied Economics* 15 (2): 1–30.

Bureau of Transportation Statistics. 2018. *Transportation Economic Trends*. US Department of Transportation, Washington, DC.

Burlig, Fiona, James B. Bushnell, David S. Rapson, and Catherine Wolfram. 2021. "Low Energy: Estimating Electric Vehicle Electricity Use." *American Economic Review: Papers and Proceedings* 111:430–35.

Carleton-Hug, Annelise, and J. William Hug. 2010. "Challenges and Opportunities for Evaluating Environmental Education Programs." *Evaluation and Program Planning* 33:159–64.

Carloni, Dorian, and Terry Dinan. 2021. "Distributional Effects of Reducing Carbon Dioxide Emissions with a Carbon Tax." Working Paper 2021–11, Congressional Budget Office, Washington, DC.

Carson, Rachel. 1962. *Silent Spring*. Boston: Houghton-Mifflin.

Chernick, Howard, and Andrew Reschovsky. 1997. "Who Pays the Gasoline Tax?" *National Tax Journal* 50 (2): 233–59.

Congressional Budget Office. 2020. *The Budget and Economic Outlook: 2020 to 2030.* Washington, DC: Congressional Budget Office.

Davis, Lucas W. 2019. "How Much Are Electric Vehicles Driven?" *Applied Economics Letters* 6 (1): 1–6.

Davis, Lucas W., and James M. Sallee. 2020. "Should Electric Vehicle Drivers Pay a Mileage Tax?" In *Environmental and Energy Policy and the Economy,* Vol. 1, ed. M. Kotchen, J. Stock, and C. Wolfram, 65–94. Chicago: University of Chicago Press.

Davis, Stacy C., and Robert G. Boundy. 2019. "Transportation Energy Data Book: Edition 39." ORNL-5198, Oak Ridge National Laboratory, Oak Ridge, TN.

Department of Energy. 2021. *Transportation Energy Data Book,* Edition 39, table 6.2. Energy Vehicle Technologies Office, Oak Ridge National Laboratory, Oak Ridge, TN. https://tedb.ornl.gov/data.

Dwyer, Michael. 2022. "Electric Vehicles and Hybrids Surpass 10% of US Light-Duty Vehicle Sales." Today in Energy. US Energy Information Administration, February 9.

Ewing, Jack, and Peter Eavis. 2022. "Electric Vehicles Start to Enter the Car-Buying Mainstream." *New York Times,* November 13.

Fox, William F. 2020. "The Influence of Autonomous Vehicles on State Tax Revenues." *National Tax Journal* 73:199–234.

Glaeser, Edward L. 2014. "The Supply of Environmentalism: Psychological Interventions and Economics." *Review of Environmental Economics and Policy* 8 (2): 208–29.

Holland, Stephen P., Erin Mansur, and Andrew J. Yates. 2020. "The Electric Vehicle Transition and the Economics of Banning Gasoline Vehicles." Working Paper no. 26804, NBER, Cambridge, MA.

Hula, Aaron, Andrea Maquire, Amy Bunker, Tristan Rojeck, and Sarah Harrison. 2021. "The 2021 EPA Automotive Trends Report: Greenhouse Gas Emissions, Fuel Economy, and Technology Since 1975." Report no. EPA-420-R-21-023, US Environmental Protection Agency, Ann Arbor, MI.

IHS Markit. 2022. "Average Age of Vehicles in the US Increases to 12.2 Years, According to S&P Global Mobility." https://www.spglobal.com/mobility/en/research-analysis/average-age-of-vehicles-in-the-us-increases-to-122-years.html.

Jacqz, Irene, and Sarah Johnston. 2022. "Unequal Electric Vehicle Adoption, Air Pollution, and Subsidy Policy." Working paper, Department of Economics, Iowa State University.

Kirk, Robert S., and William J. Mallett. 2020. "Funding and Financing Highways and Public Transportation." Report R45350, Congressional Research Service, Washington, DC.

Langer, Ashley, Vikram Maheshri, and Clifford Winston. 2017. "From Gallons to Miles: A Disaggregate Analysis of Automobile and Externality Taxes." *Journal of Public Economics* 152:34–46.

Levin, Laurence, Matthew S. Lewis, and Frank A. Wolak. 2017. "High Frequency Evidence on the Demand for Gasoline." *American Economic Journal: Economic Policy* 9 (3): 314–47.

Levinson, Arik. 2019. "Energy Efficiency Standards are More Regressive Than Energy Taxes: Theory and Evidence." *Journal of the Association of Environmental and Resource Economics* 6 (S1): S7–S36.

Lowry, Ira S. 1960. "Filtering and Housing Standards: A Conceptual Analysis." *Land Economics* 36 (4): 362–70.

Mehrotra, Neil, Matthew A. Turner, and Juan Pablo Uribe. 2023. "Does the US Have an Infrastructure Cost Problem? Evidence from the Interstate Highway System." Working Paper no. 30989, NBER, Cambridge, MA.

Metcalf, Gilbert E. 1999. "A Distributional Analysis of Green Tax Reforms." *National Tax Journal* 52 (4): 655–81.

———. 2022. "The Distributional Impacts of a VMT-Gas Tax Swap." In *Environmental and Energy Policy and the Economy*, Vol. 4, ed. Tatyana Deryugina, Matthew Kotchen, and James Stock. Chicago: University of Chicago Press.

Muehlegger, Erich, and David S. Rapson. 2018. "Subsidizing Low- and Middle-Income Adoption of Electric Vehicles: Quasi-Experimental Evidence from California." Working Paper no. 25359, NBER, Cambridge, MA.

National Transportation Database. 2021. "Complete Monthly Ridership (with Adjustments and Estimates)." Federal Transit Administration, Washington, DC.

Poterba, James M. 1991. "Is the Gasoline Tax Regressive?" *Tax Policy and the Economy* 5:145–64.

Rapson, David S., and Erich Muehlegger. 2021. "The Economics of Electric Vehicles." Working Paper no. 29093, NBER, Cambridge, MA.

Small, Kenneth A., and Kurt van Dender. 2007. "Fuel Efficiency and Motor Vehicle Travel: The Declining Rebound Effect." *Energy Journal* 28 (1): 25–52.

Small, Kenneth A., Clifford Winston, and Carol A. Evans. 1989. *Road Work: A New Highway Pricing and Investment Policy*. Washington, DC: Brookings Institution.

Stone, David. 2018. "Electrified Vehicles Continue to See Slow Growth and Less Use Than Conventional Vehicles." Today in Energy, US Energy Information Administration, May 22.

US Internal Revenue Service. 2021. "SOI Tax Stats—Individual Statistical Tables by Size of Adjusted Gross Income." https://www.irs.gov/statistics/soi-tax-stats-individual-statistical-tables-by-size-of-adjusted-gross-income.

van Dender, Kurt. 2019. "Taxing Vehicles, Fuels, and Road Use: Opportunities for Improving Transport Tax Practice." Taxation Working Paper no. 44, Organisation for Economic Co-operation and Development, Paris.

Vickrey, William. 1952. "The Revision of the Rapid Transit Fare Structure in the City of New York." Technical Monograph #3, Mayor's Committee on Management Survey, New York City.

Wang, Qi, Geng Niu, Xu Gan, and Qiaoling Cai. 2022. "Green Returns to Education: Does Education Affect Environmental Attitudes and Behaviors in China?" *PLoS One* 17 (2): 1–20.

Weatherford, Brian A. 2012. "Mileage-Based User Fee Winners and Losers." Dissertation, RAND Corporation, Santa Monica, CA.

Tax-Avoidance Networks and the Push for a "Historic" Global Tax Reform

Katarzyna Bilicka, *Utah State University and NBER,* United States of America
Michael Devereux, *Oxford University,* United Kingdom
Irem Güçeri, *Oxford University,* United Kingdom

Executive Summary

In this paper, we investigate the use of intellectual property (IP) in multinationals' tax-avoidance strategies. Income arising from intangible property is generally taxed in the location in which such income is received. Many multinationals (MNCs) therefore use tax havens as a base for IP ownership. We leverage a universe of global patent applications and transactions, combined with financial and ownership information, to investigate whether firms locate their patents in tax havens. We find evidence of disproportionate use of havens for both new patent applications and purchase of existing patents. Tax havens such as the Cayman Islands and Liechtenstein have substantially more patents per inhabitant than the largest patenting nations, such as China and the United States. Some 5% of patents in the European markets are held in tax havens, and 30% of global cross-border patent transactions within MNCs have buyers located in tax havens. MNCs that meet the size threshold requirements for the proposed Global Minimum Tax are particularly active in developing patents: they constitute 2.6% of affiliates but are responsible for 42% of all patent applications and 45% of tax haven ones. The Global Minimum Tax could therefore have an important impact on incentives to locate patents in low-tax jurisdictions.

Tax Policy and the Economy, volume 37, 2023.
Published by The University of Chicago Press for the National Bureau of Economic Research. https://doi.org/10.1086/724353

I. Introduction

Tax avoidance by multinational corporations (MNCs) relies on highly complex and global subsidiary networks. Profitable innovative companies with a large portfolio of intangible assets are able to use these networks intensively to reduce their tax liability in high-tax jurisdictions. In the aftermath of the global financial crisis, governments' need for tax revenue, together with evidence of very low taxes being paid by MNCs in high-tax jurisdictions, has triggered significant proposals to reform the international tax system (fig. 1).

The G20/OECD proposal for a Global Minimum Tax (GMT, or "Pillar 2") has now been agreed upon in principle by more than 140 countries. These countries have further agreed to pass relevant domestic legislation by the end of 2022 for implementation to start in 2023.[1] Although the original timetable has slipped, and doubts remain about whether the GMT will eventually be implemented by a critical mass of countries, this would constitute the most fundamental reform of international taxation in a century. The policy debate surrounding this unprecedented international tax-reform agenda emphasizes the superior ability of companies with intensive research and development (R&D) and innovation to move capital easily around the world.

In this paper, we ask: How do profitable MNCs manipulate the location of their intellectual property (IP), and in particular patents, to shift

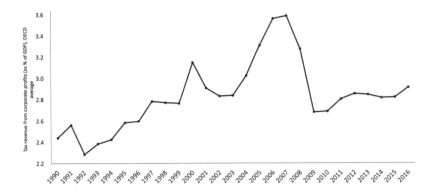

Fig. 1. Taxes on income, profits, and capital gains of corporates (as % of gross domestic product [GDP]). Data are from Organisation for Economic Cooperation and Development (OECD). This figure plots the average percent of tax on income, profits, and capital gains of corporations in the OECD. Each fraction is computed annually as a percentage of GDP of each country. A color version of this figure is available online.

profits to tax havens? We provide policy-relevant information on tax-avoidance networks through the use of IP and subsidiary-ownership relations, and we also briefly consider the likely impact of tax reforms on the patterns of data we describe.

To address our question, we use a novel patent data set, the Orbis IP database, that covers patent applications globally. Many authors in the past have worked with PATSTAT data that cover patent application data collected by the European Patent Office (e.g., Griffith, Miller, and O'Connell 2014; Berkes, Manysheva, and Mestieri 2022) and data from the US Intellectual Property Office (e.g., Bloom, Schankerman, and van Reenen 2013; Acemoglu et al. 2018). The Orbis IP data set includes information from both these sources. In addition, it expands the coverage beyond Europe and the United States to help us understand the global nature of IP networks. We match this data set with the company ownership data set from Orbis. These data allow us to link subsidiary locations of multinational firms to their parent companies and consequently to firms potentially affected by GMT. As such, the matched data cover the location of subsidiaries and consequently firm activities, as well as patents they hold around the globe, which allows us to consider links between the location of IP and firm activity.

We begin our discussion of profit-shifting networks with a description of the different ways in which multinationals can use IP to reduce their taxable income in high-tax jurisdictions. One prominent strategy is for MNCs to locate the ownership of IP in a low-tax jurisdiction. In some cases, the IP is located in a tax haven where there is little or no R&D activity. Although we present striking evidence on patent applications by, and patent transfers to, tax-haven affiliates of multinationals, we only show a small piece of a larger puzzle in IP-related tax-avoidance activity, because there need not be direct IP ownership by the tax-haven affiliate for it to facilitate profit shifting. Instead, a cost-sharing agreement between the parent company (or a suitably-linked affiliate entity) and the tax-haven affiliate can be used to effectively make the tax-haven affiliate the beneficial owner with rights over a significant share of the royalty income on an IP. Such an arrangement results in a very low effective tax rate on income related to the IP, but it cannot be identified by patent ownership or transfer data.

We have three sets of main findings. The first set of results is on global patenting activity broadly: we show that a large share of patenting and patent ownership in the world is predominantly in countries that have strong innovation ecosystems. More than 80% of firms (including affiliates of MNCs) that apply for cross-border patents reside in China, Japan, the United States, South Korea, and large European Union countries. We also find that a large share of patenting activity is carried out by what we call "Pillar 2 firms," referring to the group of MNCs that will be liable to the GMT (or Pillar 2 of the OECD/G20 Inclusive Framework) when it comes into effect.[2] Furthermore, patenting activity is overwhelmingly concentrated at the top of the firm size distribution: more than 80% of patent applications are made by MNCs that are in the top quartile of the turnover size distribution.

In our second set of results, we show the importance of low-tax jurisdictions in patent ownership. We distinguish between two types of low-tax jurisdictions: (1) tax havens where low or no R&D takes place and (2) "investment hubs" where the local innovation ecosystem is strong. A disproportionate share of patenting activity takes place in both of these types of low-tax jurisdictions. We find that almost 4% of all patent applications filed by Pillar 2 firms in 2019 ended up being held by affiliates of those firms located in tax havens. This used to be around 2% in the early 1990s. This number is the sum of patents applied for by affiliates located in tax havens plus patents that are eventually purchased by tax-haven affiliates of those Pillar 2 firms. For example, affiliates based in the Cayman Islands apply for almost double the number of patents per resident of that jurisdiction. In contrast, affiliates based in Sweden apply for just 0.07 patents per resident of that jurisdiction.

We show the importance of IP transfers from high-tax to low-tax jurisdictions early in the life of a patent at a low value to be one of the important IP-based profit-shifting strategies. We document a substantial rise in the share of intragroup patent transfers where the buyer is a tax-haven entity. We find this pattern to be prevalent for both Pillar 2 firms and smaller companies. We also show that patents that are transacted at least once are of higher value and have a higher probability of being applied for by a tax-haven affiliate relative to the patents that are never bought or sold.

Our third set of results explores heterogeneity in the role of tax havens across firms with different geographical locations, patent characteristics, and firm characteristics. First, affiliates located in Europe have a much higher proportion of patent applications that end up being held in tax havens, with on average 5% of those applications, compared with 2% for firms located in Asia. Second, tax-haven affiliates play a more significant role in patents that have a higher predicted value and more forward citations. Furthermore, we find that the share of tax-haven applicants is actually lower for granted patents relative to patents that are not granted. At the same time, patents that are eventually granted are more likely to be transacted into a tax haven. Third, we find that the role of tax havens in patent applications and transactions does not vary significantly across different-sized MNCs by turnover, but that MNCs with large subsidiary networks use tax havens much more prominently. Affiliates in tax havens are much more likely to be involved in patent transactions as buyers if they are members of large subsidiary networks even if they have a relatively small size by turnover. This evidence supports the notion that the turnover-based size threshold for the Pillar 2 minimum tax may not catch important tax-minimizing MNCs.

Our work relates to several strands of the literature. First, there has been a recent rise in the use of patent data to address important research questions on taxation, innovation, and productivity. Authors have documented the innovation boom of the twentieth century, driven by innovations from United States, Japanese, and European firms (Akcigit et al. 2018; Berkes et al. 2022). Although various components of the innovation ecosystem and technology spillovers are the primary driver of location choice for innovation (Bloom et al. 2013; Feng and Jaravel 2020), innovating firms and individuals both respond to tax incentives, either provided through reduced rates or favorable tax base provisions (Akcigit, Grigsby, and Nicholas 2017; Akcigit, Hanley, and Stantcheva 2022). In this paper, we expand this work in two dimensions. First, we use a global data set that encompasses all previously used patent data sets to give us a more comprehensive picture of the global patenting activities of firms. Second, we focus on the specific role that tax havens play in the location of IP and uncover a disproportionate number of patents held in those low-tax jurisdictions.

Second, we contribute to the literature that specifically focuses on the international aspect of the location of intangible assets and IP. Evidence suggests that MNCs specifically locate their intangible assets (Grubert and Slemrod, 1998; Desai, Foley, and Hines 2006; Dischinger and Riedel 2011) and patents (Grubert 2003; Karkinsky and Riedel 2012; Griffith et al. 2014) in low-tax jurisdictions. We contribute by documenting the patent-related paths through which MNCs shift profits to tax havens and quantify the importance of tax havens as locations for patents. This helps us understand one of the mechanisms of profit shifting by MNCs in greater depth. There is a recent related literature that studies the effects of patent-box policies (Griffith et al. 2014; Alstadsaeter et al.

2018) that target IP by offering low tax rates for holding IP in an otherwise high-tax-rate country. The evidence suggests that firms have incentives to use these IP boxes for profit-shifting purposes rather than to promote R&D (Knoll and Riedel 2019; Gaessler, Hall, and Harhoff 2021; Knoll et al. 2021; Schwab and Todtenhaupt 2021). Our work is closely related to this literature, as we study the MNCs' responses to incentives for IP-related income.

More broadly, our work relates to the rich literature on the profit-shifting activities of MNCs. This literature is vast and focuses on several dimensions. The first is the role of various profit-shifting strategies that enable MNCs to minimize their taxable profits. These include debt shifting (Desai, Foley, and Hines 2004; Huizinga, Laeven, and Nicodeme 2008), abuse of transfer pricing (Cristea and Nguyen 2016; Davies et al. 2018; Koethenbuerger, Mardan, and Stimmelmayr 2019), and patent location (Dischinger and Riedel 2011). Second, this literature attempts to estimate the extent of profit shifting by MNCs by emphasizing the role of tax havens as conduit countries (Hines and Rice 1994; Gumpert, Hines, and Schnitzer 2016; Dowd, Landefeld, and Moore 2017). A recent review paper by Riedel (2018, 178) reported estimates of shifting in the range of 5–30% of taxable profit and concluded that it is "too early to draw final conclusions on the quantitative importance of international tax-avoidance activities."[3] Several papers in this area use top-to-bottom approaches using macroeconomic indicators (Tørsløv, Wier, and Zucman 2022), and bottom-up approaches using country-by-country data (Fuest et al. 2022; Garcia-Bernardo and Janský 2022; Garcia-Bernardo, Janský, and Zucman 2022), corporate tax returns data (Bilicka 2019), and financial data. More recent work in this literature quantifies the distortions to gross domestic product, productivity, and financial flows that profit shifting generates (Coppola et al. 2021; Guvenen et al. 2022), estimates the effects of tax-avoidance restrictions on real activities of MNCs (Suárez Serrato 2018; Bilicka, Qi, and Xing 2022), and tries to understand what factors and which actors enable firms to shift profits more effectively across borders (Bilicka and Scur 2021; Bustos et al. 2022). Our technical companion paper—Bilicka, Devereux, and Güçeri (2022)—builds a model of tax policy and investment that incorporates unobserved heterogeneity in MNCs' profit-shifting capability and different costs of setting up tax-minimization networks, including those that involve IP, as discussed in this paper. In Bilicka et al. (2022), we quantify the policy trade-off between raising tax revenue by combating tax avoidance (via, for example, a GMT) and attracting investment (fig. 1).

II.   How Do Firms Use IP to Shift Profits?

The principles of taxation of profit of multinational companies are primarily set out in the Organisation for Economic Cooperation and Development (OECD) model tax treaty. This approach, which dates back to the 1920s, sets out a compromise between countries in their taxing rights over multinational profits. Very broadly, the approach distinguishes between a place of residence (the location of the investor) and a place of source (where the economic activity takes place). The compromise is that "active" income is taxed in the "source" country, and passive income is taxed in the "residence" country. This distinction, combined with the approach of "separate accounting" whereby tax is levied on the profit deemed to arise in each separate entity within the multinational, is at the heart of most of the problems of the system. In this paper, we focus on one particular problem: that this system makes it relatively easy for multinationals to shift profit to low-tax jurisdictions.

Use of tax havens. There are three main ways in which multinationals can take advantage of specific rules to move profits to low-tax jurisdictions: transfer pricing, debt shifting, and location of IP. We focus on the location of IP, and more specifically patents. Article 12(1) of the OECD model tax treaty states that royalties arising from the use of IP are to be taxed exclusively in the residence country, provided the recipient is the beneficial owner of the payment. That is, the source country has no rights to tax the underlying income from which royalties are paid. The tax-avoidance opportunity arises when the beneficial owner of the royalty payment is, for example, a subsidiary of a multinational company located in a tax haven. In this case, the profit arising from the IP, or patent, is likely to be taxed primarily in the haven at a low, or even zero, rate.

That raises the question of how the beneficial ownership of the IP can be located in a haven. There are essentially three ways to achieve this. We summarize these in panel A of table 1 and discuss each in turn.[4] The first is the most straightforward. If R&D is undertaken by a subsidiary in the haven itself, then it is reasonable for that subsidiary to apply for a patent and to be the beneficial owner. There are some low-tax jurisdictions with a strong innovation ecosystem, such as Switzerland, Hong Kong, and Singapore. We would expect there to be large numbers of patent applications in these locations.

Second, suppose that R&D is undertaken by a firm in country A and is successful in creating IP, for which the firm applies for a patent. The firm

Table 1
Location of Innovation and Patents

Panel A: Different IP-Shifting Strategies for Shifting Income to Tax Havens			
	(1)	(2)	(3)
	Location of		
Type	Innovation	Patent	Can We Observe It?
1	Tax haven	Tax haven	Yes: patent application filed in tax haven
2	Any country	Tax haven	Yes: transaction with haven buyer occurs
3	Any country	Any country	No: cost-sharing agreement not recorded in patent data

Panel B: Types of IP Location		
	(1)	(2)
	Location Types	Description
1	Location of protection	Where the invention has market protection. Litigation takes place in this jurisdiction in cases of breaches in IP protection.
2	Location of application	Where the relevant IP office for reviewing and handling the administration of patent applications is located. The application may seek protection in the local or foreign jurisdictions. This is separate from the location of inventors, who may be resident in different jurisdictions around the world.
3	Location of applicant	Where the entity that owns a patent is resident for tax purposes.
4	Location of buyer/seller of a patent	Where the entity that buys or sells the patent is resident for tax purposes.
5	Location of beneficial owner of a patent	Where the entity that has the right to receive all, or part of, the income stream arising from licensing the patent.
6	Location of the subsidiary in a high-tax jurisdiction that pays royalties for the right to use the IP	The high-tax locations typically make financial transfers to low-tax jurisdictions to lower tax burden in high-tax locations.

Note: Panel A column 1 is the location where the innovation or research and development takes place. Column 2 is the ultimate location of the patent. Column 3 tells us whether we can observe this type of intellectual property (IP) in our data set and where would we observe a tax haven in that context.

could then sell the patent (even a patent that is not yet granted) to its subsidiary in a haven. In principle, such a sale would need to take place at an "arm's-length price," and the profit on the sale would be taxed in country A. However, it is extremely difficult to value patents, which, by definition, are unique. Uncertainty around the true value enables multinationals to choose a low price, avoiding at least some tax in country A. Having undertaken this transaction, however, the beneficial owner of the patent is the subsidiary in the haven. In either of these two cases, the data used in this study would identify that ownership, and in the second case, would also provide details of the sale to the haven (although not the value declared for tax purposes).

The third route is more complex, and there are a number of variations available. However, the basic approach is a variant of the second above. Under what is known as a cost-contribution arrangement, or cost sharing, the haven subsidiary can finance part of the R&D taking place in country A. By agreement with the entity in country A, it would then have the legal right to receive part of the resulting income stream. For example, if the haven subsidiary provided 90% of financing of the R&D, it could claim rights to 90% of the income. In effect, the haven subsidiary would have beneficial ownership of 90% of the income stream for tax purposes. However, in this case, the haven subsidiary would not apply for the patent, nor would it purchase the patent. The data used in this study cannot identify such arrangements.[5] As a result, the data cannot be used to estimate the full extent of profit shifting through the manipulation of rights to the royalty income stream. There may be many patents with beneficial owners located in a tax haven that we do not capture in our analysis, suggesting that the evidence we provide is a modest lower bound of the role of low-tax jurisdictions for IP location.

Furthermore, not observing a royalty flow between two high-tax jurisdictions does not necessarily imply that tax minimization is not taking place; it could be the case that the royalty income is eventually passed onto a tax-haven subsidiary. The presence of an intermediary can be a form of "treaty shopping" to avoid withholding taxes.

Cross-border transfers of royalty flows are subject to a withholding tax at the source in the absence of special arrangements (e.g., the European Union) or double taxation treaties between the source and recipient countries. In figure 2, we demonstrate the taxes levied on the income of different affiliates of an MNC with IP. Consider two companies located in two EU countries. The entity in location (1) carries out R&D and develops a patent, and the entity in location (2) holds an exclusive license to the patent

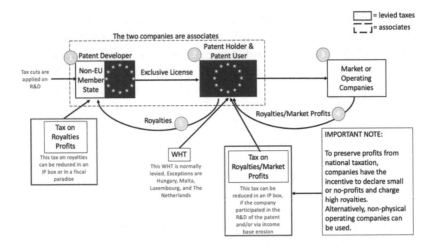

Fig. 2. How does taxation of IP ownership work? Data are from Organisation for Economic Cooperation and Development (OECD). This figure describes various levels of taxes imposed on MNCs with intellectual property (IP) ownership. EU = European Union; R&D = research and development; WHT = withholding tax. A color version of this figure is available online.

and pays royalties to the entity in location (1) while selling the product in the market marked by location (3). Profits arising from the sale of the product in location (3) may be taxable in either location (2) or (3). The entity in location (2) can substantially reduce its taxable profit through the royalty payments it makes to the patent-developing entity. If the ownership (or beneficial ownership) is transferred to a low-tax entity, then the royalty flows are taxed at a low or zero rate. The tax base in location (2) is reduced significantly.[6]

Use of IP-box regimes. Another important scheme for reducing tax liability on IP-related profit is the so-called IP-box regime, particularly in Europe. Many high-tax jurisdictions in Europe such as the United Kingdom and France apply a reduced corporate income tax rate on income that arises from patents. The reduced tax rate in the United Kingdom and France is 10%, which is much lower than the corporate tax rate on ordinary income.[7] There are substantial heterogeneities across patent-box regimes, along the dimensions of (i) the patent-box tax rate, (ii) the type of IP that can be included in the tax base (examples are nonpatent IP such as trademarks), (iii) whether IP transferred to a country after it was developed can be included in the base or whether the IP needs to be developed locally, and (iv) how much of the R&D spending on the patent was made in the IP-box jurisdiction. This R&D development condition is part of Action 5 in the OECD's Base Erosion and Profit Shifting (BEPS) process under the "nexus requirement" of IP-box policies (OECD 2019). We include descriptive evidence on patents in these IP-box regimes in the appendices, but we leave a more detailed exploration of those to future work.

III.   Previous Reforms and the GMT

There have been many attempts over the past decade to limit the use of IP for profit shifting. For example, an important reform in 2011 made it more difficult for US multinationals to engage in cost-contribution arrangements. However, agreements before 2011 were "grandfathered," meaning that any IP eventually arising from R&D undertaken within an existing agreement would continue to fall under the pre-2011 arrangements. That offers considerable scope for income arising in the past decade to be traced to earlier agreements. In 2013–15, the BEPS project also sought to limit this form of profit shifting. In essence, the approach taken was to limit taxing rights to any countries where some real "functions and activities" took place. Hence, it would not be enough simply to have a "brass plate" subsidiary in a haven that only existed to collect income. Instead, it has become necessary to effectively locate staff in these locations who are at least nominally charged with managing the income stream. These regulations, at the very least, increase the cost of locating IP in tax havens. As such, we would expect the importance of tax havens for locating IP to start declining within a few years of 2011.

In October 2021, 137 countries from the OECD's Inclusive Framework agreed on the broad principle of levying a 15% minimum tax on the "excess profit" of subsidiaries of large multinational companies. The basic approach agreed is that, if the overall effective tax rate of all subsidiaries of a multinational in a particular jurisdiction is below 15%, then there will be a "top-up" tax to lift the total tax paid to 15% of "excess profit." This top-up tax may be collected in the jurisdiction itself through a "qualified domestic minimum top-up tax." If the jurisdiction chooses not to implement such a tax, then the country of the multinational's headquarters becomes entitled to levy the tax through an "income inclusion rule." If it does not do so, then other countries in which the multinational operates may do so through an "under-tax payments rule." At the time of writing, the aim is to introduce these rules in 2024. In principle, this should have a significant impact on the incentive to shift profit to tax havens. Suppose, for example, that the "high-tax" country has a statutory corporation tax rate of 20%. Then shifting $100 to a zero-rate haven saves $20 in tax. Following the introduction of the minimum tax, then at the margin, the $100 transferred would be liable to $15 of tax, reducing the potential gain to only $5. There are still many unanswered questions as to how the proposed minimum tax will work, and indeed the extent to which countries actually implement it. In the context of this paper, the GMT has the potential to affect the structure of global networks for IP location, as it would limit the potential tax savings from those arrangements as well.

IV.   Data Construction and Description

In this section, we describe the data sets we use in this paper and provide an overview of how the sample for the analysis was constructed. The paper combines insights from the Orbis Intellectual Property Dataset, Orbis Financial, and Orbis ownership data sets.

A.   Data Sets We Use

Patent applications and applicants. Orbis IP database includes the universe of global patent applications going back to the 1800s. To obtain comprehensive information on each patent, patent owner, transactions, and values, we use four patent data sets. First, we use the patent headers, which contain the universe, 133 million, of all global patent applications. The vast majority of these patent applications, 112 million, were filed after 1980. This data set contains information on patent publication number; the country in which the patent is applied for and published in; the date of the application, publication, and granting; and the number of citations.[8] Second, we use the Orbis lookup data set that provides a bridge between patent applications and patent applicants. The patent applicant is a subsidiary that files the patent application to the IP office. This data set identifies 86 million applicant-patent pairs.

Patent transactions. The third data set we use is a universe of patent transactions between 1980 and 2020. This data set includes 83 million patent transactions related to 8 million patents.[9] This data set includes a wealth of information related to each transaction, specifically on the dates, deal types, names, and locations of buyers and sellers and the relationship between the buyer and seller; that is, whether it is an intragroup transaction. We use the information on the date of each transaction if it was completed, and disregard all transactions that were announced but not completed. We also extract information on who the buyer and the seller were, whether the transaction was intragroup, and whether it occurred before the patent was granted or not.

The transactions data form a panel that traces the history of transactions related to each patent. For our purposes, we collapse this data set at the patent level and construct the following relevant variables: the number of transactions, the number of intragroup transactions, and the number of tax-haven buyers. We also obtain information on the country of the first seller and the last buyer to track the patents that crossed borders while transacted. After removing observations where the deal was not completed and where we have no information on the buyer and the seller countries, we are left with almost 6 million patents that were successfully transacted and for which we know their source and destination countries.

Patent values. For a subset of patents, Orbis also estimates the value of each of those patents across the years 2010–20. This information is collected for only about 1.1 million patents. Orbis does not collect actual values, but rather uses an estimation approach to construct these values. There are 26 indicators that are taken into account, which include, for example, the strength of the invention, the number of inventors mentioned in the application, heterogeneity of applications, and intended worldwide protection. The valuation does not take into account transactions that occur. However, given that the value is simply an estimate rather than the true value, we do not use the time dimension of these data, but extract information on the first value of the patent and the last value of the patent and collapse the data set at the patent level.

Orbis financial and ownership data. In this paper, we are interested in two groups of firms. First, we look at the global patenting activity of all firms and then zoom in on those firms that will potentially be subject to the new set of Pillar 2 regulations and the GMT. We define Pillar 2 firms as those that had more than €750 million of turnover in 2019. We do not track changes in Pillar 2 status; hence, it is plausible that some of the firms we consider in this subsample were below the Pillar 2 regulatory thresholds in years before 2019. Inversely, it is possible that by the time GMT comes into effect, more firms will be subject to the regulations imposed.

For the subset of Pillar 2 firms, we collect data on their financial and ownership structure from Orbis. We first extract from a list of firms that in 2019 had more than €750 million of turnover. Orbis has 13,500 entities that report having a global consolidated turnover over that value. Of those firms, 9,200 are global ultimate owners of those MNCs, and the additional 4,000 are wholly owned by another corporation that also reports having more than 750 million turnover. We only consider the 9,200 MNCs as our Pillar 2 sample. For those 9,200 MNCs, we collect consolidated financial information for the parent firm in 2019: assets, turnover (revenue), Standard Industrial Classification code, employment, profits, and tax liability. This allows us to calculate their overall effective tax rates (ETRs), which are the ratio of tax liability to profit and loss before taxes.

Furthermore, for each of those MNCs, we collect information on their wholly owned subsidiaries 10 levels down, using the latest static Orbis ownership structure from 2020. This gives us 1.5 million subsidiaries of those MNCs. We do not track the historical ownership, and we do not collect ownership for non-Pillar 2 firms. Both the financial and ownership coverage for the smaller firms in Orbis are of much lower quality.

B.   Sample Construction and Description

We start with the universe of patent applications and match this data set with the patent-applicant bridge from Orbis. We have applicant information for two-thirds of all patents in our data set. This leaves us with just more than 2 million patent applicants that applied for 86 million patents between 1900 and 2020. We then match the transaction data set, and we find a match for almost 6 million patents. Hence, in our sample, 7% of all patents were transacted at least once, and 1% were transacted within a firm. For 60% of the patents that were ever transacted, at least one transaction occurred before the patent was granted. We also know the patent value for just more than 1 million patents.

For some of our analysis, we focus on patent applications that are filed in a location different than the location of the subsidiary. We call these cross-border applications. About 46% of all applications are cross-border, and these are filed by about 35% of all firms. The locations of patents we have in these data correspond to the types of IP locations that we outline in table 1. In particular, we have data on and, consequently, focus on the location of the application (type 2), the location of the applicant (type 3), and the location of the buyer/seller (type 4).

In the analysis that follows, we limit the scope of this data set to include only patent applications after 1990. There are two reasons to do so. First, this paper is focused on the exploration of profit shifting, which was relatively limited before the 1990s. Second, the coverage in our data set improves after 1990. There were 95.5 million patent applications since 1990; hence, we capture the majority of this data set with this approach. We provide a longer time series of all patent applications dating back to 1900 in figure C1.

V.   Which Firms Innovate and Where?

We start our analysis with a brief description of the global innovation activity. In figure 3, we plot the evolution of patent applications over time, aggregating the total number of applications according to the application year. In panel A, we plot separately time trends for all firms and for firms subject to Pillar 2 restrictions. In panel B, we calculate the share of patent applications filed by Pillar 2 firms; that is, firms with a global turnover in excess of €750 million. There has been a large increase in patent applications since early 2000, mainly driven by non-Pillar 2 firms. For example, in 2018 there were 4 million patent applications filed by all firms, of which Pillar 2 firms filed just under 40%. The share of patent applications filed by Pillar 2 firms has declined substantially since 2004. This suggests that innovation, as proxied by patent applications, has shifted away from these large Pillar 2 firms toward smaller players.

Out of 2 million firms that apply for patents in our data set, just under 65,000 belong to MNCs that will likely be subject to Pillar 2 regulations. This is around 2.6% of all firms. However, 28% of all patent applications are filed by headquarters of Pillar 2 MNCs, and a further 15% are filed by their subsidiaries. As such, these 2.6% of affiliates are responsible for 43% of all patent applications in the data set. Pillar 2 firms and their subsidiaries also are responsible for 45% of all tax-haven patent applications and 55% of all cross-border patent applications. In table 2 for a subsample of Pillar 2 firms, we show that patenting activity is highly concentrated even among those largest firms. Some 40% of all patent applications filed by Pillar 2 firms are filed by the largest 5% of those firms.

The key question we address in this paper is the extent to which the patent holder (through a new application or through a purchase of an existing patent) is in a tax-advantaged location. To the extent that a multinational can undertake innovation in a high-tax country, but hold the resulting patent in a haven, then the country of the holder of the patent does not necessarily identify where the innovation took place. In principle, we would also like to identify where innovation activity occurs. We have data on two types of locations. First, we know where applications are filed. We take this to be a proxy of where the protection is offered to the patent. For example, an American business could apply in a European country for a patent from the European Patent Office, for protection in European

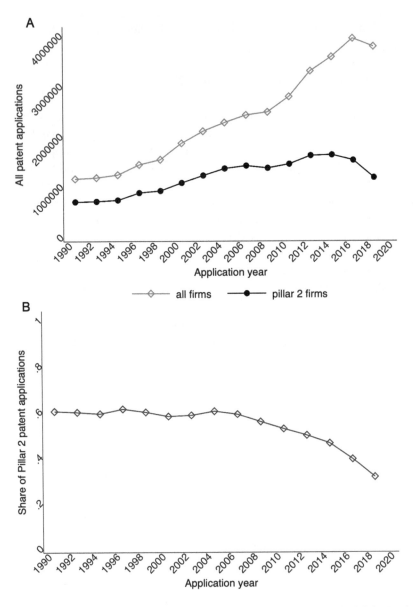

Fig. 3. The evolution of patent applications over time: 1990–2020. Matched Orbis intellectual property data and Orbis ownership data. These figures demonstrate the evolution of the patenting activity of global firms. Each point in panel *A* corresponds to a 2-year average of aggregated patent applications for each of 1990/91 up until 2019/20. In panel *B*, we plot the share of patents applied for by Pillar 2 firms in all patents applied for in each year. We then average this across 2 years, similar to panel *A*. The full data set includes 2 million unique firms owning 86.5 million unique patents. Pillar 2 firms are headquarters and subsidiaries of multinational corporations that have more than €750 million of turnover in 2019 and constitute 65,000 of the 2 million firms. A color version of this figure is available online

Table 2
Concentration of Patenting Activity: MNC Turnover Distribution

MNC Turnover Distributions (pct)	Patents (1)	Tax-Haven Applications (2)	Tax-Haven Applicants (3)	Trans (4)	Haven Buyers (5)
0–25th	3.66	3.49	4.2	2.55	1.53
25th–50th	5.08	4.93	5.17	5.19	5.5
50th–75th	11.62	12.29	15.87	11.65	10.41
75th–90th	19.42	16.76	13.11	25.89	28.26
90th–95th	19.4	17.1	15.26	30.02	38.39
95th+	40.82	45.44	46.38	24.71	15.91

Note: This table shows the fraction of patent applications according to the size distribution of multinational corporation (MNC) turnover. We include only Pillar 2 firms here. Column 1 shows the overall fractions of patents held, column 2 fractions of tax-haven patent applications, column 3 fractions of tax-haven patent applicants, column 4 fractions of cross-border transactions, and column 5 fractions of tax-haven buyers. Each column adds up to 100%. Each row represents size bin of MNCs turnover. For example, 95th+ includes firms with global turnover in the 95th percentile of the distribution of Pillar 2 MNCs; i.e., the top largest firms.

markets. Second, we know the location of the applicant. The latter is likely to be a better proxy for where innovation takes place. However, the location of the patent does not need to reflect the location of innovation. Hence, we only focus on patent locations in what follows.

Table 3 summarizes the top 10 application locations and the top 10 countries where the applicants reside. In panel A, we summarize these for all applications, and in panel B, we summarize these for cross-border applications; that is, where the application is in a different country from the applicant. This table is in fact dominated by large, innovating countries. First, 25% of all patent applications since 1990 have been filed in China, followed by 18% in Japan; the United States is third with 14.5% of all patent applications. These three countries together capture almost 60% of the entire patent application market. Second, these three countries also constitute 65% of all countries where firms applying for patents reside. This suggests that the majority of innovation is happening in China, Japan, and the United States. The presence of other Asian countries, such as South Korea and Taiwan, in the top 10 highlights the increasing importance of Asia as an innovation hub.[10]

The market for cross-border patent applications looks quite different. The country with the highest number of cross-border patent applications is Spain; presumably, these are applications for protection in the European market more generally. There is a stark difference in the behavior of

Table 3
Top Patent Application Locations and Applicants

Application Locations	No. of Applications	% of Applications	Applying Countries	No. of Applications	% of Applications
		Panel A: All Applications			
China	17,487,640	25.47	Japan	17,615,342	25.66
Japan	12,546,851	18.27	China	14,764,226	21.5
United States	10,085,166	14.69	United States	12,614,601	18.37
Spain	5,616,475	8.18	Germany	4,955,506	7.22
South Korea	4,291,348	6.25	South Korea	4,646,528	6.77
Germany	2,755,246	4.01	France	1,856,880	2.7
Taiwan	1,627,020	2.37	United Kingdom	1,624,560	2.37
Australia	1,489,301	2.17	Taiwan	1,503,463	2.19
Canada	1,296,701	1.89	Switzerland	1,106,986	1.61
United Kingdom	969,817	1.41	Italy	1,015,381	1.48
		Panel B: Cross-Border Applications			
Spain	5,616,475	17.85	United States	8,039,684	25.56
United States	5,510,249	17.52	Japan	6,745,245	21.44
China	3,499,120	11.12	Germany	3,586,348	11.4
Japan	1,676,754	5.33	South Korea	1,551,921	4.93
Germany	1,386,088	4.41	France	1,420,996	4.52
Australia	1,356,484	4.31	United Kingdom	1,173,826	3.73
Canada	1,199,048	3.81	Switzerland	1,088,923	3.46
South Korea	1,196,741	3.8	Netherlands	946,884	3.01
Taiwan	897,256	2.85	Italy	795,914	2.53
India	591,577	1.88	China	775,706	2.47

Source: Matched Orbis intellectual property data for years 1990–2020.
Note: Application locations are defined as countries where firms apply for patents. Applying countries are locations of subsidiaries. Panel A summarizes the top 10 locations for all patent applications. Panel B does the same for cross-border patents. Cross-border patents are defined as those where the application country is different than the country of residence of the subsidiary applying for a patent.

US and Chinese firms. US firms applied for 12.6 million patents worldwide, of which more than 8 million were cross border—more than 63%. By contrast, Chinese firms applied for 14.7 million patents worldwide, but only around 775,000 of these (5.2%) were cross-border. A similar pattern applies to the location of patent applications. Just more than 10 million applications were made in the United States, of which 5.5 million (55%) were by firms outside the United States. By contrast, of the 17.5 million applications made in China, only 3.5 million (20%) were made by firms located outside China.

A notable factor country in this table is Switzerland, typically regarded as a tax haven. Swiss firms applied for just more than 1.1 million patents. Of these, more than 98% were cross-border, applied for outside Switzerland. Firms in the Netherlands, also a tax-friendly environment, to a large extent made patent applications outside the country as well.

VI. The Role of Tax Havens: Applications and Transactions

In this section, we discuss the role of tax havens in the possible tax-minimization practices of firms.[11] There are two primary ways in which tax havens may play a role in profit shifting for firms in our data set: (1) as a residence location of firms applying for patents and (2) as a residence location for firms purchasing existing patents (whether or not they have been granted).[12]

We begin by looking at the evolution of both of these channels in aggregate. In figure 4 panel A, we present the total number of new patents held in tax havens each year, from either channel, as a proportion of the total number of new patents. The figure shows that tax havens play an increasing role in patenting activity of Pillar 2 firms, as the share of patents that end up in tax havens doubled from 2% to 4% since 1990. To put this in context, the population of these tax havens is around 70 million people, which is about 0.88% of the global population.

In panels B and C, we disaggregate this total number of new patents into those that were applied for by firms in tax-haven countries and those that were purchased by firms in those countries. In panel B, we show the large role of tax havens as patent applicants with an increase in the number of applications that they file from 20,000 a year in the early 1990s to almost 1 million in 2012. These applicants constitute up to 3.5% of all applicants globally. We see an increasing role of tax-haven applicants for Pillar 2 MNCs, with the share of patent applications filed by their tax-haven subsidiaries more than doubling, from 1.5% in 1990 to 3.5% by the end of the sample. Evidence from table C1 suggests a large role of Switzerland, with more than 54% of all applications filed. This likely means that some firms choose to file patents in Europe using their Swiss subsidiaries. Singapore, Ireland, and Hong Kong all together represent 85% of those tax-haven applicants, with a much smaller role for small tax havens such as the Cayman Islands.

Nevertheless, the Cayman Islands population is around 66,000, but firms resident in the Cayman Islands filed more than 100,000 patent applications, more than 1.5 patents per inhabitant. In China, the largest patenting

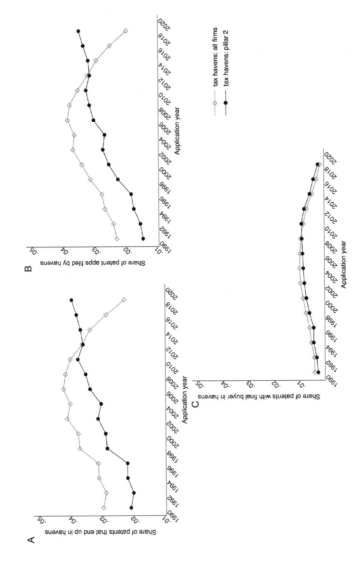

Fig. 4. The importance of tax havens: 1990–2020. Matched Orbis intellectual property data and Orbis ownership data. These figures demonstrate the evolution of the patenting activity of global firms in tax havens. In panel A, we include a number of patents that eventually end up in a tax haven as a share of all patent applications in each year. This consists of two aspects of tax-haven ownership: (1) the number of patents applied for by tax-haven subsidiaries and (2) the number of patents that are eventually bought by tax-haven subsidiaries, even if they were applied for by non-haven-located firms. In panels B and C, we break this share into the two aspects, showing share of (1) in panel B and share of (2) in panel C. A color version of this figure is available online.

country since 1990, the number of patents applied for per inhabitant is 0.012. In table 4, we compute a ranking of the top 10 countries by patent applications of their resident firms. To do that, we aggregate the number of patent applications by firms resident in those countries 1990–2020 and scale this number by the population of those countries in 2021. In the top 10, we have six tax havens, with the top three countries being the Cayman Islands, Liechtenstein, and the British Virgin Islands. It is unlikely that large innovation activity takes place in those countries, and the large share of patent applications per inhabitant suggests a prevalence of profit shifting using IP.

In panel C of figure 4, we explore the extent to which patents are applied for elsewhere but are purchased by firms in tax havens. Our findings indicate that the share of patents purchased by firms in tax havens is about 1%. First, note that only 7% of all patents in our data set are transacted at all. This suggests that a large share of those that are transacted ends up in tax havens. We explore this further in figure 5. Second, note that the older patents tend to be transacted more, simply because of the longer lifespan.

Transaction data. To understand the trends in the transaction data and the importance of transactions for patents, we investigate the transaction data separately. We compare patents that were transacted at least once

Table 4
Top 10 Patent-Applying Countries Scaled by Population

Country	Population (thousands)	No. of Patent Apps	No. of Patent Apps by Population
Cayman Islands	66	116	1.75
Liechtenstein	38	38	.99
British Virgin Islands	30	21	.69
Bermuda	64	14	.22
Japan	125,700	17,600	.14
Switzerland	8,698	1,107	.13
Luxembourg	639	80	.12
Finland	5,542	519	.09
South Korea	51,745	4,647	.09
Sweden	10,416	733	.07

Source: World Bank population data matched with Orbis intellectual property data.
Note: We compute the total number of patents applied for by affiliates (both subsidiaries and headquarters) resident in each country 1990–2020 and divide this number by the 2021 population of each country. We rank these and in this table present the top 10 countries together with the number of patent applications per population. Patent and population numbers are in thousands, rounded to the nearest thousand.

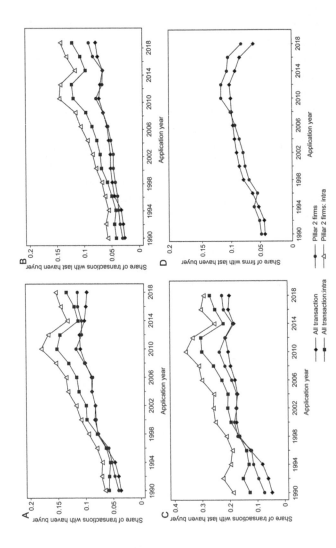

Fig. 5. Importance of tax havens in patent transactions. Matched Orbis intellectual property data and Orbis ownership data. These figures present the evolution of the share of transactions with tax havens in the transaction data. Panels A–C show the share of tax haven transactions in all transactions. We aggregate all transactions and attribute them to the patent without distinguishing the transaction year. Panel D shows the share of firms in the transaction data that have a final tax-haven buyer. In panel A, we look at any tax-haven buyer; in panel B, at only last tax-haven buyers; and in panel C, we consider the subset of cross-border transactions only. Intrafirm patents are those transacted between related parties. Haven buyers means that the firm that bought the patent was located in a tax haven. A color version of this figure is available online.

to those that were never transacted. We present the results in table 5. First, the value and number of citations of patents that have been transacted at least once are much higher than those of patents that were never transacted. Second, and perhaps more important in our setting, the share of tax-haven resident firms that apply for patents is almost triple in the subsample of patents that were transacted relative to those that never were.

In figure 5, we present the share of transactions with a tax-haven purchaser. We distinguish between all transactions and transactions of patents initially applied for by Pillar 2 firms. We further consider all transactions and all intrafirm transactions separately. This results in four distinct lines in this figure. In panels A and B, we show the number of transactions with tax-haven purchasers as a proportion of all transactions. In panel C, we show the number of cross-border transactions with tax havens as a proportion of all cross-border transactions. In panel D, we do not use the number of transactions but create a dummy equal to 1 when a final buyer is in a tax haven, and zero otherwise. Hence, this panel shows the share of patents that had a final tax-haven buyer, rather than the share of transactions with a final haven buyer.[13]

The findings are striking. First, panel A shows that the share of transactions with tax-haven buyers has almost tripled for patents in our sample that have at least one transaction. In 2010, at the highest point in our data, more than 17% of all patent Pillar 2 intrafirm transactions had a tax-haven buyer, and more than 10% of all transactions had a tax-haven buyer too. Panel B shows that in almost 15% of all Pillar 2 intrafirm transactions, the tax haven was the final buyer of the patent. When we consider only cross-border transactions, these numbers are even higher. Panel C demonstrates that in 2010, 40% of all patent Pillar 2 intrafirm

Table 5
Transacted and Never-Transacted Patents: Differences

	Value First Trans	Value Last Trans	No. of Cits	% of Haven Applications	% of Haven Applicants
Never transacted	209,356	528,105	20	.50	2.57
Transacted at least once	385,763	763,303	51	.05	7.34

Source: Matched Orbis intellectual property data and Orbis ownership data.
Note: This table compares the average values, number of citations, percentage of tax-haven applications, and percentage of applicants within sample of patents that were never transacted and those that were transacted at least once. The first value is the value of the patent the first year it appears in the value data set, and the last value is the value of the patents in 2020, or the last year it appears in the value data set. Applicants define locations where subsidiaries are. Tax-haven countries are listed in the appendices.

cross-border transactions had a tax-haven buyer, and more than 30% of all cross-border transactions had a tax-haven buyer too (not shown). Similarly, in about 35% of all Pillar 2 intrafirm transactions, the tax haven was the final buyer of the patent. Finally, in panel D we consider the number of patents that end up with a tax-haven buyer as a share of all patents that are transacted at least once, and we find that, of all patents for Pillar 2 firms that are transacted, more than 12% end up in tax havens.

These results suggest that in almost half of the instances when a patent is transacted cross-border within a firm, the final destination is a tax haven. These results likely explain a large share of patents that end up in tax havens. The role of tax havens as patent buyers is also greater for intrafirm transactions, especially for patents applied for by Pillar 2 firms.

In table C2, we show that the majority of tax-haven buyers are located in Switzerland, Singapore, and Ireland. However, a relatively large fraction of patents is bought by firms residing in the Cayman Islands, Barbados, Bermuda, and the British Virgin Islands. Patents sold to tax havens are mostly sold there by firms residing in the United States (56% of all instances), followed by German firms (10%), with the remainder of countries playing a relatively minor role.

VII.   Exploring Heterogeneities

So far, we have examined the role of tax havens without distinguishing between the different characteristics of the patents. In this section, we consider heterogeneity for patents applied for by Pillar 2 firms only. Corresponding results for all firms are in the appendices.

A.   By Patent Characteristics

Locations. We begin an exploration of heterogeneity by differentiating patents according to where the application takes place. We take this to be an indicator of the market in which the patent offers protection. As we have already seen, there are clearly very different trends and behaviors in different countries. Specifically, in figure 6, we differentiate patents by whether they are applied for in four locations: Europe, Asia, the United States, or the rest of the world. This figure considers only Pillar 2 firms; the position for all firms is shown in figure C2.[14]

The first three panels of figure 6 repeat the results of figure 4, but separately for each of these four markets. Panel A, therefore, shows the final ownership in tax havens of patents in each market, including both initial

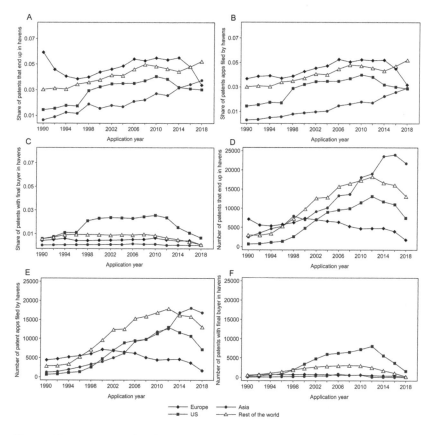

Fig. 6. The importance of tax havens for Pillar 2 firms: geographical variation. Matched Orbis intellectual property data and Orbis ownership data. These figures demonstrate the evolution of the patenting activity of Pillar 2 firms in tax havens. The geographical breakdown is at the application country level. In panels *A–C*, we present the share of patents, and in panels *D–F*, we present the number of patents. In panel *A*, we include a number of patents that eventually end up in a tax haven as a share of all patent applications in each year. This consists of two aspects of tax-haven ownership: (1) the number of patents applied for by tax-haven subsidiaries and (2) the number of patents that are eventually bought by tax-haven subsidiaries, even if they were applied for by non-haven-located firms. In panels *B* and *C*, we break this share into the two aspects, showing share of (1) in panel *B* and share of (2) in panel *C*. We repeat this for panels *D–F*, using just the raw numbers of patents. For corresponding graphs for all firms, see the appendices. A color version of this figure is available online.

applications and purchases by firms in tax havens. There is clearly considerable variation both across markets and over time. Just under 1% of patents in Asian markets were held in tax havens in 1990, but by 2020, that proportion had tripled to around 3%. At the other extreme, 6% of patents in European markets were held in tax havens in 1990. This has fallen a little since and has varied over time. But consistently, this proportion has been more than 5%. The proportion of patents in markets in the rest of the world has also grown strongly, to around 5%.

Panels B and C confirm that the primary way patents are held in tax havens is through the initial application. This is inevitable, because relatively few patents are traded. However, an exception to this pattern is for patents in the US market. In this case, around 2% of the patents have been purchased by firms in havens. Panels D, E, and F show the total number of patents as opposed to the share. The rapid growth in the number of patents in China, in particular, means that the relative importance of havens appears different when considering absolute numbers. In absolute terms, more patents in the Asian markets are held in havens.

We explore heterogeneity in transactions further in figure 7, which can be directly compared with figure 5. Specifically, panel A of figure 7 shows the location breakdown for all Pillar 2 firms transactions (in panel A of figure 5, the line designated with circles). Panel B of figure 7 shows the location breakdown for all Pillar 2 firms transactions with last haven buyer (in panel B of figure 5, the line designated with circles). The numerator varies across those two panels, but the denominator is the same; that is, all transactions by Pillar 2 firms. There is clearly important variation across markets. The tax-haven share of purchases of patents in Asian markets has fallen considerably over the past 20 years to close to zero. By contrast, the comparable figure for the rest of the world has been around 20%, and the figure for Europe jumped to around 35% in 2018. The share of haven purchasers is a little lower for final transactions of a patent.

Patent value and granting. In table 6, we explore heterogeneity in other patent characteristics, focusing on patent values and whether the patent was granted. In panel A, we divide all patent applications into four bins according to the first value of the patent. In panel B, we do the same using the last value of the patent.[15] In panel C, we use citations to proxy how valuable the patent is. In panel D, we consider differences between patents that were eventually granted and those that were not. In each of those panels and within each of the value bins, we compute the share of tax-haven applications, applicants, transactions, and intrafirm transactions in all applications in that particular bin. We include total patents and transactions for reference as well.

Starting with panel A, we show that the share of tax-haven applicants in all applicants for least valuable patents is 1.7%, and the share of tax-haven applications in all patent applications for those patents is 0.21%. At the same time, the more valuable the patent is, the higher the share of tax-haven applicants and applications. Looking across bins of the different first values of the patent, we do not see much heterogeneity in the transactions with tax havens.

In panel B, we consider the last value of the patent, which arguably may be a better proxy for how valuable the patent is in Orbis data. We find a very similar pattern for tax-haven applicants and applications as

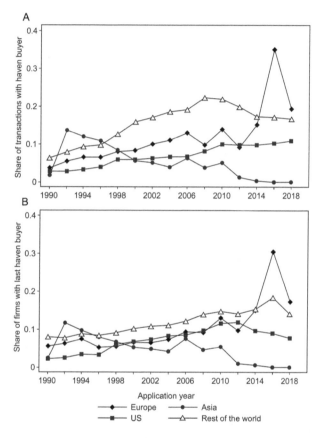

Fig. 7. Importance of tax havens in patent transactions: geographical variation. Matched Orbis intellectual property data and Orbis ownership data. These figures present the evolution of the share of transactions with tax havens in the transaction data, disaggregated by the country where the patent was applied for. For example, the Europe line shows the share of tax-haven buyers for patents that were applied for in Europe. Panel A shows the share of tax-haven transactions in all transactions. We aggregate all transactions and attribute them to the patent without distinguishing the transaction year. Panel B shows the share of firms in transaction data that have a final tax-haven buyer. Haven buyers means that the firm that bought the patent was located in a tax haven. A color version of this figure is available online.

Table 6

Heterogeneities According to Patent Characteristics: The Role of Tax Havens

	Tax-Haven Applications		Tax-Haven Applicants		Tax-Haven Transactions		Tax-Haven Intra Transactions		Total Patents	Total Transactions
Panel A: First Value Quantiles										
Q1	54,361	.21%	440,429	1.68%	518,200	24.95%	148,608	7.15%	26,253,111	2,077,098
Q2	44,662	.69%	264,078	4.10%	290,905	22.34%	123,542	9.49%	6,444,865	1,301,922
Q3	81,681	.75%	447,938	4.09%	622,472	24.91%	252,801	10.11%	10,942,391	2,499,375
Q4	105,267	.75%	599,788	4.27%	1,239,612	24.25%	360,530	7.05%	14,035,835	5,112,200
Panel B: Last Value Quantiles										
Q1	70,874	.34%	437,353	2.10%	271,108	16.73%	81,527	5.03%	20,780,147	1,620,385
Q2	35,325	.42%	264,375	3.16%	352,937	21.16%	109,165	6.55%	8,361,954	1,667,825
Q3	48,141	.35%	396,969	2.87%	975,743	27.25%	264,406	7.39%	13,821,984	3,580,112
Q4	131,631	.89%	653,536	4.44%	1,071,401	25.99%	430,383	10.44%	14,712,117	4,122,273
Panel C: Citations Quantiles										
Q1	568	.01%	100,785	2.36%	148,766	21.36%	52,477	7.54%	4,264,081	696,440
Q2	497	.01%	119,898	2.93%	230,031	24.60%	69,084	7.39%	4,091,416	935,275
Q3	166	0%	127,175	3.70%	403,702	26.90%	98,550	6.57%	3,437,930	1,500,995
Q4	20	0%	158,453	4.13%	813,924	27.09%	230,779	7.68%	3,840,325	3,004,482
Panel D: Granted vs. Not Granted										
Ungranted	151,179	.42%	1,129,083	3.10%	1,287,721	22.81%	449,664	7.97%	36,404,963	5,644,673
Granted	175,243	.53%	925,076	2.80%	1,454,450	24.98%	466,461	8.01%	33,051,290	5,821,988

Source: Matched Orbis intellectual property data and Orbis ownership data for years 1990–2020.

Note: This table summarizes the distribution of tax-haven and patent-box applications and applicants across quartiles of first patent value (panel A), last patent value (panel B), citations (panel C), and whether the patent was eventually granted or not (panel D). Within each quartile, we calculate the share of tax-haven patent applications in applications in all applications in that quartile. As such, in Q1 row 1 column 1, number should be interpreted as a share of tax-haven patent applications in all patent applications within the least valuable patents according to the first value. Applications are locations where firms apply for patents. First value is the value of the patent the first year it appears in the value data set, and last value is the value of the patents in 2020, or the last year it appears in the value data set. Applicants define locations where subsidiaries are. Tax-haven and patent-box countries are listed in the appendices.

in panel A; that is, there are fewer applicants from and applications to tax-haven countries within the group of least valuable patents as a share of all patent applications. In this panel, we also see a variation in the transactions with tax-haven buyers. For the most valuable patents, 26% of all transactions had a tax-haven purchaser, and only 16.7% of all transactions for the least valuable patents had a tax-haven purchaser. A similar pattern can be observed for the fraction of final tax-haven purchasers. We observe similar patterns across patents with more citations in panel C.

In panel D, we compare the importance of tax havens for patents that were granted versus those that were eventually not. We find that the share of tax-haven applicants is actually lower in cases when a patent was granted, 2.8% versus 3.1%. At the same time, patents that are eventually granted are more likely to be transacted into a tax haven: 25% of them have a tax-haven purchaser, and 22.8% of patents that are not eventually granted have one.

B. By Firm Characteristics

We then consider heterogeneity in behavior across multinational firms with different observable characteristics. In table 7, we split firms in several dimensions. In panel A, we consider size, measured by turnover, splitting the sample into quartiles, but also examine the top 10% and top 5% firms by turnover. There is some variation by the size of a firm, but the differences are not striking. For example, 2.3% of patents of the second quartile of firms are by haven applicants, compared with 4.3% for the top 5% of firms. Larger firms also have a slightly higher share of haven purchases in all transactions.

Panel B shows a similar position based on the number of subsidiaries a multinational has. This may well depend on how aggressive the firm chooses to be in its tax position. As such, in panel C, we disaggregate firms by the number of tax-haven affiliates they have. First, the use of havens seems to rise with the measure of firm size. Interestingly, the top 1% make a smaller use of havens than the next 9%. This may reflect a greater sophistication in tax planning for the very largest firms, which may be exploiting cost-contribution arrangements, or other arrangements, to separate the ownership of the patent and the right to receive the royalty income. Second, as panel D indicates, the more tax-haven affiliates the firm has, the more likely it is to use these affiliates as patent applicants and final destinations for patent applications. Specifically, firms with more than 20 tax-haven affiliates have 1.8% of their patent applications filed in tax havens, 12.4%

Table 7
MNC Patenting According to Firm Characteristics: Shares

Characteristics	Haven Applications (%)	Haven Applicants (%)	Haven Buyers (%)
Panel A: Turnover Distribution			
0–25th	.7	3.1	11.6
25th–50th	.5	2.3	10.4
50th–75th	.7	4.2	12.3
75th–90th	.8	3.8	10.4
90th–95th	.6	4.1	13.8
95th+	.5	4.3	11.8
Panel B: Number of Subsidiaries			
Fewer than 25 subsidiaries (25th percentile)	.5	1.8	7.1
25–71 subsidiaries (25th–50th percentile)	.5	2.3	9.1
71–201 subsidiaries (50th–75th percentile)	.7	3.9	12.4
201–495 subsidiaries (75th–90th percentile)	.8	4.9	11.6
495–1,000 subsidiaries (90th–99th percentile)	.9	6.1	14.7
More than 1,000 subsidiaries (99th percentile)	.7	3.2	12.5
Panel C: Number of Tax-Haven Affiliates			
No haven affiliates	.4	0	2.8
1 haven affiliate	.2	.5	3.2
2–5 haven affiliates	.6	2.2	8.1
5–10 haven affiliates	.6	4.6	13.7
10–20 haven affiliates	.9	7.5	17.4
More than 20 haven affiliates	1.8	12.4	19.8
Panel D: ETRs			
Above 15 ETR	.6	3.0	11.2
Below 15 ETR	.8	5.0	12.5

Source: Matched Orbis intellectual property data and Orbis ownership data.
Note: This table summarizes the shares of patents in each of the categories: in column 1 share of tax-haven applications, column 2 share of tax-haven applicant countries, and column 3 share of tax-haven buyers in cross-border transactions. To calculate these shares, we collapse the data set at the multinational corporation (MNC) level across all years 1990–2020. We consider four types of attributes: panel A, turnover distribution quintiles, panel B, MNCs with below or above 15% effective tax rate (ETR), panel C, MNCs with different numbers of tax-haven affiliates, and panel D, MNCs with different numbers of wholly owned subsidiaries.

of their applications filed by tax-haven resident firms, and almost 20% of their transactions with a tax-haven buyer. In contrast, for firms with no tax-haven affiliates, these fractions are 0.4%, 0%, and 2.8%, respectively.

In panel D, we calculate the consolidated MNC-level ETRs, as the ratio of tax liability to profit and loss before taxes. We then divide MNCs into those with ETRs above and below 15%. We use 15% because this is the new GMT rate agreed on by Pillar 2 regulations. Firms with an ETR below 15% apply for patents in havens 5% of the time, compared with only 3% for firms with an ETR above 15%. Similarly, the share of patents that are transacted into tax havens is 12.5% for those firms with ETR below 15% and a lower 11.2% for those first with higher ETRs. These results suggest that by using tax havens for IP location, these MNCs are likely reducing their overall ETRs.

VIII. Conclusions

The evidence we provide in this paper suggests that tax havens play an important function as a location of IP. Using a novel global data set on patent applications and transactions, we demonstrate the disproportionate role that these low-tax jurisdictions play as patent applicants and patent transfer destinations, especially for the most valuable patents.

Our findings have several implications for the future of global policies targeting profit shifting via the use of IP. First, the use of tax havens for locating IP has increased almost continuously since the 1990s for the largest firms, in spite of large global reforms that target profit shifting of these large MNCs. This means that previous initiatives have not made it more costly or more difficult for MNCs to use IP to minimize their tax liabilities. Second, the role of firms applying for patents in Asian countries in both general patenting activity and the use of tax havens has increased in the past decade, while the role of firms in Europe and the United States has declined. This suggests that policies that target profit shifting may be more effective in Europe and the United States and less effective in Asia. Third, the role of tax havens in patent applications and transactions does not vary significantly across MNCs with different turnovers.

In principle, the GMT could have a significant impact on MNCs' incentive to shift profit to tax havens, although there are still many unanswered questions as to how the proposed tax will work and the extent to which countries will actually implement it. Essentially, under the GMT, the marginal tax rate on an additional dollar of profit in a haven will be at least 15%. Shifting profit from a country with, say, a 20% rate would save only 5% on the profit shifted. If the haven currently does not tax the income at all, then that represents a very significant reduction in the benefit of shifting. In turn, that represents a very significant reduction in the incentive to locate patents in the haven in the first place. However, our findings point toward an important aspect of GMT that may limit its effectiveness in combating IP-based profit shifting: the turnover-based size threshold may not catch important tax-minimizing, IP-intensive MNCs. Our evidence suggests that the use of tax havens as a patent location destination has increased most rapidly among the firms potentially subject to GMT (i.e., the Pillar 2 firms). However, this tax-haven usage does not substantially vary across the turnover distribution of Pillar 2 firms. As such, it is likely that firms below the GMT suggested turnover threshold may be involved in as much profit shifting using IP located in tax havens.

In our technical companion paper, Bilicka et al. (2022), we use the findings from the current paper to discuss possible adverse effects of profit shifting on overall investment by MNCs. In particular, we build a model in which MNCs invest in an intangible "tax-avoidance asset." We have in mind the legal structure of the MNC, including the location of IP in tax-haven countries or networks that allow for the relocation of such IP to tax havens. As such, we allow for unobserved heterogeneity across different types of firms with regard to access to different tax-avoidance strategies or networks that they prefer to have. We also allow for corner solutions in which firms can choose to shift all profits to tax havens. This results in the most tax-aggressive MNCs being substantially more responsive to changes in tax regimes than the least aggressive firms. A consequence of firms' investing in a tax-avoidance asset is a lower cost of capital for investment. This suggests that any regulation that will increase the cost of profit shifting, such as GMT, is likely going to reduce investment in productive assets. Together, the current paper and the technical paper highlight the trade-offs that policy makers are facing in combating profit shifting.

Appendix A

IP-Regime Countries

Many countries in the world offer special regimes for IP, with reduced rates on patents and R&D-related activities. These incentives are extremely heterogeneous across countries. Nevertheless, the picture of IP incentives would not be complete without looking at the role these countries play in patenting activities of firms. We list countries that offer IP-regime incentives in appendix B. In figure A1, we show that these countries indeed capture a large share of the innovation market, with more than 25% of applications filed in IP-regime countries and about 30% of applicants residing in those countries. The role of these countries as application destinations and applicant countries has been increasing since the 1990s. However, note that these countries include China, South Korea, and India, Asian countries with large real activities and growing innovation markets. Hence, these trends are unlikely to proxy for tax-minimization activities.

Similarly, the IP-regime countries play a large role as destinations for patent transfers. In figure A1, we document that these countries are destinations for patents in about 15% of patent transactions and 30% of cross-border patent transactions in 2019. However, evidence from these figures suggests a declining role of IP-regime countries, especially relative to tax havens, as destinations for patent transactions. In the early 1990s, almost 70% of all cross-border buyers were located in countries that offer special IP regimes. In 2019, this fraction was 30%. IP-regime countries are more important as final transaction destinations for intrafirm transactions, as evidenced by panels B and D, especially since 2000, when a large number of these incentives came about.

In figure A3, we look closely at four distinct IP regimes introduced across different countries (Shehaj and Weichenrieder 2021). We pick the regime introductions that fall within our sample period and specifically target patents, rather than R&D activities more broadly. First, we consider the United Kingdom, which introduced a patent-box regime in 2013 with a low tax rate on patents at 10%. Second, we consider the Netherlands, which introduced a patent-box regime in 2007 at a rate of 10% for patents. Third, we consider Hungary, with a regime for royalties and capital gains introduced in 2013 with low tax rates of 9.5% and 4.5%, respectively. Fourth, we consider India, which introduced a patent-related incentive in 2016 at a rate of 10%. We show that special IP regimes were introduced in three out of those four countries (European ones) as the share of cross-border patent applications filed in those countries was declining. After the introduction of those special IP regimes, the share of the cross-border market captured by the applications in those countries stopped declining. In the case of India, the share of patent applications was generally following an increasing trend, but since 2010, 6 years before the regime introduction started declining as well. These results, although not causal, suggest a role of special IP regimes in countries trying to protect their patenting activities.

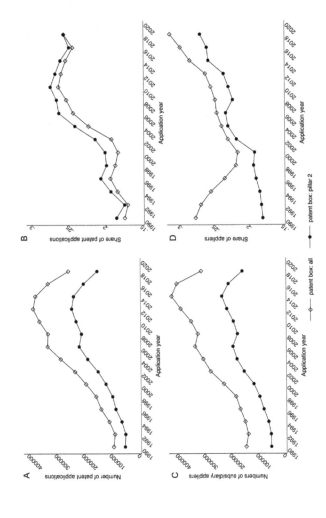

Fig. A1. The importance of IP-regime country applicants and applications. Matched Orbis intellectual property (IP) data and Orbis ownership data. These figures demonstrate the evolution of the patenting activity of global firms in tax havens. In panel A, we include a number of applications filed in patent-box countries by firms resident outside of those countries. In panel B, we include a share of these applications. In panel C, we include a number of applications filed by firms resident in patent-box countries outside of those countries. In panel D, we include a share of these. A color version of this figure is available online.

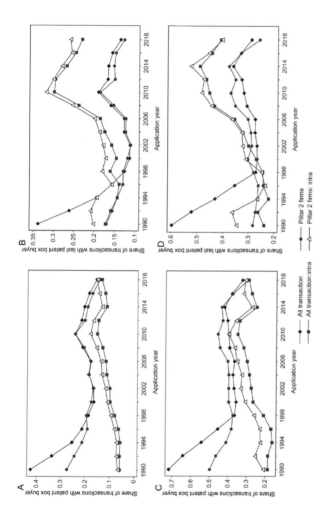

Fig. A2. Importance of IP-regime country buyers. Matched Orbis intellectual property (IP) data and Orbis ownership data. In all panels, we show the share of transactions with a patent box buyer country. In panel *A*, we include all transactions. In panel *B*, we only include final transactions. In panel *C*, we focus on cross-border transactions. In panel *D*, only include final cross-border transactions. These figures present the evolution of the number of patent transactions using the patent-level aggregated data. This means that we aggregate all transactions and attribute them to the patent without distinguishing the transaction year. Intrafirm patents are those transacted between related parties. Haven buyers means that the firm that bought the patent was located in a tax haven. We consider only cross-border transactions, which constitute 25% of all transactions. A color version of this figure is available online.

91

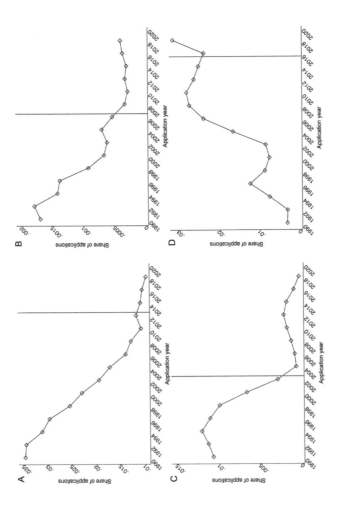

Fig. A3. The effect of IP regimes on patenting activity. Matched Orbis intellectual property (IP) data and Orbis ownership data. These figures demonstrate the evolution of the patenting activity around the introduction of IP regimes, in 2013 for the United Kingdom (panel A), in 2007 for the Netherlands (panel B), in 2003 for Hungary (panel C), and in 2016 for India (panel D). In each figure, we plot the share of patent applications in each of the respective countries as a fraction of all cross-border patent applications. A color version of this figure is available online.

Appendix B

Examples of Intellectual Property Holding Relationships and Withholding Taxes

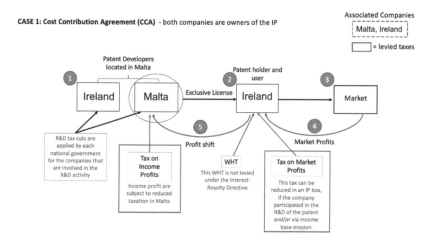

Fig. B1. Example, cost-sharing agreement. Data are from Organisation for Economic Co-operation and Development. This figure describes various levels of taxes imposed on multinational corporations with a cost-contribution (sharing) agreement for intellectual property (IP). R&D = research and development; WHT = withholding tax. A color version of this figure is available online.

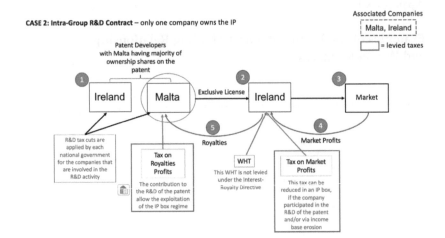

Fig. B2. Example, IP transfer. Data are from Organisation for Economic Cooperation and Development. This figure describes various levels of taxes imposed on multinational corporations with intragroup research and development (R&D) contracts for intellectual property (IP). WHT = withholding tax. A color version of this figure is available online.

Appendix C

Additional Figures and Tables

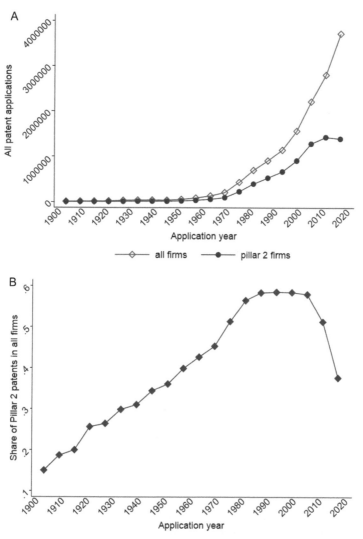

Fig. C1. The evolution of patent applications over time: 1900–2020. Matched Orbis intellectual property data and Orbis ownership data. Each point in panel *A* corresponds to a 2-year average of aggregated patent applications for each of 1900/01 up until 2019/20. In panel *B*, we plot the share of patents applied for by Pillar 2 firms in all patents applied for in each year. These figures demonstrate the evolution of the patenting activity of global firms starting in 1990. The data set includes 2 million unique firms owning 86.5 million unique patents. A color version of this figure is available online

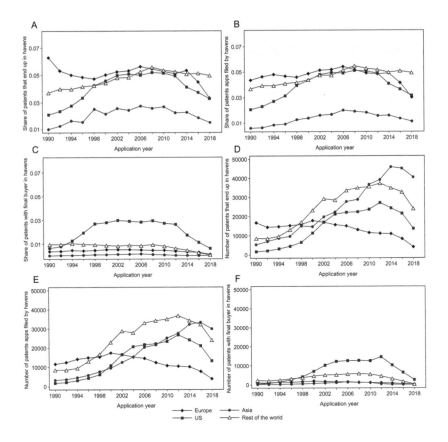

Fig. C2. The importance of tax havens for all firms: geographical variation. Matched Orbis intellectual property data and Orbis ownership data. These figures demonstrate the evolution of the patenting activity of all firms in tax havens. In panels *A–C*, we present the share of patents, and in panels *D–F*, we present the number of patents. In panel *A*, we include a number of patents that eventually end up in a tax haven as a share of all patent applications in each year. This consists of two aspects of tax-haven ownership: (1) the number of patents applied for by tax-haven subsidiaries and (2) the number of patents that are eventually bought by tax-haven subsidiaries, even if they were applied for by non–haven-located firms. In panels *B* and *C*, we break this share into the two aspects, showing share of (1) in panel *B* and share of (2) in panel *C*. We repeat this for panels *D–F*, using just the raw numbers of patents. For corresponding graphs for all firms, see the appendices. A color version of this figure is available online.

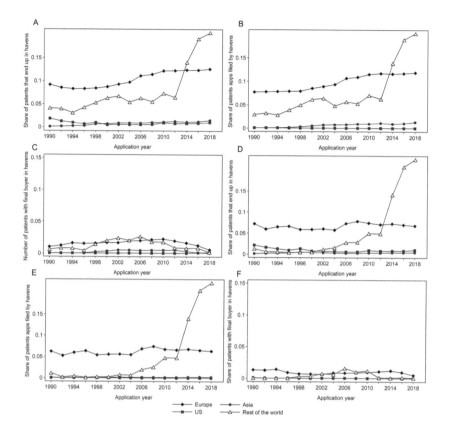

Fig. C3. The importance of tax havens for Pillar 2 firms: geographical variation by applicant and headquarters countries. Matched Orbis intellectual property data and Orbis ownership data. These figures demonstrate the evolution of the patenting activity of Pillar 2 firms in tax havens. The geographical breakdown is at the applicant country level in panels *A–C* and at the country of the parent of the applicant level in panels *D–F*. In all panels, we present the share of patents. In panels *A* and *D*, we include a number of patents that eventually end up in a tax haven as a share of all patent applications in each year. This consists of two aspects of tax-haven ownership: (1) the number of patents applied for by tax-haven subsidiaries and (2) the number of patents that are eventually bought by tax-haven subsidiaries, even if they were applied for by non-haven-located firms. In the remaining panels, we break this share into the two aspects, showing share of (1) in panels *B* and *E* and share of (2) in panels *C* and *F*. A color version of this figure is available online.

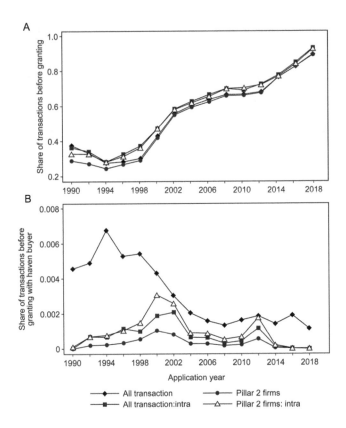

Fig. C4. Evolution of patent transactions over time: patent transactions before granting. Matched Orbis intellectual property data and Orbis ownership data. In panel *A*, we show the share of patent transactions that happened before the patent was granted. In panel *B*, we show the share of patent transactions with tax haven buyer countries that happened before the patent was granted. These figures present the evolution of the number of patent transactions using the patent-level aggregated data. This means that we aggregate all transactions and attribute them to the patent without distinguishing the transaction year. Intrafirm patents are those transacted between related parties. Transactions before granting are defined as those that occurred after the patent was applied for but before it was granted. A color version of this figure is available online.

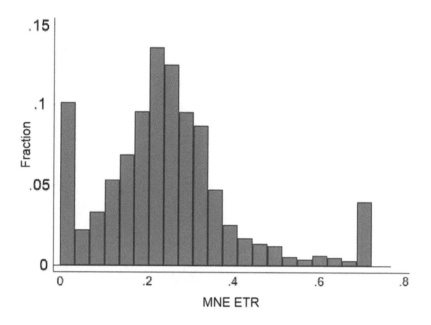

Fig. C5. Distribution of parent-level ETRs. Matched Orbis intellectual property data and Orbis ownership data. This figure plots the distribution of parent-level effective tax rates (ETRs) for Pillar 2 firms. We exclude firms that have negative tax and set ETR to zero when profits are negative but tax paid is positive. MNE = multinational enterprise. A color version of this figure is available online.

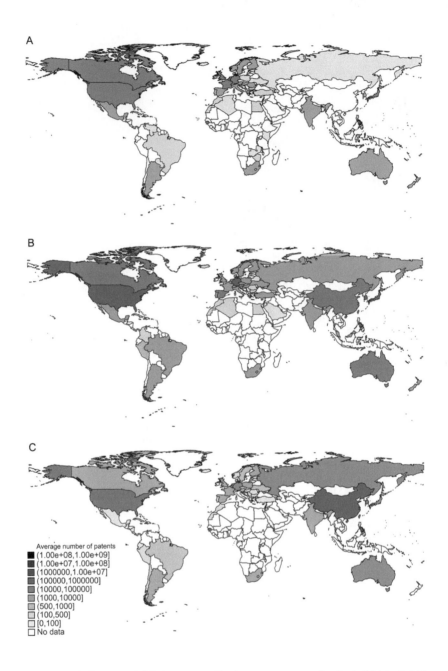

Fig. C6. The location of global patent applications across years: all patents. Matched Orbis intellectual property data and Orbis ownership data. These maps plot the total number of patent applications in various locations. These include patent applications in the country where the subsidiary applying for the patent is located too. Panel *A* shows the distribution in 1980, panel *B* in 2000, and panel *C* in 2018. A color version of this figure is available online.

Table C1

Top Patent Locations and Countries: Tax Havens and Patent Boxes

Application Locations	No. of Applications	% of Applications	Applying Countries	No. of Applications	% of Applications
		Panel A: Tax Havens			
Hong Kong	128,727	38.89	Switzerland	1,106,986	54.28
Singapore	119,302	36.04	Singapore	216,924	10.64
Switzerland	29,163	8.81	Ireland	195,042	9.56
Ireland	20,428	6.17	Hong Kong	184,167	9.03
Cyprus	15,261	4.61	Cayman Islands	116,432	5.71
Costa Rica	8,091	2.44	Luxembourg	79,728	3.91
Luxembourg	3,684	1.11	Liechtenstein	37,790	1.85
Panama	2,326	.7	British Virgin Islands	20,934	1.03
San Marino	2,281	.69	Barbados	18,613	.91
Jordan	1,403	.42	Bermuda	14,116	.69
		Panel B: Patent-Box Countries			
China	3,499,120	49.53	South Korea	1,551,921	19.44
South Korea	1,196,741	16.94	France	1,420,996	17.8
India	591,577	8.37	United Kingdom	1,173,826	14.7
United Kingdom	519,083	7.35	Netherlands	946,884	11.86
Spain	442,130	6.26	Italy	795,914	9.97
Israel	157,197	2.23	China	775,706	9.71
France	128,561	1.82	Belgium	259,818	3.25
Portugal	118,211	1.67	Singapore	208,917	2.62
Singapore	111,295	1.58	Israel	208,575	2.61
Hungary	107,051	1.52	Ireland	188,576	2.36

Source: Matched Orbis intellectual property data and Orbis ownership data for years 1990–2020.

Note: Application locations are defined as countries where firms apply for patents. Applying countries are locations of subsidiaries. Panel A summarizes country locations according to number of applications for tax-haven countries. Panel B does the same for patent-box countries. Tax-haven and patent-box countries are listed in the appendices.

Table C2
Top Patent Transaction Buyers and Sellers: Tax Havens, Patent Boxes versus All, Cross-Country Transactions

Panel A: Buyer Countries

Buyer Country	nb	%	Haven Buyer Country	nb	%	Patent-Box Buyer Country	nb	%
United States	4,591,683	25.79	Switzerland	1,297,523	37.48	Italy	1,703,149	24.27
Italy	1,703,149	9.57	Singapore	636,749	18.39	United Kingdom	1,314,819	18.74
Germany	1,395,479	7.84	Ireland	593,440	17.14	Netherlands	934,607	13.32
United Kingdom	1,314,819	7.39	Luxembourg	322,817	9.32	Ireland	636,749	9.08
Switzerland	1,297,523	7.29	Cayman Islands	268,653	7.76	France	608,522	8.67
Netherlands	934,607	5.25	Hong Kong	122,253	3.53	Singapore	593,440	8.46
Canada	878,392	4.93	Barbados	108,930	3.15	China	324,529	4.63
Ireland	636,749	3.58	Bermuda	39,720	1.15	Luxembourg	268,653	3.83
France	608,522	3.42	British Virgin Islands	18,621	.54	Belgium	189,478	2.7
Singapore	593,440	3.33	Malta	12,999	.38	Barbados	122,253	1.74

Panel B: Seller Countries

Seller Country	nb	%	Seller Country if Haven Buyer	nb	%	Seller Country If Patent-Box Buyer	nb	%
United States	6,063,486	34.06	United States	1,955,934	56.49	United States	3,208,957	45.73
Germany	2,355,900	13.23	Germany	356,074	10.28	Germany	967,735	13.79
United Kingdom	1,434,575	8.06	United Kingdom	111,219	3.21	United Kingdom	410,920	5.86
Switzerland	1,224,893	6.88	Luxembourg	103,434	2.99	Switzerland	330,619	4.71
Netherlands	791,738	4.45	Switzerland	96,518	2.79	France	302,161	4.31
France	750,448	4.22	Japan	77,154	2.23	Japan	268,662	3.83
Canada	686,326	3.86	France	70,846	2.05	Netherlands	228,887	3.26
Japan	510,058	2.87	Australia	63,522	1.83	Italy	152,079	2.17
Italy	452,263	2.54	Bermuda	62,738	1.81	Canada	151,313	2.16
Singapore	392,442	2.2	Singapore	59,193	1.71	Luxembourg	118,659	1.69

Source: Matched Orbis intellectual property data and Orbis ownership data.
Note: The numbers are transaction counts across all sample years. Panel A shows summaries of transactions ranking buyer countries according to the number of transactions, first for all countries, then for tax-haven buyer countries only, followed by patent-box buyer countries only. Panel B shows summaries of transactions ranking seller countries according to the number of transactions, first for all buyers, then when the buyer is a tax haven, followed by when a buyer is patent-box country. nb is the number of transactions; % is the percent of all transactions. Tax havens and patent-box countries are defined in the appendices.

Table C3

Evolution of Top 10 Buyer Countries: Haven versus All

				Panel A: Tax Haven Buyers				
Country	No. of trans: 2000	% Trans	Country	No. of trans: 2010	% Trans	Country	No. of trans: 2019	% Trans
CH	20,900	82.32	CH	54,960	42.97	SG	143,065	39.04
IE	1,578	6.22	IE	29,706	23.23	CH	106,956	29.18
LU	1,175	4.63	LU	15,737	12.3	IE	47,171	12.87
SG	817	3.22	SG	15,096	11.8	BM	20,576	5.61
BM	184	.72	KY	3,241	2.53	BB	17,490	4.77
HK	128	.5	BM	2,557	2	LU	16,591	4.53
LI	121	.48	HK	2,366	1.85	HK	8,455	2.31
BS	87	.34	VG	1,709	1.34	MT	4,623	1.26
KY	85	.33	BB	609	.48	KY	426	.12
BB	83	.33	VC	540	.42	LI	301	.08
				Panel B: All Buyers				
US	245,392	39.6	US	2,181,937	66.59	US	7,475,583	80.98
DE	110,209	17.79	DE	401,826	12.26	CA	410,951	4.45
IT	106,984	17.27	JP	109,232	3.33	DE	250,405	2.71
GB	45,810	7.39	GB	104,833	3.2	SG	143,065	1.55
CH	20,900	3.37	CN	68,838	2.1	NL	133,431	1.45
JP	16,750	2.7	CH	54,960	1.68	GB	110,674	1.2
NL	13,287	2.14	FR	50,191	1.53	CH	106,956	1.16
BE	11,086	1.79	BR	37,054	1.13	CN	97,855	1.06
FR	10,720	1.73	NL	35,532	1.08	FR	83,400	.9
CA	6,127	.99	IE	29,706	.91	JP	81,207	.88

Source: Matched Orbis intellectual property data and Orbis ownership data.

Note: This table includes only the transactions where the buyer is located in a tax haven. The first 10 countries are in order of the most transactions across all time periods. At the bottom, we summarize the number and fraction of transactions where both buyer and seller are tax-haven countries.

Appendix D

Lists of Countries

Table D1
List of Tax-Haven Countries

Andorra	Dominica	Malta	Samoa
Anguilla	Dominican Republic	Marshall Islands	San Marino
Antigua and Barbuda	Gibraltar	Mauritius	Seychelles
Aruba	Grenada	Micronesia	Singapore
Bahamas	Guernsey	Monaco	Switzerland
Bahrain	Hong Kong	Montserrat	Tonga
Barbados	Ireland	Nauru	Turks and Caicos
Belize	Isle of Man	Netherlands	Islands
Bermuda	Jersey	Antilles	Vanuatu
British Virgin Islands	Lebanon	Niue	
Cayman Islands	Liberia	Panama	
Cook Islands	Liechtenstein	Saint Martin	
Costa Rica	Luxembourg	Saint Vincent and	
Cyprus	Macao	Grenadines	
Djibouti	Maldives	Saint Kitts and Nevis	

Table D2
List of Patent-Box Countries

Barbados	Macao
Belgium	Mauritius
China	Netherlands
Colombia	Portugal
France	Singapore
Hungary	South Korea
India	Spain
Ireland	Thailand
Israel	Turkey
Italy	United Kingdom
Luxembourg	Uruguay

Endnotes

Author email addresses: Bilicka (kat.bilicka@usu.edu), Devereux (michael.devereux@ sbs.ox.ac.uk), Güçeri (irem.guceri@bsg.ox.ac.uk). We thank Joseph Andrus and Steve Shay for our discussions on the legal aspects of the use of IP for profit shifting. We are grateful for excellent research assistance from Martina Beretta. Irem Güçeri acknowledges financial support through the Oxford University Press John Fell Fund. For acknowledgments, sources of research support, and disclosure of the authors' material financial relationships, if any, please see https://www.nber.org/books-and-chapters/tax-policy-and-economy-volume-37/tax-avoidance-networks-and-push-historic-global-tax-reform.

1. See Organisation for Economic Cooperation and Development agreements in July 2021 and October 2021.

2. In this paper, we define them as firms with total revenue of more than €750 million in 2019, the largest MNCs in the world.

3. See also, e.g., Desai et al. (2006), Slemrod and Wilson (2009), Egger, Eggert, and Winner (2010), Dharmapala and Riedel (2013), and Dischinger, Knoll, and Riedel (2014). Part of the reason for uncertainty with respect to the degree of profit shifting is that the counterfactual of the tax that would have been levied in the absence of profit shifting is not well defined. The traditional approach to estimating this counterfactual is that of Hines and Rice (1994), who implicitly estimate profit in a jurisdiction based on the use of capital and labor located there. But that is only partially the basis for the international allocation of taxing rights, which also allocates rights to jurisdictions in which valuable assets are owned or lending originates. Other approaches taken in the literature are reviewed elsewhere. See, e.g., Dharmapala (2014) and Riedel (2018).

4. The "location of a patent" may refer to one of many places, as a patent can technically be located in multiple jurisdictions for different purposes. In panel B of table 1, we provide a list of potential location options. In Sections V and VI, we use these definitions in our analysis. Note that the locations of protection and application are mostly irrelevant from a profit-shifting perspective. In this paper, we do not exploit the inventor's location information.

5. McDonald (2008) shows that for a sample of US MNCs in 2002, 17% had a cost-sharing agreement in place.

6. In appendix B, we provide detailed graphs visualizing two additional cases of taxation of IP when firms enter into cost-sharing and intragroup agreements.

7. In many cases, the patent-box tax rate is half or less than half the main corporate tax rate. Details for 2021 can be found at https://taxfoundation.org/patent-box-regimes-europe-2021.

8. In addition, the data set includes information on contracting countries; that is, where the protection is applied for (but only for European Patent Office patents, approximately 2 million of our patents) and the expiration date of the patent. We do not use these in the paper.

9. The source of these data is Zephyr, which is a Bureau van Dijk data set that covers mergers and acquisitions.

10. In figure C6, we show a map with the location of all patents across the years 1980, 2000, and 2018.

11. We list all the tax-haven countries we consider in appendix D. The definition of tax haven follows prior literature (Hines and Rice 1994; Tørsløv et al. 2022) and includes countries with low corporate tax rates.

12. We do not present separate evidence on the share of patent applications in tax havens. Firms do apply for patents in tax havens, but their role is minimal relative to other countries. We find just under 20,000 applications filed in tax havens in a given year. This has been increasing over the years from 10,000 in the 1990s. However, these applications consist of at most 0.8% of all patent applications in a given year and that share has been relatively flat. This is consistent with the location of the application being the market where firms seek protection for their innovation. Because tax havens are not big markets, conceptually they should not be important application locations. To verify that, in table C1 we show that more than 85% of applications in tax havens are filed by the largest four: Hong Kong, Singapore, Switzerland, and Ireland.

13. Results between panels B and D are different because in many cases, patents are sold to a number of different subsidiaries, which affects both the numerator and denominator of our ratios.

14. In figure C3, we show additional results considering the location of the applicant and the location of the parent of the applicant. Here, the role of subsidiaries located in Europe as well as European MNCs is dominant. This suggests that likely a large share of patents applied for in the United States or in Asia that end up in tax havens are owned by European firms.

15. Note that these values are rounded estimates from the Orbis IP value data set, in which the 5th and 25th percentile of values is the same: that is, 5,000. The 50th percentile is 10,000 and the 95th one is 1,097,000. This is why the number of patents in each bin is heavily skewed toward the bottom value quantile.

References

Acemoglu, D., U. Akcigit, H. Alp, N. Bloom, and W. Kerr. 2018. "Innovation, Reallocation and Growth." *American Economic Review* 108 (11): 3450–91.

Akcigit, U., J. Grigsby, and T. Nicholas. 2017. "Immigration and the Rise of American Ingenuity." *American Economic Review* 107 (5): 327–31.

Akcigit, U., J. Grigsby, T. Nicholas, and S. Stantcheva. 2018. "Taxation and Innovation in the 20th Century." Working Paper no. 24982, NBER, Cambridge, MA.

Akcigit, U., D. Hanley, and S. Stantcheva. 2022. "Optimal Taxation and R&D Policies." *Econometrica* 90 (2): 645–84.

Alstadsaeter, A., S. Barrios, G. Nicodeme, A. M. Skonieczna, and A. Vezzani. 2018. "Patent Boxes Design, Patents Location, and Local R&D." *Economic Policy* 33 (93): 131–77.

Berkes, E., K. Manysheva, and M. Mestieri. 2022. "Global Innovation Spillovers and Productivity: Evidence from 100 Years of World Patent Data." Working Paper no. 2022-15, Federal Reserve Bank of Chicago, Chicago.

Bilicka, K. A. 2019. "Comparing UK Tax Returns of Foreign Multinationals to Matched Domestic Firms." *American Economic Review* 109 (8): 2921–53.

Bilicka, K. A., M. Devereux, and I. Güçeri. 2022. "Tax Policy, Investment and Profit-Shifting." Technical report photocopy, NBER, Cambridge, MA.

Bilicka, K. A., Y. Qi, and J. Xing. 2022. "Real Responses to Anti-Tax Avoidance: Evidence from the UK Worldwide Debt Cap." *Journal of Public Economics* 214:104742.

Bilicka, K. A., and D. Scur. 2021. "Organizational Capacity and Profit Shifting." Technical report, NBER, Cambridge, MA.

Bloom, N., M. Schankerman, and J. van Reenen. 2013. "Identifying Technology Spillovers and Product Market Rivalry." *Econometrica* 81 (4): 1347–93.

Bustos, S., D. Pomeranz, J. C. S. Serrato, J. Vila-Belda, and G. Zucman. 2022. "The Race between Tax Enforcement and Tax Planning: Evidence from a Natural Experiment in Chile." Technical report, NBER, Cambridge, MA.

Coppola, A., M. Maggiori, B. Neiman, and J. Schreger. 2021. "Redrawing the Map of Global Capital Flows: The Role of Cross-Border Financing and Tax Havens." *Quarterly Journal of Economics* 136 (3): 1499–556.

Cristea, A. D., and D. X. Nguyen. 2016. "Transfer Pricing by Multinational Firms: New Evidence from Foreign Firm Ownerships." *American Economic Journal: Economic Policy* 8 (3): 170–202.

Davies, R. B., J. Martin, M. Parenti, and F. Toubal. 2018. "Knocking on Tax Haven's Door: Multinational Firms and Transfer Pricing." *Review of Economics and Statistics* 100 (1): 120–34.

Desai, M. A., C. F. Foley, and J. R. Hines. 2004. "A Multinational Perspective on Capital Structure Choice and Internal Capital Markets." *Journal of Finance* 59 (6): 2451–87.

———. 2006. "The Demand for Tax Haven Operations." *Journal of Public Economics* 90 (3): 513–31.

Dharmapala, D. 2014. "What Do We Know about Base Erosion and Profit Shifting? A Review of the Empirical Literature." *Fiscal Studies* 35 (4): 421–48.

Dharmapala, D., and N. Riedel. 2013. "Earnings Shocks and Tax-Motivated Income-Shifting: Evidence from European Multinationals." *Journal of Public Economics* 97 (C): 95–107.

Dischinger, M., B. Knoll, and N. Riedel. 2014. "There's No Place Like Home: The Profitability Gap between Headquarters and Their Foreign Subsidiaries." *Journal of Economics and Management Strategy* 23 (2): 369–95.

Dischinger, M., and N. Riedel. 2011. "Corporate Taxes and the Location of Intangible Assets within Multinational Firms." *Journal of Public Economics* 95 (7–8): 691–707.

Dowd, T., P. Landefeld, and A. Moore. 2017. "Profit Shifting of U.S. Multinationals." *Journal of Public Economics* 148:1–13.

Egger, P., W. Eggert, and H. Winner. 2010. "Saving Taxes through Foreign Plant Ownership." *Journal of International Economics* 81 (1): 99–108.

Feng, J., and X. Jaravel. 2020. "Crafting Intellectual Property Rights: Implications for Patent Assertion Entities, Litigation, and Innovation." *American Economic Journal: Applied Economics* 12 (1): 140–81.

Fuest, C., S. Greil, F. Hugger, and F. Neumeier. 2022. "Global Profit Shifting of Multinational Companies: Evidence from CBCR Micro Data." CESifo Working Paper Series 9757, CESifo.

Gaessler, F., B. Hall, and D. Harhoff. 2021. "Should There Be Lower Taxes on Patent Income?" *Research Policy* 50 (1): 104–29.

Garcia-Bernardo, J., and P. Janský. 2022. "Profit Shifting of Multinational Corporations Worldwide." arXiv preprint, https://arxiv.org/abs/2201.08444.

Garcia-Bernardo, J., P. Janský, and G. Zucman. 2022. "Did the Tax Cuts and Jobs Act Reduce Profit Shifting by US Multinational Companies?" Working Paper no. 30086, NBER, Cambridge, MA.

Griffith, R., H. Miller, and M. O'Connell. 2014. "Ownership of Intellectual Property and Corporate Taxation." *Journal of Public Economics* 112:12–23.

Grubert, H. 2003. "Intangible Income, Intercompany Transactions, Income Shifting, and the Choice of Location." *National Tax Journal* 56 (1): 221–42.

Grubert, H., and J. Slemrod. 1998. "The Effect of Taxes on Investment and Income Shifting to Puerto Rico." *Review of Economics and Statistics* 80 (3): 365–73.

Gumpert, A., J. R. Hines, and M. Schnitzer. 2016. "Multinational Firms and Tax Havens." *Review of Economics and Statistics* 98 (4): 713–27.

Guvenen, F., R. J. Mataloni Jr., D. G. Rassier, and K. J. Ruhl. 2022. "Offshore Profit Shifting and Aggregate Measurement: Balance of Payments, Foreign Investment, Productivity, and the Labor Share." *American Economic Review* 112 (6): 1848–84.

Hines, J. R., and E. M. Rice. 1994. "Fiscal Paradise: Foreign Tax Havens and American Business." *Quarterly Journal of Economics* 109 (1): 149–82.

Huizinga, H., L. Laeven, and G. Nicodeme. 2008. "Capital Structure and International Debt Shifting." *Journal of Financial Economics* 88 (1): 80–118.

Karkinsky, T., and N. Riedel. 2012. "Corporate Taxation and the Choice of Patent Location within Multinational Firms." *Journal of International Economics* 88 (1): 176–85.

Knoll, B., and N. Riedel. 2019. "Patent Shifting and Anti-Tax Avoidance Legislation." *ifo DICE Report* 17 (4): 25–29.

Knoll, B., N. Riedel, T. Schwab, M. Todtenhaupt, and J. Voget. 2021. "Cross-Border Effects of R&D Tax Incentives." *Research Policy* 50 (9): 104326.

Koethenbuerger, M., M. Mardan, and M. Stimmelmayr. 2019. "Profit Shifting and Investment Effects: The Implications of Zero-Taxable Profits." *Journal of Public Economics* 173:96–112.

McDonald, M. 2008. "Income Shifting from Transfer Pricing: Further Evidence from Tax Return Data." Office of Tax Analysis Occasional Papers, US Department of the Treasury. https://home.treasury.gov/system/files/131/TP-2.pdf.

OECD (Organisation for Economic Cooperation and Development). 2019. *Harmful Tax Practices—2018 Progress Report on Preferential Regimes.* https://www.oecd-ilibrary.org/content/publication/9789264311480-en.

Riedel, N. 2018. "Quantifying International Tax Avoidance: A Review of the Academic Literature." *Review of Economics* 69 (2): 169–81.

Schwab, T., and M. Todtenhaupt. 2021. "Thinking Outside the Box: The Cross-Border Effect of Tax Cuts on R&D." *Journal of Public Economics* 204:104536.

Shehaj, P., and A. J. Weichenrieder. 2021. "Corporate Income Tax, IP Boxes and the Location of R&D." WU International Taxation Research Paper Series 2021-10, Vienna University of Economics and Business.

Slemrod, J., and J. D. Wilson. 2009. "Tax Competition with Parasitic Tax Havens." *Journal of Public Economics* 93 (11–12): 1261–70.

Suárez Serrato, J. C. 2018. "Unintended Consequences of Eliminating Tax Havens." Working Paper no. 24850, NBER, Cambridge, MA.

Tørsløv, T., L. Wier, and G. Zucman. 2022. "The Missing Profits of Nations." *Review of Economic Studies*, forthcoming.

Experience Rating as an Automatic Stabilizer

Mark Duggan, *Stanford University and NBER,* United States of America

Audrey Guo, *Santa Clara University,* United States of America

Andrew C. Johnston, *University of California at Merced and NBER,* United States of America

Executive Summary

Unemployment-insurance taxes are experience rated, penalizing firms that dismiss workers. We examine whether experience rating serves as an automatic stabilizer in the labor market. Taking advantage of the variation in layoff penalties across states, we utilize detailed data on state tax schedules and assess whether firms are less responsive to labor-demand shocks when facing higher layoff penalties. Our findings show that average layoff penalties from UI reduce firm adjustments to negative shocks by 11%. This indicates that experience rating contributes to labor market stabilization. For example, during the Great Recession, experience rating preserved nearly a million jobs.

I. Introduction

Unemployment insurance (UI) is considered an automatic stabilizer because it provides benefits in proportion to unemployment. In the United States, UI may also stabilize the labor market through its unique tax system. Employer UI taxes are *experience rated*, which means firms are penalized with tax hikes when workers claim UI, and firms are rewarded with lower tax rates when they refrain from layoffs. Firms considering whether to dismiss workers during a downturn, therefore, may do more to avoid layoffs in the presence of experience rating, potentially stabilizing the labor market.

Tax Policy and the Economy, volume 37, 2023.

We examine whether experience rating dampens the effect of macro-economic shocks on labor demand. To this end, we create measures of the 1-year marginal tax cost (MTC) of layoffs and exploit variation in experience rating across industries and states. Exposure to experience rating differs by state primarily because states have (i) different maximum rates that shield high-layoff firms from the full cost of their layoffs, (ii) different tax schedules that vary in the steepness of penalties, and (iii) different benefit generosities, which generate differences in the cost of layoffs. Exposure to experience rating differs also by industry (within a state) because industries vary in their use of layoffs. Historical layoff rates place firms at different locations on the tax schedule where marginal penalties differ. We collect detailed information on the tax schedules of each state and the average tax rate of each industry within a state in each year to estimate the MTC firms face.

To test whether experience rating changes firm responses to shocks, we calculate demand shocks as the national employment change in an employer's (three-digit North American Industry Classification System [NAICS]) industry. We use a leave-out measure to capture plausibly exogenous demand changes outside the employer's own state. Our findings demonstrate that on average, a positive (negative) 10 percentage point national industry shock increases (decreases) employment in an industry by 9 percentage points. We exploit differences in experience rating arising across states and industries, as outlined above, and find that employment is less responsive to national shocks when firms face more exposure to experience rating. The average MTC (a firing penalty equal to $89 per worker for a 10% layoff) reduces employers' downsizing by 9%. That is, if a 10% shock would have reduced employment by 9% without experience rating, the average exposure to experience rating reduces the response to 8%.

We also examine dimensions of heterogeneity in the effect of experience rating on firm adjustment. Experience rating dampens adjustments to negative shocks but not positive shocks. What this suggests is that experience rating increases employment during downturns without a symmetric reduction in employment during expansions. We also find more pronounced dampening effects in less-risky industries. This suggests that high-risk businesses are more likely to ignore marginal UI taxes when making separation decisions. The estimated effects are also larger and more statistically significant in benefit-ratio states compared with reserve-ratio states, where our measure is a better approximation of total tax costs. This also implies our MTC for reserve ratio states is measured with some error, so our estimated stabilization effects are likely understated. Back-of-the-envelope estimates imply that experience rating prevented the layoffs of 852,000 workers in 2008, which was about 8% of the unemployed population. Thus, it appears that experience rating is a stabilizing force over the business cycle.

We contribute to previous work using quasi-experimental methods to estimate the macroeconomic effects of experience rating on labor demand. Lester and Kidd (1939) first discussed the diverse implications of experience rating in the labor market. The modern literature begins with Feldstein (1976), who presents a model that imperfect experience rating implicitly subsidizes—and increases—unemployment through temporary layoffs. Feldstein (1978) substantiates the model with data and finds that layoff subsidies through imperfect experience rating are responsible for half of temporary-layoff unemployment (where half of unemployment was from temporary layoffs at the time).

Later work by Topel (1983) and Card and Levine (1994) provides further support to Feldstein's hypothesis. Topel finds that layoff subsidies by incomplete experience rating increase temporary-layoff unemployment by 30%. Card and Levine find that experience rating is associated with lower rates of temporary layoff, especially in recessionary years, and less seasonal fluctuation in temporary layoffs. Anderson (1993) expands the scope to look beyond temporary layoffs. She combines a model of employment adjustment with administrative data and documents that greater experience rating leads to less seasonal adjustments in employment. In later work, Anderson and Meyer (2000) examine Washington state's adoption of experience rating in 1985 on labor demand and wages, finding that industry-level tax hikes are passed on to workers in the form of lower wages, and experience rating reduces worker turnover.

Recent work on UI taxation is relatively sparse, because major policy changes are rare and administrative data are decentralized. Johnston (2021) exploits the kink in the UI tax schedule using administrative tax data from Florida. He finds that UI taxes reduce hiring and employment but have no effect on exit or wages. Guo (2023a) examines firms with establishments in multiple states to compare behavior across experience-rating regimes. She finds that during downturns, manufacturing plants were more likely to exit states with higher UI tax costs. Guo (2023b) analyzes a set of state-level tax increases that occurred after the Great Recession and finds that tax increases lowered employment growth within exposed firms. Auray and Fuller (2020) explore the effect experience rating can have on UI claims, and Lachowska, Sorkin, and Woodbury (2022) use administrative data from Washington state to measure firm level take-up and appeal rates. They find that appeals behavior is negatively correlated with worker claim rates, suggesting firm influence on claiming. Huang (2022) and Duggan, Guo, and Johnston (2022) find that larger UI tax bases increase labor demand for part-time and low-wage workers.[1]

In summary, the previous literature has found that greater experience rating provides the benefit of reducing the prevalence of temporary layoffs but imposes a cost during economic recoveries, as tax increases cause employers to be more likely to exit and less likely to hire. In this paper, we explore whether experience rating also provides the benefit of an automatic stabilizing effect during economic downturns, by dampening firms' response to negative shocks. Our outcome of interest is not the prevalence of layoffs themselves but rather the responsiveness of firms to economic shocks. Another contribution is to create updated measures of the MTC for the past 2 decades. Variation in UI tax costs has grown substantially since the 1980s and 1990s, as some states have indexed their tax bases to grow with average income and many states have not, leading to declining real tax bases over time.

II. Background

Under federal regulation, each state in the United States administers a UI program, under which separated workers can receive weekly benefits while they search for new work. Laid-off workers receive a weekly payment that replaces approximately half of their earnings for up to 6 months in normal times. To receive benefits, workers are supposed to substantiate that they are unemployed "for no fault of their own," usually requiring that the worker was laid off for economic reasons and neither quit nor was fired for cause.[2] In 2019, the year prior to the COVID-19 pandemic, more than 5 million Americans received UI benefits, with an average weekly payment of $370, with substantial variation across states. After the onset of the pandemic, 24 million Americans received UI benefits in the first half of 2020.[3]

When workers receive UI benefits, payments to workers are charged to the account of their former employer, operated by each state's department of labor. The firm pays a variable payroll tax that is designed, approximately, to recover the cost of benefits paid out to the firm's former employees. Past work typically finds that the portion of UI taxes that is stable over time and market-wide is borne by employees in the form of lower wages, and the portion of UI taxes that changes over time or varies by firm within a market is borne by the firm in lower profits.

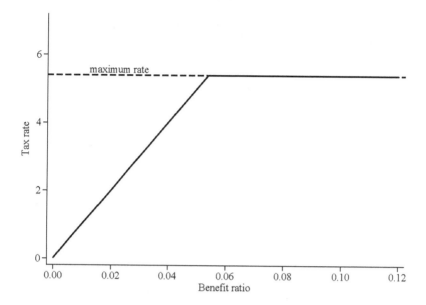

Fig. 1. Sample benefit-ratio unemployment insurance tax formula. Administrative data are from Florida's Department of Economic Opportunity. A color version of this figure is available online.

Figure 1 illustrates a sample UI tax schedule for the state of Florida, which uses a benefit-ratio formula. Tax rates rise linearly with the benefit ratio until the rate would exceed the maximum, generating a kink in the tax schedule. The slope is defined by a yearly updated parameter that state bureaucrats select, and in some years the slope increases dramatically to stabilize a flagging trust fund. The slope of the tax schedule denotes the rise in UI tax rates for each percentage point increase in the employer's benefit ratio, defined below:

$$BR_{ft} = \frac{\sum_{i=-3}^{-1} \text{Claims}_{f,t-i}}{\sum_{j=-3}^{-1} \text{Taxable Payroll}_{f,t-j}}.$$

The numerator sums the total UI benefits claimed by the firm's employees over the past 3 years, and the denominator sums the total taxable payroll in the past 3 years. Intuitively, firms with relatively more workers who claim UI benefits for a long time will have large values in the numerator, and their counterparts with few layoffs have low values. As this equation shows, a layoff will typically increase a firm's tax rate for 3 years. Some benefit-ratio states have a longer 5-year look-back period, meaning a layoff will elevate a firm's tax rate for 5 years. After the look-back period has passed, the layoff no longer affects firm tax rates in benefit-ratio states.

Another experience-rating regime many states use is the reserve-ratio system, defined below. The key difference from the benefit ratio is the persistence of UI claims in the numerator of the tax formula:

$$RR_{ft} = \frac{\sum_i \text{Contributions}_i - \sum_i \text{Claims}_{f,t-i}}{\frac{1}{3}\sum_{j=-3}^{-1} \text{Taxable Payroll}_{f,t-j}}.$$

In reserve-ratio states, each employer has a running reserve balance, equal to all previous UI contributions (taxes paid) minus all previous UI claims. This balance can be positive or negative, with negative balances resulting in tax rates close to the maximum. This means that a large layoff will increase a firm's tax bill for many more years than in benefit-ratio states, where claim history is automatically erased after the 3-year look-back period, and a small layoff may only increase taxes for a year. Figure 2 illustrates a sample UI tax schedule for Missouri, which uses a reserve-ratio formula. Here and in other reserve-ratio states, the tax changes in a step function with the reserve ratio, with larger discontinuities if the firm's account is negative. Either the benefit- or reserve-ratio formulas are used in all but three states in the United States.

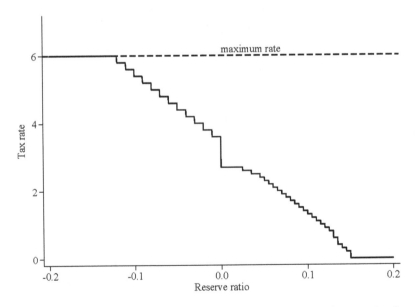

Fig. 2. Sample reserve-ratio unemployment-insurance tax formula. Administrative data are from Missouri's Department of Economic Opportunity. A color version of this figure is available online.

Thus, experience rating in UI presents policy makers with a trade-off. The benefits of experience rating center on the fact that layoff taxes serve as a Pigouvian tax that corrects the fiscal externality of layoffs. Experience rating stabilizes employment, gives employers an incentive to flag ineligible UI claims and prevents employers from using unemployment insurance to provide paid vacation for employees at the expense of the community (Doornik, Schoenherr, and Skrastins 2022). The costs of experience rating are that it tends to increase taxes on firms that are already struggling, that taxes fall most heavily on middle-class-employing employers (such as construction and manufacturing), and that firms may discourage eligible workers from claiming benefits (Auray and Fuller 2020; Lachowska et al. 2022). Another concern is that experience rating may cause employers to avoid hiring workers that are prone to layoff, or those that when dismissed are likely to remain unemployed for long periods of time and thus accrue a large tax bill. A core criticism of experience rating is that it internalizes the negative externality of layoffs but fails to internalize the positive externality of new hires.

Penalties for layoffs vary substantially across states, because UI is administered at the state rather than federal level. States vary considerably in the way they tax firms to finance UI, primarily through differences in the taxable wage base and the maximum tax rate.[4] A simple measure of exposure to experience rating is the state's maximum rate multiplied by its taxable wage base. This product reflects the highest possible per-worker penalty borne by individual firms in the state. For example, California currently has the lowest possible taxable wage base ($7,000 per worker per year), with a maximum rate of only 6.2%. Therefore, it is easy for firms to hit the maximum rate, and the maximum penalty a Californian firm can pay for layoffs is only $7,000 × 6.2% = $434 per worker. By contrast, neighboring Oregon has a taxable wage base of $47,700 and a maximum rate of 5.4%, so the maximum penalty a firm in Oregon can pay is $47,700 × 5.4% = $2,576 per worker—almost six times the penalty possible in California. Raising either the maximum tax rate or the taxable wage increases the possible penalty proportionately. Another state-specific factor affecting the potential penalties employers face is the generosity of UI benefits; more generous benefits mechanically translate into higher potential benefit charges from laid-off workers. In 2019, maximum weekly benefits ranged from a low of $235 in Mississippi to a high of $795 in Massachusetts. Meanwhile, minimum benefit eligibility is more similar across states, as most states require less than $5,000 of earnings within the preceding year to qualify for benefits.

Exposure to experience rating also varies, even within a state, based on a firm's placement on the tax schedule. Firms close to the minimum rate can face the full penalty, and potential penalties fall as the firm approaches the maximum rate. Once a firm is at the maximum rate, added layoffs impose no immediate MTC.[5] Thus, firms that routinely lay off workers (including seasonal employment) will consistently be close to the maximum rate, leading to minimal threat of additional tax increases. We harness both dimensions of variation in experience rating to understand how it affects the firm's decision to downsize.

Experience rating acts as a classic Pigouvian tax, internalizing the fiscal costs of UI to the firms that generate layoffs, which encourages more socially efficient decisions. In the presence of exogenous negative shocks, firms may have strong private incentives to reduce costs by downsizing their workforce. It may be, however, that experience rating helps to blunt the influence of downturns by encouraging firms to maintain some of the employees that they would otherwise have let go. Understanding the degree to which experience rating buttresses employment during downturns is the object of this paper.

III. Data

We use employment data from the public-use Quarterly Census of Employment and Wages (QCEW) for the period 2001–19. We start in 2001 because it is the first available year of UI tax data by NAICS industry, and we end our analysis with the last year prior to the COVID-19 pandemic. The QCEW is sourced from state UI programs and reports establishment counts, employment, UI tax contributions, and taxable wages. Dividing tax contributions by taxable wages allows us to calculate average industry tax rates for each geographic area.

Observations are reported at multiple levels of aggregation, and for our analysis, we use employment counts at the state by three-digit NAICS level. Cells with too few establishments to pass disclosure requirements are withheld, and we also exclude public administration. To prevent industries from entering and exiting the sample endogenously, we drop any state-industry cells that do not have a continuous panel of nonmissing data. We also drop any industry for which a single state ever accounts for more than 30% of national employment. This drops a total of 14 industries (15%), most of which are very small or industries with missing data, and results in 79 three-digit industries remaining in our analysis.

Although our QCEW data span all 50 states plus Washington, DC, empirical tax schedules are sourced from the Department of Labor's ETA 204 Experience Rating Reports and are not available for all years and states.[6] Thus, our analysis sample of QCEW data matched to state tax schedules includes 46 out of 51 states, and 86% of state-years, because some states failed to report in certain years. Completely missing states are Alaska, Delaware, North Carolina, North Dakota, and Oklahoma; because Alaska, Delaware, and Oklahoma use neither a benefit-ratio nor reserve-ratio formula, they are not required to report to the Department of Labor.

Figure A1 illustrates the composition of our analysis sample, by state. Of the 46 states in our sample, nine have full industry coverage throughout the sample period (79 industries up to 2006 and 78 industries thereafter), and only nine states have more than 10% of industry-years missing. Missing industry-years is highly correlated with state population, as there is a disclosure threshold for the public-use QCEW. Meanwhile, full coverage of MTC information is available for 28 states. Figure A2 illustrates the composition of our analysis sample, by NAICS sector. Agriculture is the most underrepresented sector, with only 63% of its industries reporting employment at the state level; mining is the second most underrepresented with 81%, followed by information with 84%.

Table 1 provides summary statistics of our state-industry analysis sample. There are a total of 228,799 state-industry-year-quarter cells, composed of 46 states, up to 72 quarters, and up to 79 industries. There is substantial variation in employment counts, both due to state population and industry size. Therefore, we estimate regressions weighting

Table 1
Summary Statistics (2001–2018)

	Mean	SD
Total employment	31,584	67,875
Total establishments	2,266	7,253
Average weekly earnings (2018$)	1,007	528
Employment change (%)	.30	7.96
Own industry shock (%)	.072	4.66
Marginal tax cost (2018$)	83.77	43.64
Tax base (2018$)	14,266	8,788
Taxable wages (%)	35.90	29.55
UI tax rate (%)	2.41	1.47
N	228,799	

Note: Observations are at the state, three-digit industry, year, and quarter level; includes 46 states, up to 79 industries, and up to 72 quarters. UI = unemployment insurance.

by employment, because state-industry cells with greater employment will reflect the employment decisions of a greater number of employers. Taxable wages are also relatively low, making up only 36% of earnings on average; because average annual earnings are around $52,000, the average state tax base is only $14,300. Recall how California has the lowest possible tax base of $7,000, and Oregon's tax base is $47,700 as of 2022.

IV. Research Design

Our goal is to estimate whether a firm's employment decisions are influenced by the degree of experience rating in their UI tax rates. If laying off workers subjects the firm to large potential tax increases, will this dampen their responses to negative labor-demand shocks?

A. Measuring Marginal Tax Costs

To create a well-defined measure of experience rating, we calculate the 1-year MTC of laying off 10% of average employment. This definition of a MTC is consistent with the measure proposed by Pavosevich (2020), which combines the state tax formula with expected UI benefit claims. It is important to note that because the MTC is only calculated for the first year, this measure is a lower bound of the potential UI tax costs from a layoff; in actuality, a layoff resulting in UI claims will result in tax increases for at least 3 consecutive years (in benefit-ratio states) if not longer (in reserve-ratio states). However, should employers heavily discount the future, this 1-year MTC is a good indication of the short-run tax increases they expect to face and will be strongly positively related to the actual present value of the tax cost.

Because both the BR (benefit ratio) and the RR (reserve ratio) are only a function of actual UI benefit claims, there does not exist a one-to-one relationship between layoffs and tax increases. Therefore, we make assumptions about how likely laid-off workers are to claim UI benefits, and for what benefit duration. Although UI benefit claiming will vary across states and across the business cycle, our baseline calculation assumes benefit-eligible weekly earnings of $870 (the nominal average in our sample), a constant 32% take-up rate, and a duration of 16 weeks (both of which are chosen to equal the US average during our sample period).[7]

Assuming stable employment over the past 3 years, the 1-year MTC for industry k in state s at time t is then calculated as follows:

$$\text{MTC}(\tau)_{skt} = \Delta\text{BR}_{st} \times \text{slope}(\tau)_{skt} \times \text{Tax Base}_{st}$$

$$= \frac{0.1 \times \text{Emp} \times E[\text{Claims}]}{3 \times \text{Tax Base} \times \text{Emp}} \times \text{slope}(\tau) \times \text{Tax Base}$$

$$= \frac{0.1 \times E[\text{Claims}]_{st}}{3} \times \text{slope}(\tau)_{skt}, \text{ where } E[\text{Claims}] = 0.32 \times \text{benefit}_{st} \times 16.$$

(1)

The ΔBR denotes the change in benefit ratio from a 10% layoff, which produces expected UI claims of $E[\text{Claims}]$. States with reserve-ratio formulas will have a similar calculation, using ΔRR instead of ΔBR, except the denominator is made up of average payroll over the past 3 years, rather than the total. The MTC is a function of the current tax rate τ because both the distance to the maximum rate and slope (τ) depend on the employer's current position on the UI tax schedule, which we define as the average industry tax rate. We also show robustness to using a measure with full take-up of UI benefits, and any other adjustments to E[Claims], such as increases in duration or benefit generosity, would scale analogously.[8]

Using empirical tax schedules collected from states by the US Department of Labor, we estimate either a linear or cubic best-fit line for each UI tax schedule, with the possibility of a discontinuity. Figure 3 displays

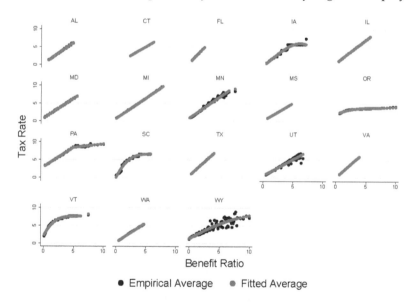

Fig. 3. Empirical tax schedules (2014), benefit-ratio states. Data are from Department of Labor 204 Experience Rating Reports. Unemployment-insurance tax rates are an increasing function of employer's benefit ratio. Fitted average based on either linear or cubic best-fit line. A color version of this figure is available online.

the variation in tax schedules across benefit-ratio states in 2014. We plot the empirical average reported by states, as well as the fitted average, as a function of the benefit ratio. Although the majority of these tax schedules have a constant slope, like the example graph shown for Florida, some states—such as Pennsylvania, South Carolina, and Vermont—have nonlinear schedules. The slopes of state tax schedules may also vary over time; for example, in 2014 Florida's tax schedule had a constant slope of 1.75 for firms that fall below the maximum tax rate, but in 2018, the slope was close to 1. We chose to estimate a constant linear slope for all states, because our analysis is at the industry rather than employer level. With nonlinear schedules, employers within an industry face different slopes depending on where they are located on the tax schedule, so the industry's average MTC would not be able to capture this nonlinearity in slope.

Figure 4 displays the variation in schedules for reserve-ratio states, which tend to have flatter slopes. Although benefit-ratio slopes range from roughly 0.3–3, reserve-ratio slopes rarely exceed 1. This is largely due to the persistence of benefit claims in reserve-ratio formulas. Although benefit-ratio formulas only include UI claims made in the past

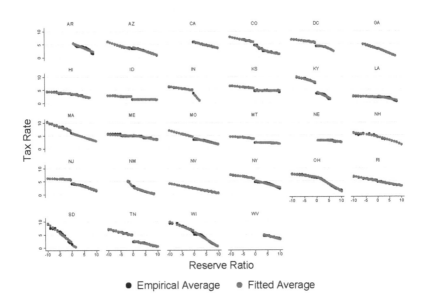

Fig. 4. Empirical tax schedules (2014), reserve-ratio states. Data are from Department of Labor 204 Experience Rating Reports. Unemployment-insurance tax rates are a decreasing function of employer's reserve ratio. Fitted average based on either linear or cubic best-fit line, with possible discontinuities at zero. A color version of this figure is available online.

3 years (and in some states up to 5 years), UI claims appear permanently in reserve-ratio formulas, as firms will continue to have a negative reserve balance until all of their previous UI charges have been repaid through tax contributions; this disparity is not captured by the simple 1-year MTC measures we calculate. Reserve-ratio states are also more likely to have nonlinear tax schedules with kinks and discontinuous jumps around zero (when a firm moves from a positive to a negative reserve balance). We are not able to capture the impact of being close to this discontinuity, as our analysis averages all employers within an industry; this produces another potential dimension of measurement error in the MTC for reserve-ratio states.

Employers already at the maximum rate will experience a slope of zero despite an increase in their benefit ratio. And for τ close to the maximum, we bound the MTC by the distance to the state maximum tax rate. Thus, states with a steep tax schedule or with high maximum tax rates will have higher values of MTC on average. Moreover, within the same state, a firm that is close to the maximum tax rate will have a lower potential penalty. In our analysis sample, approximately 0.5% of state-industry cells are affected by the maximum rate cutoff in any given year; the share affected is highest in 2010–11 when it was 1.6% and is close to zero in 2001–3.

There is considerable variation in the value of the MTC, from a 10th percentile of $39 to a 90th percentile of $135 (in 2018 dollars). In our analysis sample, the mean employment-weighted 1-year MTC from a 10% layoff is $89. This means that on average, a 10% layoff is expected to increase next year's UI tax costs by $89 per worker in 2018 dollars. Figure 5 plots the mean per-worker UI tax and MTC, by NAICS sector. Averaging across all states, there is not much correlation between MTC and average taxes paid, as most tax schedules are linear and very few industries are close enough to the maximum for it to be binding. The construction industry pays by far the highest UI taxes, at more than $700 per worker annually. Meanwhile, stable industries such as education and health care have some of the lowest costs per worker. For high-turnover sectors such as hospitality/food and retail trade, the low UI tax costs are primarily due to low take-up rates of UI.

B. Calculating Economic Shocks

To estimate firms' responses to an exogenous shock to labor demand, we also construct national measures of industry employment change. For

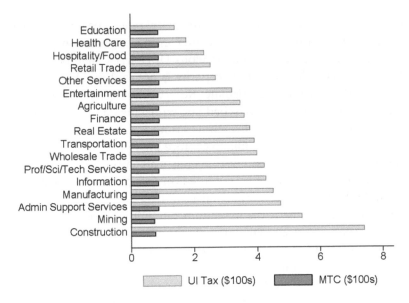

Fig. 5. Mean 1-year per-capita unemployment-insurance (UI) tax and marginal tax cost (MTC) by North American Industry Classification System (NAICS) sector. Average per-capita tax calculated by dividing quarterly UI contributions by employment and then summing over Q1–Q4. Values are inflation-adjusted to 2018 dollars. A color version of this figure is available online.

each state-by-three-digit NAICS industry, we generate leave-one-out national measures of employment change using monthly employment from the QCEW. We define ownind$_{skm}$, which measures the shock to a given three-digit industry k in state s based on the rest of the nation's year-over-year industry growth from month m in a given year to month m in a given year y:

$$\text{shock}_{skmy} = 100 \times \frac{E_{skm,y+1} - E_{skmy}}{E_{skmy}}, \quad \text{where } E_{skmy} = \sum_{i \,!=s}(\text{employment}_{ikmy}).$$

Thus, shock$_{skmy}$ calculates year-over-year percentage changes of national employment, leaving out the own state's employment in that industry. These measures are initially constructed at the monthly level, before quarterly measures shocks$_{skt}$ are calculated by taking the average of the monthly measures (t refers to a given year-quarter). Figure 6 assesses the correlation between the calculated industry employment shocks and the actual industry employment change in each geographic area. The two measures are highly correlated; a 1 percentage point national industry shock results in 89% pass-through to industry employment at the state

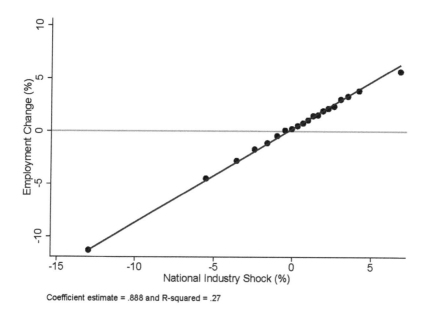

Coefficient estimate = .888 and R-squared = .27

Fig. 6. Correlation between national industry shock and employment-change measures. $N = 228,799$. Binned scatterplot and linear best-fit line of national industry shock by year-over-year employment change. A color version of this figure is available online.

level. This suggests that local industry employment is highly responsive to the industry's national employment shocks.

C. *Estimating Equation*

To identify the impact of experience rating on the sensitivity of employment to economic shocks, we measure year-over-year employment changes (from quarter t to the same quarter the following year) for each quarter in our sample period from 2001 to 2018. We then estimate the following regression specification:

$$\text{Emp}\Delta_{skt} = \alpha_s + \delta_t + \gamma_k \times \text{year}_t + \beta_0 \text{shock}_{skt} \tag{2}$$
$$+ \beta_1 \text{MTC}_{skt} + \beta_2 (\text{MTC}_{skt} \cdot \text{shock}_{skt}) + \varepsilon_{skt}.$$

Here t denotes year-quarter, k denotes industry, and s denotes state. MTC_{kst} varies not only by state and quarter but also by industry, because we use average industry tax rates from the QCEW to identify how far firms are from the maximum tax rate. The coefficient of interest is β_2, which measures the additive response from facing a higher MTC (i.e., greater experience rating). The baseline response to a 1 percentage point national industry shock is estimated by β_0. To the extent that an industry's position on the tax schedule (and thus MTC) is influenced by current economic conditions, we also include industry-by-year fixed effects. A key identifying assumption of this approach is that the value of the current MTC is orthogonal to other unobserved factors that might influence employment changes in the state-industry cell, after controlling for state, industry-year, and year-quarter fixed effects.

Our analysis also assumes that firms bear some of the UI tax burden. If employers were able to pass 100% of UI tax increases through to workers in the form of lower wages, they may not respond at all to experience rating. However, the existing literature on UI tax incidence (Anderson and Meyer 2000; Johnston 2021; Guo 2023a) has found clear evidence of imperfect pass-through at the firm level. In theory, the assignment of firm-specific tax rates prevents firms from fully passing on tax increases in a competitive labor market where there are other firms facing lower rates.

V.   Results

Table 2 reports regression estimates from equation (2). Our preferred specification in column 2 estimates that the average 1-year MTC of $89 lowers responsiveness to national shocks by 0.09 percentage points, or 9% relative to the β_0 estimate from column 1 ($(0.89 \times 0.0986)/0.958$). In addition, one standard deviation increase in MTC lowers responsiveness to national shocks by 0.04 percentage points, or 4%. Columns 3 and 4 estimate specifications with state-by-industry and state-by-year fixed effects; because our MTC measures do not vary much within a given state and year, the inclusion of state-by-year fixed effects absorbs much of our identifying variation. Nevertheless, the magnitudes of β_2 remain quite stable across these additional specifications, providing additional evidence that in states where industries face high marginal tax costs, responsiveness to the national economic shock is dampened.

We also explore heterogeneity of firm responses using subgroup analysis. Table 3 reports regression estimates along three dimensions of heterogeneity: (1) how experience rating affects adjustment when shocks are positive or negative, (2) in high- and low-risk industries (based on average tax rates), and (3) whether the state uses a reserve-ratio or benefit-ratio formula. Columns 1 and 2 show that the impact of the MTC is asymmetric: UI reduces downsizing during contractions but does not reduce growth during expansions. Whereas a standard model of the labor market

Table 2
Interaction of Industry Shocks with Marginal Tax Cost (2001–2018)

	Dependent Variable: Employment Change (%)			
	(1)	(2)	(3)	(4)
Industry shock	.958**	.139	.199	.182
	(.0472)	(.236)	(.230)	(.221)
MTC × shock (100s)	−.0798+	−.0986*	−.107*	−.0839+
	(.0426)	(.0429)	(.0477)	(.0433)
MTC (100s)	.101	.155	.271**	−.179
	(.100)	(.0950)	(.0984)	(.180)
R^2	.501	.527	.563	.559
Mean of dep. variable	.870	.870	.870	.870
Industry-by-year FE		X	X	X
State-by-industry FE			X	
State-by-year FE				X
N	228,799	228,799	228,797	228,799

Note: MTC = marginal tax cost. Observations are at state, three-digit industry, year, and quarter level; includes state, industry, and year-quarter fixed effects (FE) and weighted by employment. Mean (weighted) MTC = 0.89 and SD = 0.38, inflation-adjusted to 2018 dollars. Robust standard errors clustered at state-industry level are in parentheses.
+$p < .10$.
*$p < .05$.
**$p < .01$.

would imply that firing costs reduce employment in equilibrium, this finding suggests that experience rating actually increases employment over the business cycle. Restricting to negative shocks, the average 1-year MTC of $90 lowers responsiveness to national shocks by 0.11 percentage points, an increase in magnitude relative to our baseline estimate.

In columns 3 and 4, we compare industries that are at greater risk of layoffs with those that have more stable employment. We define a quarter of industries as high risk by whether their UI tax rates fell within the top quartile of industry rates. Examples of high-risk industries include all industries in the construction sector, ground transportation (which includes school-bus drivers), and administrative and support services (which includes temporary help services). These high-risk industries, which tend to be seasonal in nature, are undeterred by experience rating; they downsize when needed regardless of the MTC. Removing them from the sample actually magnifies the impact of the MTC in deterring layoffs. Among lower-risk industries, the average 1-year MTC of $90 lowers responsiveness to national shocks by 0.15 percentage points, a more than 50% increase in magnitude relative to our baseline estimate. Finally, columns 5 and 6 test for differential responses to benefit-ratio versus

Table 3
Subgroup Analysis (2001–2018)

	Dependent Variable: Employment Change (%)					
	Positive Shock	Negative Shock	High Risk	Not High Risk	Benefit Ratio	Reserve Ratio
	(1)	(2)	(3)	(4)	(5)	(6)
Industry shock	−1.304*	.523**	−.121	.0982	.426**	.138
	(.611)	(.0785)	(.174)	(.356)	(.133)	(.332)
MTC × shock	.0503	−.122**	−.0553	−.164**	−.140$^+$	−.0815
	(.106)	(.0473)	(.0710)	(.0633)	(.0812)	(.0496)
MTC (100s)	−.159	.232	.292	.317**	.369*	.129
	(.245)	(.216)	(.280)	(.108)	(.152)	(.135)
R^2	.367	.657	.635	.526	.600	.563
Emp. change mean	2.324	−3.152	.170	1.045	.957	.801
MTC mean	.890	.895	.843	.904	1.065	.754
Industry-by-year FE	X	X	X	X	X	X
State-by-industry FE	X	X	X	X	X	X
N	141,259	87,466	52,406	176,391	89,950	138,847

Note: Observations at the state, three-digit industry, year, and quarter level. Includes state, industry, and year-quarter fixed effects (FE), and weighted by employment. Marginal tax cost (MTC) inflation-adjusted to 2018 dollars. Robust standard errors clustered at state-industry level are in parentheses.
$^+p < .10.$
$^*p < .05.$
$^{**}p < .01.$

reserve-ratio formulas. The estimated magnitude is larger and more statistically significant for benefit-ratio states. As previously discussed, we expect the MTC to be less accurately measured for reserve-ratio states. Many tax schedules have discontinuous jumps around a RR of zero, and because reserves are a stock rather than flow, differential persistence of tax increases cannot be captured by our 1-year measure.

A potential concern with our MTC measure is that it does not fully capture the impact of a state's maximum tax rate on experience rating, because it does not account for larger layoffs or full take-up of UI benefits (our measure is defined for a 10% layoff with a 32% take-up rate). To account for this, we construct an alternative 1-year MTC that now assumes full take-up of UI benefits. This essentially magnifies the MTC of layoffs, making it easier for firms to hit the maximum tax rate and face no additional increases. Whereas distance from the maximum only affected 0.5% of observations in our previous MTC measure, distance from the maximum now affects 10% of state-industry cells. The mean MTC is now $262, almost triple the size of the original mean. Table 4 reports

Table 4
Interaction of Industry Shocks with Magnified Marginal Tax Cost (2001–2018)

	Dependent Variable: Employment Change (%)			
	(1)	(2)	(3)	(4)
Industry shock	1.006**	.182	.249	.214
	(.0556)	(.220)	(.214)	(.203)
MTC × shock (100s)	−.0459**	−.0498**	−.0555**	−.0407*
	(.0174)	(.0175)	(.0188)	(.0194)
MTC (100s)	−.0273	−.00274	−.0000381	−.0318
	(.0377)	(.0353)	(.0396)	(.0562)
R^2	.502	.527	.564	.559
Mean of dep. variable	.870	.870	.870	.870
Industry-by-year FE		X	X	X
State-by-industry FE			X	
State-by-year FE				X
N	228,799	228,799	228,797	228,799

Note: MTC = marginal tax cost. Observations are at state, three-digit industry, year, and quarter level; includes state, industry, and year-quarter fixed effects (FE) and weighted by employment. Mean (weighted) MTC = 2.62 and SD = 1.16, inflation-adjusted to 2018 dollars. Robust standard errors clustered at state-industry level are in parentheses.
*$p < .05$.
**$p < .01$.

estimates using this magnified MTC measure, and our previous conclusion still holds. For the average industry, experience rating dampens the responsiveness to economic shocks by 0.13 percentage points (2.62 × 0.0498), a substantially larger effect than our baseline estimates.

A final exercise we undertake is to estimate a horse race comparing the impact of marginal tax costs with two other dimensions of the state tax schedule, the maximum tax or the taxable base. We calculate the maximum tax by multiplying the tax base by the maximum rate, and consider it a measure of the costliness of large layoffs. Likewise, the tax base could potentially influence employment decisions, as previous work has shown that higher tax bases increase low-wage employment (Duggan et al. 2022; Huang 2022). Restricting to quarters with negative shocks, table A1 reports estimates for both the original employment-change outcome, as well as the change in quarterly establishment counts (to account for exit). Columns 1 and 2 show that after including either the maximum tax or the tax base as additional interactions, the coefficient on the MTC interaction is still statistically significant and very similar in magnitude (compared with column 2 of table 3). Columns 3 and 4 test for impacts on establishment exit by estimating regressions of year-over-year percentage change in the number of establishments in each state-industry cell. Although we find no impact of the MTC on establishment change, column 4 suggests that greater tax bases are correlated with greater rates of establishment exit. This is consistent with the finding in Guo (2023a) that firms are more likely to exit from high-tax states during economic downturns.

VI. Conclusion

In the United States, unemployment insurance is financed with experience-rated employer payroll taxes that increase to reflect the cost of UI benefits claimed by laid-off workers. Experience rating internalizes the fiscal costs of unemployed workers to the firms who choose to lay them off. On the other hand, state maximum tax rates cap the potential penalty firms face, to insure them from particularly negative shocks (which results in a zero MTC beyond a certain point). Insurance versus internalization is a key trade-off governments face when designing UI financing schemes. In this paper, we examine whether the internalization of layoffs helps stabilize labor demand during economic contractions. Precisely, whether experience rating reduces firm responses to exogenous shocks.

We combine detailed tax-schedule data for each state with the average tax rates of firms in each state-industry cell to calculate the MTC of an additional 10% layoff. This measure allows us to compare how firms react to exogenous shocks in environments with higher and lower penalties for layoffs. As a benchmark, we find that industries within a given state are highly responsive to national shocks; a negative (positive) 10% national shock reduces (increases) state-level employment by 9%. In the presence of the average level of experience rating ($89 per worker for a 10% layoff), employment reductions are 9% smaller, therefore aiding in stabilizing employment. This is also an asymmetric effect, as experience rating preserves employment in response to negative shocks, but does not reduce hiring in the face of positive shocks.

With the usual caveats about external validity, we use our estimates to calculate how much experience rating stabilizes employment in the United States. We find that experience rating saved 231,000 jobs in the 2001 recession and 852,000 jobs in 2008 (8% of the unemployed population).[9] Several states suspended experience rating during pandemic lockdowns. If they had not, experience rating might have had a similar stabilizing effect during the pandemic contraction.

There are two key limitations of our work. The first is that marginal tax costs are measured with error, especially in states with nonlinear tax schedules. Also, in some states, tax increases last for no more than 3 years, whereas in other states, tax increases persist until the employer has paid back the full cost of benefits. Our measure also does not account for these differences in the time a firm's rate is elevated, which means that we likely suffer a kind of measurement error that biases our estimates toward zero. It may be that we underestimate the true effect of experience rating in attenuating firm responses to shocks. The second limitation is that we are not able to fully examine potential costs of experience rating that could be destabilizing. For instance, experience rating allows taxes to rise more on ailing businesses that dismiss workers. It may be that experience rating increases the exit rates of firms that would otherwise be viable producers and employers. We explore this by measuring whether experience rating also lowers establishment growth in the wake of negative shocks, but we are unable to find conclusive evidence.

The state-level determination of tax regimes and benefit generosity is beyond the scope of this paper, but one major determinant is the choice of whether to index UI tax bases to average earnings. In the 1970s and 1980s, 17 states adopted flexible tax bases that automatically increase with earnings growth, and to this day, indexed states have significantly larger tax bases than the rest of the nation. Generous UI benefits are also correlated with greater experience rating, although there is substantial excess variation; states that do not collect enough revenues relative to benefits paid end up with insufficiently funded trust funds. By the end of 2020, due to the COVID-19 pandemic, 17 states had depleted their UI trust funds and were required to borrow from the federal government.

A more comprehensive analysis of the benefits and costs of alternative UI financing represents an important direction for future research. The design of UI financing may be just as important for labor market outcomes over the business cycle as that of UI benefits. A voluminous literature has explored this issue on the benefit side—for example, the trade-offs of a high versus low replacement rate or maximum duration of benefits. However, the current variation in UI financing across the United States is even greater than the variation in UI benefits. This is likely driven by policy uncertainty over the optimal design, and it has resulted in large funding shortfalls in many states that are not sustainable in the long term.

Appendix

Appendix Tables and Figures

Table A1
Horse Race between Marginal Tax Cost (MTC) and Max Tax or Tax Base (2001–2018)

	Employment Change (%)		Establishment Change (%)	
	(1)	(2)	(3)	(4)
Industry shock	1.089**	1.056**	.394**	.405**
	(.0642)	(.0684)	(.0591)	(.0609)
MTC × shock (100s)	−.136**	−.132*	−.0272	−.0252
	(.0516)	(.0524)	(.0450)	(.0456)
MTC (100s)	−.233	−.186	.0270	.0628
	(.210)	(.213)	(.218)	(.219)
Max tax × shock (100s)	−.00235		.00505	
	(.00302)		(.00377)	
Maximum tax (100s)	.00488		.00805	
	(.0238)		(.0236)	
Tax base × shock (1000s)		.000413		.00280
		(.00242)		(.00212)
Tax base (1000s)		−.0239		−.0489*
		(.0215)		(.0243)
R^2	.541	.541	.273	.273
Mean of dep. variable	−3.150	−3.150	−.537	−.537
N	87,484	87,484	87,484	87,484

Note: Observations are at state, three-digit industry, year, and quarter level. The table includes state, industry-year, and year-quarter fixed effects, and regressions weighted by employment. Mean (weighted) MTC = 0.90 and SD = 0.38; mean max tax = 9.85 and SD = 5.9; mean base = 13.7 and SD = 8.1; all are inflation-adjusted to 2018 dollars. Robust standard errors clustered at state-industry level are in parentheses.
*$p < .05$.
**$p < .01$.

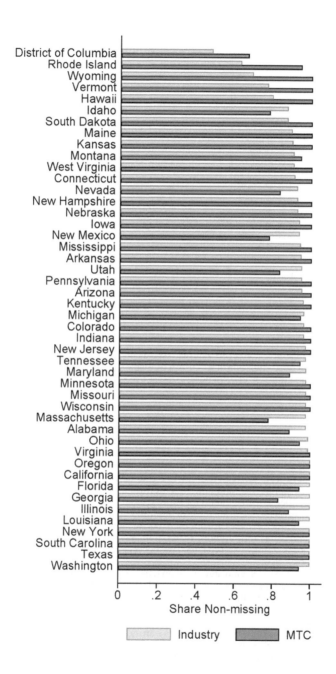

Fig. A1. Composition of analysis sample. For each state in our analysis sample, we plot the share of industries that are nonmissing and the share of years for which marginal tax cost (MTC) information is nonmissing. A color version of this figure is available online.

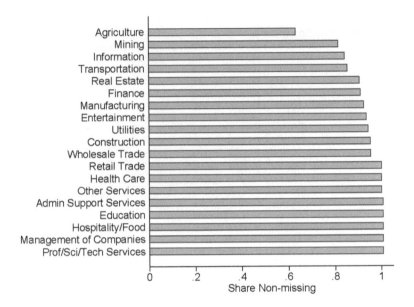

Fig. A2. Composition of analysis sample. We calculate the share of nonmissing state-quarters for each three-digit North American Industry Classification System (NAICS) industry and then plot the average of those shares by NAICS sector. A color version of this figure is available online.

Endnotes

Author email addresses: Duggan (mgduggan@stanford.edu), Guo (aguo@scu.edu), Johnston (acjohnston@ucmerced.edu). We are grateful to participants at the Tax Policy and the Economy Conference, and to Robert Moffitt for helpful comments and conversations about the paper. We are grateful for support from the National Bureau of Economic Research. Views expressed here are those of the author and should not be attributed to our employers or to NBER. Mistakes are our own. For acknowledgments, sources of research support, and disclosure of the authors' material financial relationships, if any, please see https://www.nber.org/books-and-chapters/tax-policy-and-economy-volume-37/experience -rating-automatic-stabilizer.

1. For interested readers, Guo and Johnston (2021) provide a broader discussion of the literature examining UI experience rating in the labor market.

2. Judges often overrule this requirement in practice if the claimant argues that their quit was justified or firing was unjustified.

3. See quarterly data on First Payments from the US Department of Labor, https://oui .doleta.gov/unemploy/data_summary/DataSum.asp.

4. States also can vary in the slope of their tax schedule and either "overcharge" or "undercharge" relative to the costs of marginal layoffs. States are brought to overcharging when their funds are strained.

5. In states that use a benefit-ratio system to assign tax rates, charges fall off a firm's balance after 3 years. A firm could be at the maximum rate this year, so additional layoffs would not have an immediate impact on the firm's tax rate, but layoffs could have an effect after old charges are removed from the firm's account.

6. ETA 204 reports can be accessed at https://oui.doleta.gov/unemploy/DataDownloads .asp.

7. Quarterly UI data are from https://oui.doleta.gov/unemploy/data_summary.

8. In robustness checks not reported in the paper, we also scale UI take-up by the benefit generosity in the state (defined as the ratio of the state's maximum benefit to the average $435 eligibility). Our results are robust to including this inverse relationship between generosity and take-up.

9. We arrive at the 2008 estimate by multiplying total civilian employment by our treatment coefficient for negative shocks, mean MTC in 2008, and mean industry shock in 2008: $146,000,000 \times -0.122 \times .87 \times -0.055 = 852,304$. For 2001, the calculation is $129,700,000 \times -0.122 \times 0.975 \times -0.015 = 231,417$.

References

Anderson, P. M. 1993. "Linear Adjustment Costs and Seasonal Labor Demand: Evidence from Retail Trade Firms." *Quarterly Journal of Economics* 108 (4): 1015–42.

Anderson, P. M., and B. D. Meyer. 2000. "The Effects of the Unemployment Insurance Payroll Tax on Wages, Employment, Claims and Denials." *Journal of Public Economics* 78 (1): 81–106.

Auray, S., and D. L. Fuller. 2020. "Eligibility, Experience Rating, and Unemployment Insurance Take-up." *Quantitative Economics* 11 (3): 1059–107.

Card, D., and P. B. Levine. 1994. "Unemployment Insurance Taxes and the Cyclical and Seasonal Properties of Unemployment." *Journal of Public Economics* 53 (1): 1–29.

Doornik, B. V., D. Schoenherr, and J. Skrastins. 2022. "Strategic Formal Layoffs: Unemployment Insurance and Informal Labor Markets." *American Economic Journal: Applied Economics* 15 (1): 292–318.

Duggan, M., A. Guo, and A. C. Johnston. 2022. "Would Broadening the UI Tax Base Help Low-Income Workers?" *AEA Papers and Proceedings* 112:107–11.

Feldstein, M. 1976. "Temporary Layoffs in the Theory of Unemployment." *Journal of Political Economy* 84 (5): 937–57.

———. 1978. "The Effect of Unemployment Insurance on Temporary Layoff Unemployment." *American Economic Review* 68 (5): 834–46.

Guo, A. 2023a. "The Effects of State Business Taxes on Plant Closures: Evidence from Unemployment Insurance Taxation and Multiestablishment Firms." *Review of Economics and Statistics*, forthcoming.

Guo, A. 2023b. "Payroll Tax Incidence: Evidence from Unemployment Insurance." Working paper, Santa Clara University.

Guo, A., and A. C. Johnston. 2021. "The Finance of Unemployment Compensation and Its Consequences." *Public Finance Review* 49 (3): 392–434.

Huang, P.-C. 2022. "Employment Effects of the Unemployment Insurance Tax Base." *Journal of Human Resources*, forthcoming.

Johnston, A. C. 2021. "Unemployment Insurance Taxes and Labor Demand: Quasi-Experimental Evidence from Administrative Data." *American Economic Journal: Economic Policy* 13 (1): 266–93.

Lachowska, M., I. Sorkin, and S. A. Woodbury. 2022. "Firms and Unemployment Insurance Take-up." Working Paper no. 30266, NBER, Cambridge, MA.

Lester, R. A., and C. V. Kidd. 1939. *The Case against Experience Rating in Unemployment Compensation.* Princeton, NJ: Princeton University Press.

Pavosevich, R. 2020. "The Cost of Layoffs in Unemployment Insurance Taxes." Monthly Labor Review, U.S. Bureau of Labor Statistics, Washington, DC.

Topel, R. 1983. "On Layoffs and Unemployment Insurance." *American Economic Review* 73 (4): 541–59.

How Much Lifetime Social Security Benefits Are Americans Leaving on the Table?

David Altig, *Federal Reserve Bank of Atlanta,* United States of America

Laurence J. Kotlikoff, *Boston University and NBER,* United States of America

Victor Yifan Ye, *Opendoor Technologies and Stanford Digital Economy Lab,* United States of America

Executive Summary

Americans are notoriously bad savers. Large numbers are reaching old age too poor to finance retirements that could last longer than they worked. This study uses the 2018 American Community Survey to impute retirement ages for 2019 Survey of Consumer Finances (SCF) respondents. Next, we run the SCF respondents through the Fiscal Analyzer (TFA) to measure the size and distribution of forgone lifetime Social Security benefits. TFA is a life-cycle, consumption-smoothing research tool that incorporates Social Security and all other major federal and state tax and benefit policies. The program can optimize lifetime Social Security choices. We find that virtually all American workers age 45–62 should wait beyond age 65 to collect. More than 90% should wait till age 70. Only 10.2% appear to do so. The median loss for this age group in the present value of household lifetime discretionary spending is $182,370. Optimizing would produce a 10.4% increase in typical workers' lifetime spending. For one in four, the lifetime spending gain exceeds 17%. For one in 10, the gain exceeds 26%. Among the poorest fifth of 45- to 62-year-olds, the median lifetime spending increase is 15.9%, with one in four gaining more than 27.4%.

I. Introduction

Many, if not most, Americans appear to be retiring with inadequate economic resources (Munnell 2015). Indeed, typical wealth holdings of new

Tax Policy and the Economy, volume 37, 2023.

retirees suffice to cover only a few years of median US household consumption.[1] It is no wonder then that some 40% of retirees are more than 50% financially dependent on Social Security (SS) and that roughly 13% are entirely dependent.[2] As for those in better financial shape, SS is often their second-largest retirement resource. These financial realities make retirees' failure to maximize their lifetime SS benefits particularly acute but also a potentially remediable problem. As we show, the vast majority—more than 90%—of Americans ages 45–62 should take their retirement benefits starting at age 70. Roughly 6% are, given current behavior, likely to do so, despite the far higher benefits available from patience.[3] Indeed, even as the system's full retirement age increases, retirement benefits taken at age 70 remain 76% higher, adjusted for inflation, than retirement benefits commenced at 62.

Paradoxically, there is widespread interest in getting the most from SS. Indeed, a vast number of popular articles, books, newspapers, and magazines as well as television, podcast, webinar, and radio shows have discussed and continue to discuss optimal SS benefit collection.[4] Academics have also weighed in on this issue. Bronshtein et al. (2016) provide an excellent survey of the literature and present striking calculations. Their findings concur with ours. But their study is illustrative. It considers stylized rather than actual households, which are examined here.

This paper assesses the costs to actual American workers—respondents to the 2019 Federal Reserve Survey of Consumer Finances (SCF)—of failing to maximize their lifetime benefits (LB). It uses the Fiscal Analyzer (TFA), developed by Economic Security Planning, Inc.,[5] to determine how much lifetime discretionary spending (LDS) working respondents to the SCF will likely leave on the table by failing to optimize their LB. Note that a worker's increase in LDS from maximizing their value will rarely equal their increase in LB. The reason is federal and state income taxes, Medicare B premiums, and federal and state benefits, which can decrease or increase when a household changes its SS benefit-collection strategy. Indeed, we report significantly smaller, if still very large, increases in LDS compared with LB.

TFA is a detailed life-cycle consumption-smoothing program that incorporates cash-flow (borrowing) constraints, lifespan uncertainty, and all major federal and state tax and transfer programs.[6] In addition to state-specific tax and benefit programs, all state-specific, federal benefit-program provisions are incorporated for all 51 states (including Washington, DC). TFA treats all taxes, whether nominally levied on businesses (e.g., federal corporate income taxes and employer payroll-tax contributions) or nominally collected as premiums (i.e., the Medicare Part B premium) as taxes paid by households. It also incorporates in-kind as well as in-cash benefit programs and benefit take-up rates. In-kind benefits, such as Medicaid and Medicare, are treated as consumed in the year received. All TFA results are presented in end-of-year dollars. But before conversion to real dollars, all TFA tax and benefit calculations are made in nominal terms in accord with federal and state tax/benefit programs, which are not fully indexed for inflation.

Our methodology involves five steps. First, we use the 2000–20 waves of the American Community Survey (ACS) to estimate the retirement probabilities of SCF workers ages 49–80. These probabilities are distinguished by birth year, age, education, gender, and marital status. Second, we impute these retirement hazards to SCF workers based on their characteristics and determine, via random assignment, the age at which they will retire. Retirement is defined as working 20 or fewer hours per week. Third, we assume that workers who retire prior to age 62 start their retirement benefit at age 62. We further assume that SCF workers who retire at or after age 62, but before age 70, start their retirement benefit in the year they retire. As for workers randomly assigned to retire after age 70, we assume they start their retirement benefits at 70 because there is no gain from further delay. Fourth, we run our worker sample with their designated retirement ages through TFA with its lifetime SS benefit optimization turned off.[7] Fifth, we rerun the SCF workers through TFA with its SS benefit optimization routine turned on and calculate the increase in LDS arising from lifetime-benefit optimization. We then compare differences in LDS.

To summarize our findings, ignoring cash-flow considerations, the vast majority of American workers should delay taking their retirement benefits until 70. Doing so would raise the median LDS of households headed by workers ages 45–62 by $182,370, or 10.2%. There is a major dispersion in available LDS gains. The 25th percentile LDS gain is $69,493, or 3.2%. The 75th percentile LDS gain is $289,893, or 17.2%. Among ages 45–62 in the bottom fifth of the resource distribution, the median lifetime spending gain from optimization is 15.9%, with one in four gaining more than 27.4%, and one in 10 gaining more than 37.0%.

Absent SS optimization, 40.9% of households in this age range are cash constrained, meaning perfect consumption smoothing is infeasible; that is, their living standard will rise in the future. With SS optimization, 68.4% are constrained. However, for most households ages 45–69, the reduction in current discretionary spending associated with SS optimization is small. At the median, it is $2,714, or 7.0%. These findings are, however, predicated on workers smoothly starting retirement-account withdrawals when they retire or at age 60 if they retire before 60. Under an extreme alternative assumption—workers waiting until 72, when required minimum distributions commence, to begin retirement-account withdrawals—SS optimization entails a large, in some cases very large, decline in current-year discretionary spending.

We proceed by describing TFA, our method of imputing retirement, and our procedure for imputing state residency to SCF respondents. We then present our findings, consider the extent to which SCF workers can optimize SS, examine the associated cash-flow issues, and conclude with suggestions for future research.

A.   The Fiscal Analyzer

TFA, deployed in Auerbach et al. (2017), Altig et al. (2019), Auerbach, Kotlikoff, and Koehler (2022), and Ilin, Kotlikoff, and Pitts (2022), is a life-cycle, consumption-smoothing tool that incorporates borrowing constraints and all major federal and state fiscal policies.[8] These policies are listed in table 1. Detailed TFA documentation is available in Auerbach, Kotlikoff, and Koehler (2019). To abstract from preferences, TFA

Table 1
List of Tax and Transfer Programs Included in the Fiscal Analyzer

Taxes	Personal Income Tax (federal and state)
	Corporate Income Tax (federal and state)
	FICA Tax (federal)
	Sales Taxes (state)
	Medicare Part B Premiums (federal)
	Estate and Gift Tax (federal)
Transfer programs	Earned Income Tax Credit (federal and state)
	Child Tax Credit (federal)
	Social Security Benefits (federal)
	Supplemental Security Income (SSI) (federal)
	Supplemental Nutritional Assistance Program (SNAP) (federal and state)
	Temporary Assistance for Needy Families (TANF) (federal and state)
	Medicaid (federal and state)
	Medicare (federal)
	Affordable Care Act (ACA) (federal and state)
	Section 8 Housing Vouchers (state and county)
	Child Care Assistance (state and county)

assumes that households smooth their living standards, defined as discretionary spending per household member adjusted for economies in shared living and the relative cost of children, to the maximum extent possible without borrowing or, if already indebted, additional borrowing.[9]

The relationship between a household's discretionary spending in year t, C_t, and its underlying living standard per effective adult, c_t, is given by

$$C_t = c_t(N + .7K)^{0.642}, \tag{1}$$

where N stands for the number of adults in the household and K for the number of children. The coefficient 0.642 is chosen such that two adults can live as cheaply, with respect to discretionary spending, as 1.6. TFA's default assumption is perfect living-standard smoothing, although the program can be run with any desired age-living-standard path, any age-specific child-equivalency factors, and any degree of economies in shared living. The program can also be run assuming any maximum age of life. In this study, we assume a maximum of age 100.[10]

TFA inputs include marital status, birth dates of each spouse/partner, birth dates of children, current-year labor earnings, current regular and retirement-account (tax-deductible and Roth) asset balances, current and projected future employer and employee contributions to each type of retirement account, retirement-account withdrawal start dates, SS retirement-benefit collection dates, defined benefit pensions, housing expenses, real estate holdings, household debts, rates of return on assets, and the inflation rate. All inputs not reported in the SCF are imputed. The most important such imputation, described below, is state residency.

B. TFA's Solution Method

TFA jointly determines a household's annual and LDS, taxes (including Medicare Part B premiums), transfers, life-insurance premiums, and bequest paths along each of the household's potential survivor paths.[11] Nondiscretionary spending on, for example, housing is taken as exogenous and obviously limits the scope for discretionary spending. Solving this problem raises the curse of dimensionality—too many variables for computational feasibility. The state variables here comprise survivor-path-specific regular assets, taxable and nontaxable (Roth) retirement-account assets for each household head and, if relevant, spouse/partner.[12]

A second challenge is determining taxes, transfer payments, discretionary spending, and life-insurance holdings for all years on each survivor path. The third hurdle is simultaneity. Spending, life-insurance amounts, and net taxes on all survivor paths are interdependent. Indeed, they are interdependent across paths because, subject to survivor-path-specific cash-flow constraints, TFA equalizes living standards (to restate, discretionary spending per household member with adjustments for the household's current demographic composition and economies in shared living) across all paths. The fourth and final difficulty is the most demanding: the program needs to process thousands of sample observations in batch mode in finite time.

TFA's computation method (CE) handles all of these challenges. Its computation engine, provided by Economic Security Planning, Inc., overcomes the curse of dimensionality in several ways. Most important, rather than attempt to solve an incredibly complex, single-dynamic program with a massive numbers of state variables, the CE posits three far simpler interdependent dynamic programs. The first smooths consumption assuming household heads and their spouses/partners, if present, reach their maximum ages of life. This dynamic program incorporates the household's cash-flow constraints; that is, that it cannot borrow or cannot borrow more that it has already done in the course of smoothing its living standard per household member. The second routine determines nonnegative annual life-insurance needs for household heads and any spouse/partners.[13]

Iteration across the three dynamic programs entails each program taking the output of the other programs as given inputs. This is a Gauss-Seidel solution method, but applied to routines, rather than equations. To ensure precision to many decimal places, TFA employs dampening across iterations and uses an adaptive sparse-grid method that entirely eliminates extrapolation error. Removing this error is critically important.[14]

TFA's CE overcomes the curse of dimensionality in two additional ways. First, survivor-specific paths of retirement-account contributions, account balances, and withdrawals are predetermined. Thus, although TFA's problem involves hundreds of thousands of state variables, those involving retirement accounts are predetermined. Second, the life-insurance routine is programmed to produce the same living-standard path in each year as that generated in the consumption-smoothing routine.[15] To summarize, TFA uses iterative dynamic programming to jointly (a) smooth each household's living standard per equivalent adult (the c_ts), subject to borrowing constraints, on its maximum-longevity path, (b) calculate year-specific life-insurance needs (and the requisite annual life-insurance premiums that must be paid), and (*c*) compute net taxes along its maximum-longevity path.

C. *Confirming TFA's Solutions*

Although TFA's inner workings are complex, its iterative dynamic programming and sparse-grid method permit CE convergence within seconds. TFA's solutions can be confirmed in seven ways. First, present-value (PV) lifetime budget constraints are satisfied within a dollar or two along all survival paths. Hence, apart from terminal bequests, intended and unintended, and funeral expenses, each household ends up, along each survival path, with precisely zero assets when the household ends (i.e., when the max of the maximum year of death across spouse/partners or the maximum year of death of a single household head is reached). Second, each unconstrained household's living standard (discretionary spending per effective adult) is smoothed (takes the same value) to the dollar across all future years. Third, for households that are constrained for one or more intervals, the living standard is smoothed in each interval. Furthermore, the living standard is higher in constrained intervals that occur later in time. Fourth, regular assets in the year before a borrowing constraint ends, via, for example, paying off a mortgage, are zero. This is a requirement of constrained consumption smoothing. To be more precise, bringing positive assets into years when the living standard is higher is inconsistent with consumption smoothing, which minimizes living-standard discrepancies to the maximum extent consistent with the household's borrowing constraint. Fifth, if a spouse/partner dies leaving life insurance for the surviving spouse/partner and children, the living standard of survivors is, to the dollar, identical to what they would otherwise have experienced. Sixth, if TFA does not calculate life insurance for a spouse/partner in a given year, survivors have a higher living standard if the spouse/partner dies in that year. Seventh, a household's regular assets never fall below the amount TFA is told the household can borrow. Anyone running *MaxiFiPlanner*, the commercial parent of TFA, can readily confirm each of the above solution properties.

D. *TFA's Taxes and Transfers*

Table 1 lists the tax and transfer programs incorporated in TFA. Maximization of lifetime SS benefits will change not only those benefits but also each household's path (annual amounts) of discretionary spending along each survivor path. This in turn will change the household's survivor-contingent paths of assets and paths of asset income, and thus paths of taxes and, potentially, paths of transfer payments. As suggested above, our results incorporate all such endogenous responses to optimizing lifetime SS benefits.

E. TFA's Lifetime Social Security Benefits Optimizer

Table 2 lists each of the SS benefits included in TFA's calculations. Table 3 lists the SS benefit provisions incorporated in TFA's calculation for the listed benefits. Parent benefits are the only benefits provided by SS that are not included in TFA. The reason is that the SCF provides no information about parents. The list of provisions is relatively short. The list of regulations implementing these provisions is anything but. Social Security's Handbook contains a vast number of rules—2,728 to be precise—governing its benefits. There are hundreds of thousands of rules about these 2,728 rules over the 12 benefits in the Program Operating Manual System (POMS). These literally countless rules (POMS has no numbering system, just links between rules) may well make SS the most complex fiscal policy yet devised by humans.[16] The CE, and thus TFA's SS benefit optimizer, is exhaustive. It considers all legal benefit-collection strategies of respondents and their spouses/partners and does so on a monthly basis. By legal, we mean all strategies permitted under SS rules. For example, spousal benefits that spouse X can receive on spouse Y's work record are not available to X until Y starts collecting their retirement benefit. In the case of spouses, all strategies reference all joint collection strategies.

Table 2
Social Security Benefits Included in the
Fiscal Analyzer

Retirement benefits
Spousal benefits
Divorced spousal benefits
Disability benefits
Child-in-care spousal benefits
Widow(er)s benefits
Divorced widow(er)s benefits
Child benefits
Disabled child benefits
Surviving child benefits
Father and mother benefits

Table 3
Social Security Benefit Provisions Included in the Fiscal Analyzer

---

Early benefit reductions for all benefit types
Delayed retirement credits
Earnings test (monthly and annual)
Adjustment of the reduction factor
Recomputation of benefits
Family benefit maximum
Combined family benefit maximum
Disabled family benefit maximum
Widow(er) benefit formulas for spouses who do/do not die before 62
RIB-LIM special widow(er) benefit formula
Windfall elimination provision
Government pension offset
All deeming rules
Retirement-benefit suspension and restart provisions

F. *Valuing Social Security and Other Future Resource Streams
and Modifying TFA for Use in This Study*

In addition to understanding the system's benefits and their availability, American workers need to properly value their benefits. Unfortunately, workers are often directed to consider their life expectancy rather than their maximum age of life in evaluating LB. Consider this statement on the Social Security Administration website: "Your life expectancy affects your retirement planning decisions. Knowing this, helps you determine whether you should start receiving your benefits at age 62, or wait until age 70 to receive a higher payment."[17]

Life expectancy refers, of course, to when, on average, a person will die. But no one will die precisely on time, at their expected age of death given their mortality probabilities. Each of us will die just once, and our actual, as opposed to expected, age of death can be exceptionally high. Indeed, we can die at our maximum age of life. Were Americans to simultaneously live thousands of parallel lives and die at all possible ages of death consistent with frequencies determined by their mortality probabilities, and were the thousands of these hypothesized clones to leave their bequests to their surviving clones, each American would in effect constitute their own annuity insurance company. In this case, actuarial valuation of future benefits, which is implied by a focus on life expectancy, would be appropriate. But none of us is starring in *Groundhog Day*. And just as we cannot count on experiencing average automobile accident losses, average homeowners insurance losses, average health insurance losses, or average pet insurance losses, we cannot count on dying years before we run out of money. Instead, economics teaches us to consider longevity risk in the same manner as we do all other risks. In particular, we need to entertain the entire range of outcomes, focusing particularly on the worst-case outcomes. When it comes to longevity risk, the worst outcome, financially speaking, is living to one's maximum age of life. Our need to concentrate on the extreme downside reflects our risk aversion. The worst case can be so bad as to render all other outcomes of secondary importance.

When it comes to longevity risk, we need to consider the financially catastrophic scenario: living as long as possible. The reason is simple. We must worry about our welfare if we do live to maximum age. This key insight, that our planning horizon must extend to our maximum age of life, underlies Menachem Yaari's seminal paper (Yaari 1965) on the economics of life (early-death) insurance and, the opposite side of the coin, annuity (late-death/longevity) insurance. Yaari's study also clarifies how one should value future income and spending streams in the context of lifespan uncertainty. Absent a well-functioning annuity market in which agents can purchase insurance against living to certain ages at actuarially fair or near actuarially fair rates, future income streams must be discounted on a nonactuarial basis; that is, by doing simple discounting. Again, this is the opposite of what most if not all financial companies, and indeed SS itself, seem to recommend. As for the appropriate real discount rate, we take, as our baseline, a 0.5% real return. This is roughly the average real return on long-dated Treasury Inflation Protected Securities observed in recent years. We also consider a 2% real return in our sensitivity analysis. Our assumed inflation rate, which we maintain through the analysis, is 3.0%. Hence, our base case entails a 3.515% nominal return. Our sensitivity analysis assumes a 5.060% nominal return.

TFA was designed to study average outcomes to economy-wide questions. For example, Auerbach et al. (2022), who use TFA, measure average lifetime net tax rates for households of different means within particular cohorts. That analysis averages over all survivor-path outcomes, which are calculated by TFA as a byproduct of determining life-insurance needs. For this study, we have modified TFA to consider a single survivor path, namely the one in which the respondent and any spouse/partner live to their maximum ages of life. This modification of TFA accords precisely with Yarri's directive that rational households base their spending decisions on a non-actuarially discounted lifetime budget that (a) applies simple discounting and (b) treats the budget/planning horizon as the maximum age of life. However, Yarri not only shows that households will, for budgetary purposes, assume maximum longevity. He also shows that if they are not extremely risk averse, households will gamble on the likelihood of dying before their maximum ages of life. Specifically, they will intentionally consume more when young knowing for sure that the cost of doing so is, conditional on continuing to live, a lower living standard when old.[18] Although we follow Yaari (1965) and value SS benefits for each individual household based on the maximum life scenario, we do turn on TFA's actuarial analysis at the end of the paper for purposes of studying how SS optimization would affect SS finance.

II.   The SCF, Benchmarking, and Data Imputations

The SCF is a cross-section survey conducted every 3 years.[19] The survey oversamples wealthy households in the process of collecting data from, in the case of the 2019 survey, 5,777 households.[20] These data include detailed information on household labor and asset income, assets and liabilities, and demographic characteristics.[21]

A.   Benchmarking the 2019 SCF to National Aggregates

SCF household-weighted totals of various economic and fiscal aggregates differ from their direct counterparts in the National Income and Product Account (NIPA) and Federal Reserve Financial Accounts (FA). To assure concordance, we follow the approach outlined in appendixes A and B in Dettling et al. (2015), which benchmarks the 2016 SCF based on "conceptually equivalent" values. Specifically, we set SCF benchmark factors to ensure that SCF-weighted aggregates coincide with conceptually comparable NIPA and FA aggregates. We used FA2018 Q4 aggregates for wages, self-employment income, and assets.

Benchmarking assets and net worth reported in the SCF requires several adjustments to the FA values. Using the approach outlined in appendix B of Dettling et al. (2015), our first asset adjustment was to reduce SCF-reported home market value by 7.3% to match the 2018 Q4 Federal Reserve FA measure. Second, we increase the SCF-reported equity in noncorporate businesses by 33.3% to match the 2019 Q3 Federal Reserve FA estimate. Third, we increased reported retirement-account assets by 11.3% to match the total reported for 2018 Q4 in the Federal Reserve's FA. Table 4 details aggregate values, their sources, and our benchmark adjustments. We inflate all SCF-reported wage income by 22.3% to match

Table 4
SCF Benchmarking Adjustments and Targets (in US$)

	SCF Unadjusted	Benchmarking Coefficient	SCF Adjusted	Target	% Diff
Wages	7,382[a]	1.22	9,027	9,027	.00
Self-employment income	2,237	.72	1,601	1,601	.00
Market val. of homes	28,048	.93	25,992	25,877	.44
Noncorp. business equity	9,795	1.33	13,055	13,055	.00
Regular assets	50,904	.69	35,373	35,374	.00
Retirement accounts	14,307	1.11	15,923	15,824	.62

Note: SCF = Survey of Consumer Finances.
[a] All values are presented in billion 2018 US dollars.

the NIPA 2018 measure of employee compensation and deflate all SCF-reported self-employment income by 28.4% to match the NIPA 2018 proprietorship and partnership income total. The fact that we need to inflate wage income and significantly deflate self-employment income to match national aggregates may reflect, in part, a tendency of SCF respondents to report wage earnings as self-employment income.

B. Imputing State Residency

The public-use SCF release does not provide state identifiers. The non–public-use SCF data do include state identifiers, but its household weights are national, not state-specific. They are, therefore, of no value for our purposes of appropriately allocating SCF households by state. Consequently, we allocate SCF households to different states based on a statistical match to the Current Population Survey (CPS). Specifically, we sort respondents to the 2019 CPS by state into cells based on marital status, age of household head, race (white or nonwhite), and education (high school diploma or less, some college, college diploma). Having done so, we calculate the distribution across states of CPS households with specific cell characteristics. Next, we randomly assign SCF households within their appropriate cell to one of the 51 states (including Washington, DC) based on the CPS-determined probabilities that households in their cell will live in specific states.

C. Earnings Imputations

The SCF is a cross-section survey. But assessing lifetime spending requires estimating future labor earnings. In addition, we need to estimate past labor earnings for each respondent and any spouse/partner to calculate these individuals' annual as well as lifetime SS benefits. Our imputation of labor earnings is based on prior (1967–2014) waves of the CPS. To impute annual labor earnings, we first group CPS observations by age, sex, and education. Next, we estimate annual earnings growth rates by age and year for individuals in each sex and education cell. These cell growth rates are used to "backcast" and forecast each individual's earnings history. These forecasts assume a 1% real growth rate in economy-wide earnings.

Past and future cell growth rates ignore earnings heterogeneity within cells. To deal with such heterogeneity, we assume that observed individual deviations in earnings from cell means are partially permanent and partially transitory, based on an underlying earnings process in which the permanent component (relative to group-trend growth) evolves as a random walk and the transitory component is serially uncorrelated. We also assume that such within-cell heterogeneity begins in the first year of labor force participation. In particular, suppose that, at each age, for group i, earnings for each individual j evolves (relative to the change in the average for the group) according to a shock that includes a permanent component, p, and an independent and identically distributed (iid) temporary component, e. Then, at age a (normalized so that age 0 is the first year of labor force participation), the within-group variance will be $a\sigma_p^2 + \sigma_e^2$. Hence, our estimate of the fraction of the observed deviation of individual earnings from group earnings, $(y_{i,j}^a - \bar{y}_i^a)$, that is permanent is $a\sigma_p^2 / (a\sigma_p^2 + \sigma_e^2)$. This share grows with age as permanent shocks accumulate. Using this estimate, we form the permanent component of current earnings for individual j, $\hat{y}_{i,j}^a$,

$$\hat{y}_{i,j}^a = \bar{y}_i^a + \left(\frac{a\sigma_p^2}{(a\sigma_p^2 + \sigma_e^2)}\right)(y_{i,j}^a - \bar{y}_i^a) = \left(\frac{a\sigma_p^2}{(a\sigma_p^2 + \sigma_e^2)}\right)y_{i,j}^a + \left(\frac{\sigma_e^2}{(a\sigma_p^2 + \sigma_e^2)}\right)\bar{y}_i^a, \quad (2)$$

and assume that future earnings grow at the group average growth rate. Furthermore, we make the simplifying assumption that the permanent and temporary earnings shocks have the same variance. This assumption reflects the literature (e.g., Moffitt and Gottschalk 1995; Meghir and Pistaferri 2011). Thus, equation (10) reduces to

$$\hat{y}_{i,j}^a = \left(\frac{a}{(a+1)}\right)y_{i,j}^a + \left(\frac{1}{(a+1)}\right)\bar{y}_i^a. \quad (3)$$

For backcasting, which we need to calculate SS benefits, we assume that the earnings for individual j were at the group mean at age 0 (i.e, the year of labor force entry) and diverged smoothly from this group mean over time so that the individual's estimated earnings t years prior to the current age a are

$$\bar{y}_i^{(a-t)} + \left(\frac{(a-t)}{a}\right)(\hat{y}_{i,j}^a - \bar{y}_i^a)\left(\frac{\bar{y}_i^{(a-t)}}{\bar{y}_i^a}\right) = \left(\frac{t}{a}\right)\bar{y}_i^{(a-t)} + \left(\frac{(a-t)}{a}\right)\hat{y}_{i,j}^a\left(\frac{\bar{y}_i^{(a-t)}}{\bar{y}_i^a}\right). \quad (4)$$

That is, for each age we use a weighted average of the estimate of current permanent earnings, deflated by general wage growth for group i, and the estimated age-a, group-i mean also deflated by general wage growth for group i, with the weights converging linearly so that as we go back, we weight the group mean more and more heavily, with a weight of one at the initial age, which we assume is age 20.

D. Treatment of SCF Divorcées and Widows

Unfortunately, the SCF provides no information on the earnings histories or projected earnings of former spouses. Nor does it includes any information of the earnings histories of deceased spouses or deceased ex-spouses. Consequently, we have no alternative but to treat these respondents as single in TFA.

E. Using the American Community Survey to Determine Retirement Hazards

The SCF respondents are asked about their expected ages of retirement. Not all respond, and those that do appear to be overly optimistic.[22] This squares with the tendency of workers in general to overestimate how long they will work.[23] As an alternative, we use the 2000 through 2020 waves of the ACS to impute retirement age based on two questions in the survey. The ACS asks respondents the number of weeks that they worked last year and the number of hours they are currently working in a typical week. We define "retired" as a person working more than 26 weeks in the previous year and working less than 21 hours a week this year.[24]

We segregate ACS working respondents by year of birth, age, gender, marital status, and education. We assume no retirement prior to age 50. Starting at 50, we classify as retired respondents who report working less than 21 hours per week in the current year but more than 26 weeks in the previous year. This lets us calculate, for specific cohorts with particular cell attributes, sample retirement probabilities over the 20 ACS surveys. We smooth these values and use the resultant smoothed

Table 5

Probability of Working More Than 20 Hours at Age 65, Age 50 Workers in 2020

Martial Stat.	Education	Male	Female
Single	High school or less	44.2	24.5
	Some college	43.2	34.0
	Four year college or more	45.3	35.9
Married	High school or less	56.5	17.9
	Some college	56.0	20.3
	Four year college or more	58.6	18.9

function to determine retirement probabilities. Conditional probabilities of working at age 65 and 70 for 50-year-old workers in 2020 are summarized in tables 5 and 6.

These cohort- and characteristics-specific retirement hazards are used to randomly assign retirement ages for each SCF respondent under age 80. We assume that all households retire at 80 if they have not yet been probabilistically retired. Retirement rates for age 50 workers in 2020 and age 50 workers in 2040 are summarized in tables 7 and 8, respectively. The predicted fraction of ACS respondents working after 55 increases over time. The drivers here include higher educational achievement among successive cohorts and a rise in the fraction of working women. To be precise, within each cohort we project some, but limited, increases in retirement ages through 2040, with married 50-year-old men with 4-year college degrees or more retiring at 65.9, approximately 0.6 years later than their 2020 counterparts.

Figure 1 plots our cohort-specific smoothed retirement hazard functions—the likelihood of working "full time" (more than half time) at different ages—for alternative birth cohorts. Two things are immediately clear. First, regardless of year of birth, the probability of working full time declines dramatically starting at age 50. Second, recent cohorts are

Table 6

Probability of Working More Than 20 Hours at Age 70, Age 50 Workers in 2020

Marital Stat.	Education	Male	Female
Single	High school or less	20.0	6.9
	Some college	17.3	11.0
	Four year college or more	18.4	10.5
Married	High school or less	26.6	3.9
	Some college	25.1	4.7
	Four year college or more	26.5	3.9

Table 7
Projected Average Retirement Age, Age 50 Workers in 2020

Marital Stat.	Education	Male	Female
Single	High school or less	63.0	59.4
	Some college	62.9	61.0
	Four year college or more	63.2	61.5
Married	High school or less	64.9	58.1
	Some college	64.9	58.5
	Four year college or more	65.3	58.3

more likely to work after age 60, but the differences are small and decrease with age.

Tables 7 and 8 show projected average retirement ages. The results, which are broken down by marital status and education, are striking. First, predicted average retirement ages are only slightly higher for future than for current age-50 workers. Second, single females with college educations are projected to retire roughly 2 years later, on average, than those with a high school diploma or less. Third, for males, education makes little difference in average retirement ages holding fixed marital status. Fourth, married males retire, on average, roughly 2 years later than single males across all levels of education. Fifth, males retire later than females, with the difference in average ages falling from roughly 4 years to roughly 2 years as one moves from lower to higher levels of education.

Tables 5 and 6 report the probability of working full time at ages 65 and 70 for 50-year-old workers in 2020. The tables are quite revealing. First, holding education and marital status fixed, the chances of working full time are substantially higher at age 65 than at age 70. Take, for example, married males with some college education. Their chances of being "fully employed" are 56.0% at age 65 and 25.1% at age 70. Second, females are substantially less likely than males to work full time. Third, married males are more likely to keep working full time than single

Table 8
Projected Average Retirement Age, Age 50 Workers in 2040

Marital Stat.	Education	Male	Female
Single	High school or less	63.1	59.0
	Some college	62.7	60.8
	Four year college or more	63.3	61.7
Married	High school or less	65.4	58.4
	Some college	65.1	58.9
	Four year college or more	65.9	58.5

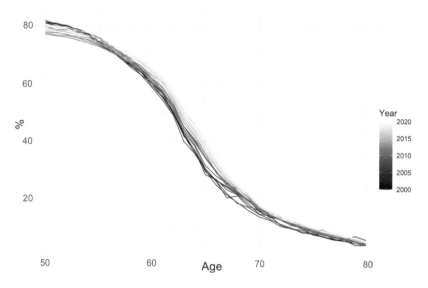

Fig. 1. Fraction of respondents working more than 20 hours per week, American Community Survey 2000–2020. A color version of this figure is available online.

males. And fourth, education significantly raises the likelihood of single, but not of married, females working full time.

III. Findings

This section presents our main results as well as sensitivity analyses.

A. Principal Findings

As indicated, we ran the 2019 SCF with TFA's SS benefit optimizer turned off and then with it turned on. We report all results in June 2022 dollars. Our maintained assumption, which may be overly strong, is that workers take their SS retirement benefit at retirement. Imputed and optimized retirement-benefit collection ages by SCF role (one for household head, two for spouse/partner) are summarized in table 9. Among all 45- to 62-year-old individuals (heads of households and spouses/partners) in the baseline, the weighted average age at which respondents start their SS retirement benefit is 66.1 and 63.6 for spouses/partners. After optimization, the average retirement-benefit collection age for household heads is 69.9 and 68.7 for spouses/partners. A large majority—91.6%—of heads of households optimize SS benefits by taking benefits at age 70. A total of 99.4% optimize by taking benefits after age 65.

Table 9
Retirement-Benefit Collection Age Distribution by Role, Survey of Consumer Finances
Respondents Ages 45–62

	Head of Household		Spouse/Partner		Total	
	Baseline	Optimized	Baseline	Optimized	Baseline	Optimized
Weighted average collection age	66.0	69.9	63.6	68.7	65.0	69.4
Percent collecting at 62	20.9	0	44.0	0	30.1	0
Percent collecting at 70	15.1	97.9	2.8	81.9	10.2	91.6
Percent collecting after 65	63.8	99.9	36.5	98.7	53.0	99.4

Table 10 reports the gains from optimizing SS for different age groups.
Consider those ages 55–62. A striking 89.0% of this group gain from optimizing SS benefit collection. The rest experience nonnegative increases in LB that come at the cost of lower lifetime non-SS benefits or higher lifetime taxes. The median LB increase for this group is 14.7%. The median PV increase in LDS is 9.5%.

The absolute median increases in LB and LDS are impressive: $181,613 and $151,962, respectively. Turn now to those ages 63–69. A total of 84.4% stand to benefit from SS optimization. For those optimizing, the gain primarily arises from suspending one's retirement benefit at full retirement age and restarting it at 70. The median lifetime-benefit increase is $117,090, producing a median LDS increase of $92,218. In percentage terms, the median LB and LDS increases are 11.2% and 6.3%, respectively. SS benefit optimization may be of particular relevance to households ages 45–62

Table 10
Distribution of Benefits from Social Security Optimization

	No. Obs.	Pct. Benefiting from Soc. Sec. Optimization	Median Inc. in PV Disc. Spending ($)	Median Pct. Inc. in PV Disc. Spending	Median Inc. in PV Social Security ($)	Median Pct. Inc. in PV Social Security
All households	5,234	75.0	116,379	6.3	158,069	13.1
Ages 21–44[a]	1,562	87.0	193,925	8.5	259,997	21.4
Ages 45–62	1,916	90.1	182,370	10.2	225,944	16.7
Ages 45–54	988	91.1	213,844	10.4	271,790	20.3
Ages 55–62	928	89.0	151,962	9.5	181,623	14.7
Ages 63–69	788	84.4	92,218	6.3	117,090	11.2

Note: PV = present value.
[a]Age refers to age of head of household as defined in the SCF.

Table 11
Social Security Benefit Increase (in $) from Optimizing by Age Cohort and Percentile Outcome

	25th	50th	75th	90th	95th	99th
Ages 21–44	113,375	259,997	401,943	538,289	614,152	759,083
Ages 45–62	103,550	221,722	358,723	492,525	563,154	697,918
Ages 45–54	127,516	271,790	403,624	535,510	621,360	713,820
Ages 55–62	86,708	181,623	312,690	438,331	513,401	641,941
Ages 63–69	50,163	117,090	197,540	288,071	339,358	435,047

because respondents in this age group may not yet have formed rigid collection plans. An astounding 90.1% can gain from optimization, producing, at the median, $225,944 and $182,370 increases in LB and LDS, respectively. This corresponds to a 20.3% rise in LB and a 10.3% rise in LDS.

Across all SCF households, 75% benefit from optimizing SS. The (weighted) median household gain is $116,379. This is an impressive figure. It represents more than 2 years of a typical American worker's earnings. Among 45- to 62-year-olds, 91.1% benefit. And, to repeat, even among 63- to 69-year-olds, 84.4% benefit, many from suspending their retirement benefit at full retirement age and restarting it at 70. Among 45- to 62-year-olds, the weighted median LDS gain is $182,370. This represents 10.2% of remaining LDS and reflects a median increase in LB of $225,944.

Tables 11 and 12 report absolute and percentage increases in LB from SS optimization. The results are strikingly large. Consider, for example, workers ages 55–62. Their median LB increase is $181,623, and the 75th percentile value is $312,690. The corresponding median percentage increases are 14.7% and 22.9%, respectively. As discussed below, higher-resource households have larger absolute LB gains, but far smaller percentage gains than lower-resource households. This explains why the household with the median absolute LB gain has a relatively small percentage LB gain.

Table 12
Percent Social Security Benefit Increase from Optimizing by Age Cohort and Percentile Outcome

	25th	50th	75th	90th	95th	99th
Ages 21–44	9.7	21.4	34.4	37.1	37.1	37.1
Ages 45–62	7.6	16.3	25.5	36.0	37.1	37.1
Ages 45–54	10.2	20.3	31.5	37.1	37.1	37.1
Ages 55–62	6.6	14.7	22.9	32.6	37.1	37.1
Ages 63–69	4.6	11.2	14.9	20.3	23.0	26.0

Table 13
LDS Increase (in $) from Optimizing Social Security by Age Cohort and Percentile Outcome

	25th	50th	75th	90th	95th	99th
Ages 21–44	65,931	193,925	327,715	455,460	523,113	704,072
Ages 45–62	69,493	182,370	289,893	410,261	470,968	603,569
Ages 45–54	88,285	213,844	334,339	447,689	516,103	651,497
Ages 55–62	51,678	151,962	256,091	369,833	423,604	557,852
Ages 63–69	20,697	92,218	172,879	249,633	303,863	398,213

Note: LDS = lifetime discretionary spending.

Tables 13 and 14 show absolute and percentage increases in LDS from SS optimization at different percentile values of the increase. Clearly, some households benefit far more than others, at least in absolute terms. For example, the ages 55–62, 75th percentile gain is $256,091, more than five times the still quite large $51,678 gain for those experiencing the 25th largest increase. For those with the 99th percentile highest gain, the amount is huge: $557,852. As for those who are retired or close to retiring—the 63- to 69-year-olds—the gains range from $20,697 at the 25th percentile to a massive $398,213 at the 95th.

Interestingly, the absolute gains available to those ages 21–44 are similar to those ages 45–62. This reflects two offsetting effects. Younger cohorts have higher earnings and, therefore, a larger absolute stake in SS. On the other hand, SS benefits are further in the future and are therefore discounted to the present over a longer period.

Table 15 breaks down percentage gains by remaining lifetime resource quintiles. The median gain for those in the bottom quintile is 15.9%. It is 1.9% for those in the top quintile. Hence, a government SS optimization mandate would be highly progressive. The 75th and 90th percentile gains are 27.4% and 37.0% for the bottom quintile. For the top quintile, they are 3.3% and 5.2%.

Table 14
Percent LDS Increase from Optimizing by Age Cohort and Percentile Outcome

	25th	50th	75th	90th	95th	99th
Ages 21–44	3.4	8.5	13.6	18.8	22.4	29.3
Ages 45–62	3.2	10.2	17.2	26.2	33.8	43.8
Ages 45–54	4.5	10.4	18.2	27.2	34.6	43.6
Ages 55–62	2.6	9.5	17.2	26.5	33.8	48.0
Ages 63–69	1.6	6.3	13.2	22.2	30.3	39.7

Note: LDS = lifetime discretionary spending.

Table 15
Percent LDS Increase from Optimizing by Total Lifetime Resources Quintile
and Percentile Outcome, SCF Households Ages 45–62

	Lifetime Res. Lower Threshold (Million US$)	25th	50th	75th	90th	95th	99th
Bottom	0	6.1	15.9	27.4	37.0	40.3	50.4
Second	1.0	6.0	13.0	20.7	27.2	31.4	43.2
Third	2.2	5.6	10.1	14.3	18.7	21.2	33.3
Fourth	4.7	2.7	6.2	10.1	13.0	15.5	18.3
Highest	15.1	.8	1.9	3.3	5.2	5.5	8.9

Note: LDS = lifetime discretionary spending; SCF = Survey of Consumer Finances.

Table 16 considers how lifetime spending increases depend on our imputed retirement/benefit-collection age. Clearly, those retiring earlier have substantially more to gain, both absolutely and in percentage terms, from optimizing. Compare, for example, 45- to 62-year-olds who retire at 62 with those who retire at 67. For the former group, there is a 19.0% median gain in LDS, with the absolute amount equaling $291,811. For the latter group, the percentage LDS median gain is 8.7%, with the absolute increase equaling $170,306. The table also shows gains to household heads retiring at age 70 and later. Indeed, the median increase is $89,868. Because SS benefits peak when collected at age 70, these gains arise from optimization of younger spouses'/partners' LB.

Table 16
Benefit from Optimizing Social Security by Age Cohort and Retirement Age

	Ages 21–44			Ages 45–62		
Imputed Retirement Age	No. Obs.	Median Inc. in PV Disc. Spending ($)	Median Pct. Inc. in PV Disc. Spending	No. Obs.	Median Inc. in PV Disc. Spending ($)	Median Pct. Inc. in PV Disc. Spending
50–59	389	242,180	14.1	229	284,445	19.7
60	41	253,654	11.2	51	319,266	21.3
61	67	344,575	13.2	67	241,177	18.9
62	62	244,579	11.0	77	291,811	19.0
63	78	258,941	12.1	115	235,609	17.1
64	76	269,922	11.2	107	216,215	13.8
65	76	241,511	9.9	122	171,773	11.7
66	98	193,379	9.0	139	173,621	10.4
67	87	164,799	6.0	122	170,306	8.7
68	92	129,210	6.0	144	151,562	6.8
69	97	69,740	3.0	136	98,585	6.0
70+	399	105,310	3.2	607	111,665	4.0

Note: PV = present value.

Table 17 considers how long household heads and, if married, spouses/ partners should delay taking their retirement benefits. The optimization algorithm recommends that 18.2% of household heads and 36.1% of spouses/partners delay collection by 8 years. Only 32.2% of household heads and 15.6% of spouses should commence benefits immediately upon retiring. These are cases in which collecting retirement benefits in the future increases lifetime net taxes (taxes net of benefits) by more than the increase in LB. Interestingly, about 4.3% of head of households and 1.2% of spouses can raise their lifetime spending by taking benefits earlier than their retirement ages.

Figure 2 shows the remarkable dispersion in absolute LDS increases. The increases are plotted against the household head's age. The black curve marks the median increase, which peaks at roughly $250,000 in the mid-forties. At the extreme, some households experience close to a $900,000 rise in LDS. One such case with $749,511 in LDS gains is shown in table 18. In this married-household case, both spouses are high earners who retire and begin collecting their retirement benefit at ages 62 and 63. By both delaying until age 70, they increase their collective present value of SS benefits by a total of $715,678.

Figure 3 displays the dispersion in optimization-based LDS increases by lifetime resources. The sample here is our ages 45–62 households. Figure 4 presents the corresponding percentage increase in LDS. Again, the dispersion is the results is remarkable. But the figures convey two additional key messages. First, the middle class and rich have far more to gain in absolute terms from maximizing LB than do the poor. Second, the poor have far more to gain in percentage terms than do the rich.

Table 17
Ages 45–62 Individuals by Optimal Years of Delay

Years Delayed	Head of Household		Spouse/Partner	
	Count	Weighted %	Count	Weighted %
<0	196	4.3	32	1.2
0	617	32.2	221	15.6
1	93	4.1	41	2.1
2	73	3.3	57	3.5
3	410	18.3	241	13.9
4	140	5.7	91	5.0
5	111	4.7	265	12.6
6	94	4.1	64	4.2
7	103	5.1	98	5.8
8	398	18.2	545	36.1

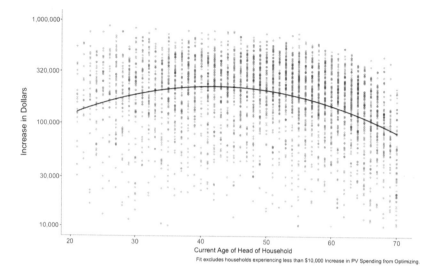

Fig. 2.   Increase in present-value (PV) discretionary spending from optimizing Social Security by age. A color version of this figure is available online.

B.   Cash-Flow Challenges to SS Optimization

Delaying SS benefit receipts will obviously reduce recipients' cash flows. Table 19 examines this issue. It shows the impact on current-year discretionary spending of optimization for all households and for

Table 18
Income and Social Security Statistics, Case 1

	Base Case	Optimized	Difference
Role 1 age	55	–	–
Role 2 age	50	–	–
Role 1 retirement age	63	63	0
Role 2 retirement age	58	58	0
Role 1 collection age	63	70	7
Role 2 collection age	62	70	8
Role 1 CY employment income ($)	148,588	148,588	0
Role 2 CY employment income ($)	428,621	428,621	0
CY disc. spending ($)	107,510	124,315	16,804
PV disc. spending ($)	4,795,150	5,544,661	749,511
Role 1 PV Social Security ($)	1,048,245	1,359,841	311,596
Role 2 PV Social Security ($)	1,104,881	1,508,963	404,082
R1 Social Security benefit at age 65 ($)	30,501	0	−30,501
R2 Social Security benefit at age 65 ($)	33,457	0	−33,457
R1 Social Security benefit at age 75 ($)	32,564	51,821	19,256
R2 Social Security benefit at age 75 ($)	33,457	58,914	25,457

Note: CY = current year; PV = present value.

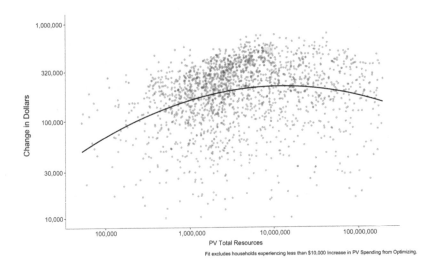

Fig. 3. Increase in lifetime discretionary spending by lifetime resources, ages 45–62. PV = present value. A color version of this figure is available online.

households benefiting from optimization. Across all households that benefit, median current-year spending drops by 3.3%, from $35,814 to $34,625.[25] This rather small response holds for separate age groups. The largest impact on medians is among those ages 63–69. These

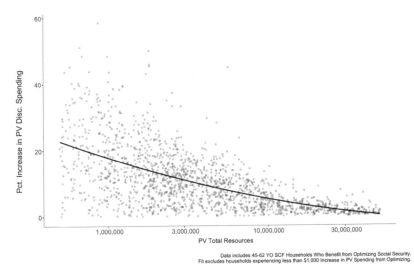

Fig. 4. Percentage increase in lifetime discretionary spending by lifetime resources, ages 45–62. PV = present value; SCF = Survey of Consumer Finances. A color version of this figure is available online.

Table 19

Weighted Median Current-Year Discretionary Spending (in $) by Age Cohort and Optimization Outcome

	All SCF Households				Households Benefiting from Optimization[a]			
	Baseline	Optimized	Diff	% Diff	Baseline	Optimized	Diff	% Diff
All households	32,772	31,854	−917	−2.8	35,814	34,625	−1,188	−3.3
Ages 21–44	31,197	30,871	−326	−1.0	34,492	33,949	−543	−1.6
Ages 45–62	34,335	33,439	−896	−2.6	38,696	35,982	−2,714	−7.0
Ages 45–54	38,077	36,299	−1,777	−4.7	41,041	38,080	−2,960	−7.2
Ages 55–62	31,177	29,418	−1,760	−5.6	34,042	33,062	−980	−2.9
Ages 63–69	31,206	29,478	−1,728	−5.5	33,490	30,597	−2,893	−8.6

Note: SCF = Survey of Consumer Finances.
[a]Sample contains households that see at least $100 improvement in PV discretionary spending from optimization.

households experience an 8.6% current-year living-standard decline. All other age groups also experience declines in median current-year spending. Hence, SS optimization comes, in general, at a modest short-term discretionary spending cost.

Table 20 details the share of households that are constrained in the baseline and under optimization. Across all households that benefit, 46.3% are constrained prior to optimization and 72.1% after optimization. Interestingly, these figures are somewhat lower for those ages 63–69, at 41.1% and 63.5%, respectively.

Table 21 reports how optimization affects the share of cash-constrained households across lifetime resource quintiles. The results are for those ages 45–62. Optimization entails a major increase in the

Table 20

Percent of Borrowing-Constrained Households by Age Cohort and Optimization Outcome

	All SCF Households			Households Benefiting from Optimization		
	Baseline	Optimized	Diff	Baseline	Optimized	Diff
All households	46.8	65.3	18.5	46.3	72.1	25.8
Ages 21–44	60.5	80.6	20.1	57.4	80.3	22.9
Ages 45–62	40.9	68.4	27.5	37.1	68.6	31.5
Ages 45–54	38.0	67.7	29.7	34.3	67.5	33.1
Ages 55–62	44.1	69.1	25.0	40.3	70.0	29.7
Ages 63–69	44.4	62.9	18.5	41.1	63.5	22.4

Table 21
Percent of Ages 45–62 Borrowing-Constrained Households by Total Lifetime Resource
Quintile and Optimization Outcome

| | All SCF Households Ages 45–62 | | | Households Ages 45–62 Benefiting from Optimization | | |
	Baseline	Optimized	Diff	Baseline	Optimized	Diff
Bottom	69.5	94.3	24.8	67.3	95.5	28.2
Second	41.6	83.3	41.6	40.8	87.5	46.7
Third	27.2	62.8	35.6	25.7	64.2	38.5
Fourth	8.9	18.7	9.8	8.6	18.8	10.2
Highest	1.1	1.2	.2	1.1	1.3	.2

Note: SCF = Survey of Consumer Finances.

share constrained in the bottom quintile, from 67.3% to 95.5% among those that benefit from this decision. In contrast, among those in the top quintile, optimization entails essentially no change in the roughly 1% of households that are cash constrained.

Lower resource quintiles are more constrained both before and after optimization. When optimized, almost all of the households (94.3%) in the bottom 20% become constrained. If we look at households who actually benefit from optimization, this rate goes up to 95.5%. Across all households, 83.3% in the second resource quintile are constrained, 62.8% in the third, and only 1.2% in the top 20%. Of the top quintile, only 1.1% are cash-flow constrained at all in the baseline case.

Table 22 reports the duration of cash-flow constraints. For all SCF working households, the baseline average (sample weighted, of course) duration is 9.9 years. For those enjoying a gain from optimization, the

Table 22
Weighted Average Cash-Flow Constraint Duration in Years

| | All SCF Households | | | Households Benefiting from Optimization | | |
	Baseline	Optimized	Diff	Baseline	Optimized	Diff
All households	9.9	18.1	8.2	9.4	20.9	11.5
Ages 21–44	13.7	29.1	15.4	11.7	29.4	17.7
Ages 45–62	8.7	16.3	7.5	8.2	16.9	8.7
Ages 45–54	9.6	18.3	8.7	9.0	18.8	9.8
Ages 55–62	7.7	14.0	6.3	7.2	14.6	7.4
Ages 63–69	8.0	10.3	2.3	7.0	9.7	2.7

Note: SCF = Survey of Consumer Finances.

average is 9.4 years. Optimization considerably extends the length of constrained spending. For all those benefiting from optimization, the average is 9.4 years before optimization. With optimization, this figure becomes 20.9 years after. For those ages 63–69, the addition to the length of their spending constraint is 2.7 years. For workers ages 45–62, the average duration rises from 8.2 to 16.9 years.

Table 23 sheds additional important light on this matter. It shows the percentage of households whose current-year discretionary spending rises, as well as the percentage for whom current-year discretionary spending falls. Across all households that benefit from optimization, 45.0% experience an immediate rise in their spending, whereas 46.8% experience an immediate decline, followed, when they become unconstrained, by an often major rise. These values are quite similar for other age groups.

C. Case Studies

Tables 18 and 24 illustrate our calculations for two sample observations. Case 1 is a very high-earning couple that has, to date, saved relatively little and will retire in their early sixties. Role 1 references the household head and Role 2 the spouse/partner. This couple enjoys a $749,511 increase in LB from SS optimization. Both spouses wait to collect until age 70. Their benefits at, for example, age 65 are zero. They would otherwise total almost $64,000. And at age 75, when they are receiving their age-70 benefit, but for the entire year, their combined annual SS benefits are close to $110,000. This couple is unconstrained. Consequently, their discretionary spending immediately rises, in this case by $16,804, or 15.6%.

Table 23
Distribution of Current-Year Discretionary Spending Change from Optimizing

	All SCF Households			Households Benefiting from Optimization		
	Pct. Better	Pct. Unchanged	Pct. Worse	Pct. Better	Pct. Unchanged	Pct. Worse
All households	32.4	33.9	33.7	45.0	8.1	46.8
Ages 21–44	35.4	24.9	39.7	40.7	13.6	45.7
Ages 45–62	39.9	15.9	44.1	45.5	4.2	50.3
Ages 45–54	40.1	13.3	46.6	44.8	3.2	52.0
Ages 55–62	39.7	18.9	41.4	46.3	5.3	48.3
Ages 63–69	42.4	20.0	37.6	50.9	3.8	45.2

Note: SCF = Survey of Consumer Finances.

Table 24
Income and Social Security Statistics, Case 2

	Base Case	Optimized	Difference
Role 1 age	51	–	–
Role 2 age	–	–	–
Role 1 retirement age	67	67	0
Role 2 retirement age	–	–	–
Role 1 collection age	67	70	3
Role 2 collection age	–	–	–
Role 1 CY employment income ($)	3,319	3,319	0
Role 2 CY employment income ($)	–	–	–
CY disc. spending ($)	11,134	10,332	–801
PV disc. spending ($)	623,631	612,144	–11,487
Role 1 PV Social Security ($)	642,116	726,383	84,267
Role 2 PV Social Security ($)	–	–	–
R1 Social Security benefit at age 65 ($)	11,611	11,611	0
R2 Social Security benefit at age 65 ($)	–	–	–
R1 Social Security benefit at age 75 ($)	15,755	19,537	3,782
R2 Social Security benefit at age 75 ($)	–	–	–
PV SNAP ($)	102,258	64,854	–37,404
PV SSI ($)	262,478	230,574	–31,903
PV Section 8 ($)	479,680	454,382	–25,298

Note: CY = current year; PV = present value; SNAP = Supplemental Nutrition Assistance program; SSI = Supplemental Security Income.

Case 2 references a single respondent whose PV of lifetime SS benefits rises by $84,267 from optimizing. But were they to do so, their LDS would fall. The reason is the loss in Food Stamps, Supplemental Security Income benefits, and Section 8 housing benefits. Hence, in our study, we treat the household as optimizing by not changing their intended collection date.

IV. Sensitivity Analysis

This section considers the sensitivity of our results to our assumed real discount rate and maximum age of life.

A. *Assuming a 2% Real Discount Rate*

As comparison of tables 10 and 25 show, assuming a 2% real (5% nominal) interest rate reduces the PV increase in median LDS to $99,797, roughly half the amount under our base case. The increase in median LB is $116,488. However, as shown in table 26, collection ages are largely the same as the base case, with about nine in 10 (90.7%) respondents

Table 25
Benefit from Optimizing Social Security by Household Type, 2% Real Interest Rate

	No. Obs.	Pct. Benefiting from Soc. Sec. Optimization	Median Inc. in PV Disc. Spending ($)	Median Pct. Inc. in PV Disc. Spending	Median Inc. in PV Social Security ($)	Median Pct. Inc. in PV Social Security
All households	5,250	74.3	56,814	3.9	73,648	10.0
Ages 21–44[a]	1,567	86.0	77,888	5.2	99,692	16.5
Ages 45–62	1,926	89.5	99,797	7.0	116,488	13.6
Ages 45–54	996	90.6	107,735	7.0	130,664	15.9
Ages 55–62	930	88.4	90,669	7.0	100,315	12.0
Ages 63–69	789	83.5	58,005	4.9	69,610	8.5

Note: PV = present value.
[a]Age refers to age of head of household as defined in the SCF.

optimizing by collecting at age 70 and more than 99% optimizing by collecting after age 65.

B. Lower Maximum Age of Life

Next, we rerun our optimization for lower maximum ages of life, specifically ages 80, 85, 90, and 95. In this analysis, we exclude households where a person's spouse is already older than the assumed maximum age of life. To put these alternative maximums in context, table 27 displays life expectancy by age and sex for cohorts ages 45, 62, and 70 in 2022. Note that today's 45-year-old males have a life expectancy of 81.7, and today's 70-year-old males have a life expectancy of 85.4. For corresponding females, life expectancies are even higher. Hence, a maximum age of life of 80 makes no sense for the population at large. Nonetheless, we include this case, as well as a case with a maximum age of life

Table 26
Retirement-Benefit Collection Age Distribution by Role, SCF Respondents Ages 45–62, 2% Real Interest Rate

	Head of Household		Spouse/Partner		Total	
	Baseline	Optimized	Baseline	Optimized	Baseline	Optimized
Weighted average collection age	66.0	69.9	63.6	68.6	65.0	69.4
Percent collecting at 62	21.1	0	44.1	.2	30.2	.1
Percent collecting at 70	14.8	97.6	2.9	80.3	10.1	90.7
Percent collecting after 65	63.4	99.9	36.5	98.6	52.7	99.4

Note: SCF = Survey of Consumer Finances.

Table 27
Conditional Life Expectancy in 2022 by Age and Gender

	Male		Female	
Age in 2022	Additional Life Expectancy	Estimated Total Years	Additional Life Expectancy	Estimated Total Years
45	36.7	81.7	40.4	85.4
62	21.5	83.5	24.4	86.4
70	15.4	85.4	17.6	87.6

of 80, to consider how individual households would respond were their actual maximum age of life 80 or were they to convince themselves that age 80 was their maximum age of life.

As shown in table 28, assuming a maximum age of life of 80, 12.5% of households ages 45–62 optimize by collecting at age 70. This is slightly higher than our no-optimization baseline, which entails 10.5% collecting at 70. Optimization nonetheless leads to later collection for most households: across all respondents, the retirement-benefit collection age increases by a year, from a baseline of 65.1–66.1. In the baseline, 29.5% of respondents collect starting at age 62; only 8% should do so after optimization even when the maximum age of life is 80. With this maximum lifespan, 82.1% of 45- to 62-year-old households will benefit from delaying collection. Hence, our findings suggest that, even if household members set an unrealistically low maximum age of life, their actual collection decisions are suboptimal.

For maximum ages of life of 85, 90, and 95, 74.4%, 86.1%, and 90.4%, respectively, of all respondents ages 45–62 optimize by collecting at age 70. And 94.2%, 98.5%, and 99.3%, respectively, should collect after 65. Taken together, these results suggest that the distribution of optimal collection ages is not particularly sensitive to our base-case assumption

Table 28
Collection Age Distribution by Maximum Age of Life, All SCF Respondents Ages 45–62

		Maximum Age of Life				
	Baseline	80	85	90	95	100
Weighted average withdrawal age	65.1	66.1	68.8	69.3	69.4	69.4
Percent withdrawing at 62	29.5	7.9	2.3	.5	.1	0
Percent withdrawing at 70	10.2	12.5	74.4	86.1	90.4	91.6
Percent withdrawing after 65	54.0	78.7	94.2	98.5	99.3	99.4

Note: SCF = Survey of Consumer Finances.

Table 29
Benefit from Optimizing Social Security by Maximum Age of Life

Maximum Age of Life	Median Increase in PV Disc. Spending					Median Pct. Increase in PV Disc. Spending				
	80	85	90	95	100	80	85	90	95	100
All households ($)	4,535	25,332	57,148	85,055	116,379	.3	1.5	3.4	4.9	6.3
Ages 21–44 ($)[a]	10,031	44,369	97,803	147,977	193,925	.4	2.2	4.8	6.9	8.5
Ages 45–62 ($)	9,607	46,186	94,352	138,434	182,370	.7	3.1	5.8	8.2	10.2
Ages 45–54 ($)	11,339	54,130	108,538	161,075	213,844	.7	3.1	5.8	8.3	10.4
Ages 55–62 ($)	8,029	38,494	79,447	116,397	151,962	.7	3.0	5.9	7.7	9.5
Ages 63–69 ($)	1,229	18,571	43,225	65,692	92,218	.1	1.6	3.6	5.0	6.3

Note: PV = present value.
[a]Age refers to age of head of household as defined in the SCF.

of a maximum age of life of 100. Even if respondents only expect to live to 90, more than five-sixths of respondents should nonetheless wait until age 70 to collect, and virtually all should wait until after 65.

Unsurprisingly, LDS gains increase with maximum age of life. As shown in table 29, at maximum ages of life of 80, 85, 90, and 95, median LDS gains from optimization for households ages 45–62 are $9,607, $46,186, $94,352, and $138,434, respectively. The corresponding percentage median increases to LDS are 0.7%, 3.1%, 5.8%, and 8.3%. Again, the base-case (maximum age of life equals 100) median percentage increase is 10.2%. Hence, even if household members only expect to live to 90, the median household still leaves close to $100,000 on the table.

The assumed maximum age of life interacts with cash-flow constraints. Absent optimization, shorter assumed maximum age of life leads to greater cash-flow constraints, as retirement accounts are withdrawn and spent over a shorter interval. This is shown in table 30. Assuming age 100 is the maximum age of life, 40.9% of households ages 45–62 are ever constrained. Assuming a maximum age of life of 80, 49.2% are constrained.

As shown in table 31, cash-flow constraints arising from optimization increase with the assumed maximum age of life. Optimization increases the share of 45- to 62-year-old households that are constrained by 7.3 percentage points, assuming a maximum age of life of 80. Assuming a maximum of 90, the share increases by 25.9 percentage points, only slightly lower than the increase of 27.5 percentage points in our base case. The story is similar for the duration of cash-flow constraints. Optimization extends the weighted average constrained duration by 1.4 years among households ages 45–62, assuming a maximum age of life of 80. Assuming

Table 30

Percent of Borrowing-Constrained Households by Age Cohort and Maximum Age of Life

Maximum Age of Life	80			85			90			95			100		
	Base.	Opt.	Diff.	Base.	Opt.	Diff.	Base.	Opt.	Diff.	Base.	Opt.	Diff.	Base.	Opt.	Diff.
All households	51.9	57.0	5.1	49.1	65.0	15.9	47.2	65.3	18.0	46.6	65.2	18.6	46.8	65.3	18.5
Ages 21–44	68.4	75.1	6.7	65.8	83.3	17.5	62.6	83.4	20.8	60.5	81.8	21.4	60.5	80.6	20.1
Ages 45–62	49.2	56.5	7.3	45.9	69.1	23.2	43.9	69.8	25.9	42.6	69.2	26.5	40.9	68.4	27.5
Ages 45–54	48.7	57.4	8.7	43.0	69.5	26.5	40.8	69.4	28.5	39.9	68.7	28.8	38.0	67.7	29.7
Ages 55–62	49.8	55.6	5.8	49.0	68.5	19.5	47.3	70.3	23.0	45.7	69.7	24.0	44.1	69.1	25.0
Ages 63–69	43.6	44.7	1.1	44.5	58.0	13.5	44.6	60.3	15.7	44.8	62.7	17.9	44.4	62.9	18.5

Table 31

Weighted Avg. Cash-Flow Constraint in Years by Age Cohort and Maximum Age of Life

Maximum Age of Life	80			85			90			95			100		
	Base.	Opt.	Diff.	Base.	Opt.	Diff.	Base.	Opt.	Diff.	Base.	Opt.	Diff.	Base.	Opt.	Diff.
All households	9.0	10.8	1.8	8.6	15.5	7.0	8.7	16.9	8.2	9.1	17.6	8.4	9.9	18.1	8.2
Ages 21–44	14.8	18.2	3.4	13.7	27.2	13.5	13.3	29.0	15.7	13.1	29.2	16.1	13.7	29.1	15.4
Ages 45–62	8.0	9.5	1.4	8.1	13.7	5.6	8.2	15.3	7.1	8.5	15.9	7.4	8.7	16.3	7.5
Ages 45–54	9.5	11.7	2.1	9.1	16.3	7.2	8.9	17.6	8.7	9.4	18.3	8.8	9.6	18.3	8.7
Ages 55–62	6.3	7.0	.7	7.0	10.8	3.8	7.4	12.7	5.3	7.5	13.3	5.8	7.7	14.0	6.3
Ages 63–69	3.7	3.6	–.1	4.7	5.9	1.2	5.8	7.6	1.7	7.2	9.6	2.4	8.0	10.3	2.3

167

a maximum of 90, the average constrained duration increases to 7.1 years. To recall, with a maximum age of 100, the average duration is 7.5 years.

V. Budgetary Costs of Optimization

How much would it cost SS were all households to optimize their lifetime-benefit collection decisions? To examine this question, we ran TFA adoption SS 2022 Trustees' Report (Social Security Administration 2022) assumptions, namely 1% real wage growth over and above age/experience-based growth, 2.4% inflation, and a 2.3% real rate of return. This analysis also considers all potential survivor paths; that is, we follow Social Security's trustees in doing an actuarial rather than an individual valuation. We also include all SCF households, from ages 21 through 99. Finally, we eliminate our sample selection that excludes those with less than $5,000 in current-year discretionary spending. We do so to provide as comprehensive and representative a data set as possible. These households may have other sources of support in the short term and still be eligible for SS.

Under these assumptions, applying SCF household weights, we obtain a baseline SS benefit trajectory for SCF cases representing 126.9 million US households.[26] For these households, the sum of current-year Old-Age and Survivors Insurance benefits from TFA is $1.03 trillion, which is slightly higher than the $0.99 trillion reported in the trustee report. Although there are a number of reasons the figures should differ somewhat, the fact that they are close is encouraging.[27]

Optimization results are summarized in table 32. Optimizing increases the present value of remaining LB of all SCF households from $56.4 to $59.8 trillion, or about a 6% increase. The absolute difference, $3.4 trillion, represents the minimum increase in SS long-term fiscal gap (the system's "infinite horizon liability"), currently $61 trillion, that would arise from optimization. Assuming that workers who enter the labor force after 2022 gain a similar proportional LB through optimization, the system's

Table 32
Total PV Benefits by Age Group in Trillion Dollars

	Current-Year OASI Benefits	PV Baseline Benefits	PV Optimized Benefits	Diff.	Pct. Diff.
All households	1.03	56.4	59.8	3.4	6.0
Ages 45–62	–	37.8	40.7	2.9	4.9

Note: OASI = Old-Age and Survivors Insurance; PV = present value.

unfunded liability would rise by roughly $6 trillion (i.e., by roughly 10%) were all households to optimize their benefit collection through time.

VI. Conclusion

SS is a critically important component of retirement-income security. Unfortunately, hundreds of millions of workers are making arguably highly inappropriate collection decisions, decisions that significantly reduce their lifetime SS benefits and, consequently, their lifetime spending. We find that virtually all US workers ages 45–62 would benefit from waiting until age 65 to collect. More than 90% would benefit from waiting until age 70. Yet only 10.2% do so, given our assumption that retirement-benefit collection begins at retirement. These age decisions are robust to alternate assumed maximum ages of life. Even assuming an unrealistically low maximum age of 85, three-quarters of workers would do best by waiting until age 70.

For those 45–62, the associated median household loss in LDS is $182,370. The 75th percentile increase is $289,893. As for the 25th percentile, the gain is $69,493—still remarkably large. These increases imply substantial percentage changes in living standards per household member. The median increase in this welfare metric is 10.4%. The 25th and 75th percentile increases are 3.2% and 17.2%, respectively.

Young as well as older workers can gain from postponing SS benefit collection. Such delay does, however, come at a higher cost: far more workers becoming cash-flow constrained. On the other hand, the typical temporary living-standard reduction is small. A modicum of workers do not gain from waiting to collect their retirement benefits. Such workers lose benefits from other transfer programs and face higher lifetime taxes, with the PV net tax increase exceeding the gain in lifetime SS benefits.

The increase in lifetime spending associated with SS lifetime-benefit maximization is typically smaller, if not considerably smaller, than the increase in LB. The reason is our fiscal system, which limits most households' living-standard gains from optimization by extracting higher taxes and reducing non-SS benefits.

There is an exceptionally large dispersion in lifetime-benefit optimization gains, ranging from several thousand dollars to close to $900,000. The percentage remaining lifetime spending gains are higher, on average, for those with low incomes. Take the poorest 20% of 45- to 62-year-olds. Their median gain from SS optimization is 15.9%. And one in four of this group experience a 27.4% or larger increase in lifetime spending.

All this said and shown, the precise gains and cash-flow constraints are highly dependent on household characteristics. Hence, one strategy does not fit all. Moreover, our results may overstate the gains from SS optimization given our maintained assumption that workers take their SS benefits as soon as they retire. On the other hand, we may understate the optimization gains because we lack the data (the earnings records on ex- or deceased spouses) needed to optimize LB for divorced spouses, widows, and divorced widows.

Finally, we estimate, using SS macroeconomic assumptions, a 6% increase in the actuarial present value of benefits owed to all current adult Americans were they all to optimize. That translates into a $3.4 trillion increase in Social Security's current colossal $61.8 trillion unfunded liability.[28] But if we assume future generations would also optimize, another $3 trillion or so could easily be added to this figure. This reflects the fact that the system's reductions for early retirement and Delayed Retirement Credits are more than actuarially fair based on current demographic and economic conditions.

Our bottom line? Social Security lifetime-benefit optimization represents a clear means of improving the welfare of retirees. High-income retirees have the most in absolute terms to gain from maximizing their LB. But low-income retirees can raise their living standards by a far higher percentage. Whether rich, middle class, or poor, what is required is simply patience: waiting to apply for the right benefits at the right time.

Endnotes

Author email addresses: Altig (dave.altig@atl.frb.org), Kotlikoff (kotlikoff@gmail.com), Ye (victorye@stanford.edu). The authors thank the Federal Reserve Bank of Atlanta, the Goodman Institute, the Alfred P. Sloan Foundation, Boston University, and Economic Security Planning, Inc., for research support. The views expressed herein are those of the authors and do not necessarily reflect the views of Economic Security Planning, Inc., the Federal Reserve Bank of Atlanta, NBER, or Opendoor Technologies. For acknowledgments, sources of research support, and disclosure of the authors' material financial relationships, if any, please see https://www.nber.org/books-and-chapters/tax-policy-and-economy-volume-37/how-much-lifetime-social-security-benefits-are-americans-leaving-table.

1. See https://www.cnbc.com/2022/07/30/vanguard-how-much-americans-have-saved-for-retirement-by-age.html and https://www.bls.gov/news.release/cesan.nr0.htm.

2. See https://www.ssa.gov/news/press/factsheets/basicfact-alt.pdf.

3. See https://money.usnews.com/money/retirement/social-security/articles/reasons-to-claim-social-security-at-age-70.

4. In 2015, Kotlikoff coauthored a 300-page book on SS rules and how best to manage them. Despite its seemingly arid content, the book became a *New York Times* best seller!

5. During its decades-long construction of TFA, Economic Security Planning received considerable government- and private-sector support from the Federal Reserve Bank of

Boston, the Sloan Foundation, The Goodman Institute, the Searle Family Trust, the National Center for Policy Analysis, the Nation Institute of Aging, and Boston University.

6. Our description of TFA draws almost verbatim from https://kotlikoff.net/wp-content/uploads/2019/03/The-Fiscal-Analyzer-Online-Appendix-6-13-22.pdf.

7. TFA's core computation engine as well as its lifetime benefit and retirement-account withdrawal optimization routines are those developed by Economic Security Planning, Inc., in the course of producing its two commercial personal financial planning tools, MaxiFiPlanner.com (https://maxifi.com) and Maximize My Social Security (https://maximizemysocialsecurity.com).

8. This TFA description borrows heavily and often verbatim from Altig et al. (2020).

9. This behavior is consistent with Leontief intertemporal preferences defined over the household's future living standard. TFA is designed to permit additional borrowing as specified by the researcher.

10. As discussed below, Yaari (1965) shows that the maximum age of life and only the maximum age of life is the correct horizon for valuing pension benefits. Given current life tables (https://www.ssa.gov/oact/STATS/table4c6.html), 2% of Americans will live beyond age 100. Hence, one could argue for an even higher maximum age of life assumption.

11. For a single person age 50, there are 50 survival paths because the person can die in any of the next 50 years. For a married couple each age 50 and each with maximum ages of life of 100, there are $50^2 = 2500$ such paths. An example is a husband dying at 69 and his spouse dying at 91.

12. These state variables are not just survivor-path-specific but year-survivor-path-specific; that is, we need to know the state vector along each survivor path in each future year. Take, for example, a 40-year-old couple that could live to 100. They have more than 200,000 survivor-contingent regular and retirement-account state variables.

13. The life-insurance program determines annual life-insurance amounts, for each potential decedent, that ensure survivors, including children, the ability to finance and thus enjoy the same living standard through their maximum ages of death or, in the case of children, departures from their parental homes, as they would have enjoyed had the spouse/partner/parent not passed away. If survivors can finance a higher living standard absent life insurance, TFA sets life insurance to zero.

14. Borrowing constraints introduce kinks in the discretionary spending functions. And dynamic programming requires interpolating backward (from year t to year $t-1$) over these functions. This propagates interpolation errors backward, producing more kinks and inaccuracies in each successive function.

15. This routine calculates and uses survivor-path, year-specific taxes and transfer payments. Thus, the maximum-longevity survival path in which the respondent and potential spouse/partner both live to their maximum ages of life provides the life-insurance routine annual living-standard targets that the life-insurance routine insures for each survivor path. The maximum-longevity survival path is, to put it euphemistically, "One ring to rule them all."

16. One measure of the system's complexity is the number of lines of efficiently written software code needed to properly apply its myriad provisions. In the CE's case, these lines of code, when printed, take up more than a ream of printing paper.

17. See https://www.ssa.gov/benefits/retirement/planner/otherthings.html?tl=1.

18. TFA accommodates this behavior via the setting of its age-living-standard index.

19. This section draws heavily and often verbatim from Altig et al. (2020).

20. The SCF combines an area-probability sample of households with a "list" sample of generally wealthier households from administrative tax records from the Internal Revenue Service. The SCF includes sampling weights to account for oversampling of wealthier households from inclusion of the list sample and for differential response rates among wealthier groups. Wealthier households have lower response rates, particularly at the highest levels (see Bricker et al. 2016). The oversampling of wealthy households allows for inference about households in the top 1% of the resource distribution. For the 2004 SCF, Kennickell (2007) shows that 15.8% of sampled households were in the top 1% of the net worth distribution for the United States, with 96.4% of these coming from the list sample. Another 38.5% of the 2004 SCF-sampled households were in the bottom 50% of the net worth distribution, with only 5.7% of these households coming from the list sample.

21. Using a multiple imputation algorithm, the Fed includes each household's record in the public-use SCF data set in five so-called replicates to account for estimation of nonreported values (item nonresponse) or for disclosure limitations. We use the first replicate for our analysis. Auerbach et al. (2017, 2022) report no significant differences in results across replicates.

22. Among 45- to 62-year-old 2019 SCF male respondents, the average age of expected full retirement is 70.3 years old, calculated using sample weights. For females, the weighted self-reported full retirement age is 68.9 years old.

23. See https://www.planadviser.com/boomers-overly-optimistic-about-work-in -retirement.

24. We include 20 hours as retired because many ACS respondents report exactly 20 hours. These respondents are likely earning less than Social Security's Earnings Test threshold and hence are likely taking SS retirement benefits.

25. Here, as elsewhere, medians are computed incorporating sample weights.

26. This represents more than 99% of US households as of 2020.

27. The PV of benefits across all SCF households is $56.4 trillion. The trustees report (Social Security Administration 2022) a $95 trillion PV in benefits but over a 75-year window. Hence, there are people who are not in our data set—current 10-year-olds, for example—who will collect over this period.

28. See https://www.ssa.gov/oact/TR/2022/VI_F_infinite.html.

References

Altig, David, Alan J. Auerbach, Patrick C. Higgins, Darryl R. Koehler, Laurence J. Kotlikoff, Michael Leiseca, Ellyn Terry, and Yifan Ye. 2019. "Did the 2017 Tax Reform Discriminate against Blue State Voters?" Working Paper no. 25570, NBER, Cambridge, MA.

Altig, David, Alan J. Auerbach, Laurence J. Kotlikoff, Elias Ilin, and Victor Yifan Ye. 2020. "Marginal Net Taxation of Americans' Labor Supply." Working Paper no. 27164, NBER, Cambridge, MA. https://www.nber.org/papers/w27164.

Auerbach, Alan J., Laurence J. Kotlikoff, and Darryl R. Koehler. 2019. "Online Appendix to the Fiscal Analyzer." https://kotlikoff.net/wp-content/uploads /2019/03/Online-appendix-6-5-19-.pdf.

———. 2022. "US Inequality, Fiscal Progressivity, and Work Disincentives: An Intragenerational Accounting." Working Paper no. 22032, NBER, Cambridge, MA.

Auerbach, Alan J., Laurence J. Kotlikoff, Darryl R. Koehler, and Manni Yu. 2017. "Is Uncle Sam Inducing the Elderly to Retire?" *Tax Policy and the Economy* 31:1–42.

Bricker, Jesse, Alice Henriques, Jacob Krimmel, and John Sabelhaus. 2016. "Measuring Income and Wealth at the Top Using Administrative and Survey Data." *Brookings Papers on Economic Activity* 1:261–331.

Bronshtein, Gila, Jason Scott, John B. Shoven, and Sita N. Slavov. 2016. "Leaving Big Money on the Table: Arbitrage Opportunities in Delaying Social Security." Technical report, NBER, Cambridge, MA.

Dettling, Lisa, Sebastian Devlin-Foltz, Jacob Krimmel, Sarah Pack, and Jeffrey Thompson. 2015. "Comparing Micro and Macro Sources for Household Accounts in the United States: Evidence from the Survey of Consumer Finances." *SSRN Electronic Journal* 01 2015. https://doi.org/10.2139/ssrn.2669590.

Ilin, Elias, Laurence J. Kotlikoff, and Melinda Pitts. 2022. "Is Our Fiscal System Discouraging Marriage? A New Look at the Marriage Tax." Technical report, NBER, Cambridge, MA.

Kennickell, Arthur B. 2007. "Look and Listen, but Don't Stop: Interviewers and Data Quality in the 2007 SCF." *Proceedings of the Survey Research Methods Section, American Statistical Association.* https://www.federalreserve.gov/econresdata/scf/files/asa20072.pdf.

Meghir, Costas, and Luigi Pistaferri. 2011. "Earnings, Consumption and Life Cycle Choices." In *Handbook of Labor Economics*, vol. 4, ed. David Card and Orley Ashenfelter, 773–854. Amsterdam: Elsevier.

Moffitt, Robert A., and Peter Gottschalk. 1995. "Trends in the Autocovariance Structure of Earnings in the US, 1969–1987." Working paper, Johns Hopkins University Department of Economics, Baltimore, MD.

Munnell, Alicia H. 2015. "Falling Short: The Coming Retirement Crisis and What to Do about It." Report no. 15-7, Center for Retirement Research at Boston College.

Social Security Administration. 2022. "The 2022 Annual Report of the Board of Trustees of the Federal Old-Age and Survivors Insurance and Federal Disability Insurance Trust Funds." https://www.ssa.gov/OACT/TR/2022.

Yaari, Menahem E. 1965. "Uncertain Lifetime, Life Insurance, and the Theory of the Consumer." *Review of Economic Studies* 32 (2): 137–50.

Effects of the Earned Income Tax Credit for Childless Adults: A Regression Discontinuity Approach

Jonathan Meer, *Texas A&M University and NBER,* United States of America

Joshua Witter, *PXT Central Science, Amazon,* United States of America

Executive Summary

Most antipoverty policy in the United States focuses on families with children, but efforts to assist childless adults have gained traction in recent years. We examine the impact of the earned income tax credit on the labor force outcomes of childless adults using the age-25 eligibility discontinuity. We find no impacts on labor force participation and employment outcomes, which may be due to lack of information about the credit, lack of behavioral response due to its small size, or that childless adults already have very high labor force participation rates.

I. Introduction

The earned income tax credit (EITC) is one of the primary antipoverty tools in the United States, transferring more than $60 billion to 25 million low-income working households in 2019 (Internal Revenue Service 2019). The EITC is thought to encourage employment for low-income households because people only become eligible if they have positive earnings. Previous research has focused almost exclusively on the impacts of the EITC on households with children; see Hoynes and Rothstein (2016) for a review, and recent work by Neumark and Shirley 2017; Wilson 2020; Kleven 2019; Kuka and Shenhav 2020; Neumark and Williams 2020; and Schanzenbach and Strain 2021, *inter alia*. Most studies find positive impacts on employment among single mothers with lower levels of education,

Tax Policy and the Economy, volume 37, 2023.

and often significant economic and social benefits, such as reductions in recidivism (Agan and Makowsky 2018), improved mother and infant health (Evans and Garthwaite 2014; Hoynes, Miller, and Simon 2015; Markowitz et al. 2017), boosts in educational achievement and attainment (Michelmore 2013; Bastian and Michelmore 2018), increases in intergenerational mobility (Jones, Simeonova, and Akee 2020), changes in marriage and fertility (Eissa and Hoynes 2000; Holtzblatt and Rebelein 2000; Baughman and Dickert-Conlin 2009; Maag and Acs 2015; Bastian 2017), and more. Studies looking at the employment effects of married couples find that total labor force participation increases for men and decreases for women. Overall, the combined labor supply of married couples seems to decrease because the increases from married men do not offset declines from married women (Eissa and Hoynes 2004). Research looking at the impacts of the EITC on adults without children, however, is sparse.

In large part, the focus on households with children is because the maximum amount of the federal credit is far lower for those without children, just $560 in 2022, as compared with $6,935 for filers with three or more children. Furthermore, the credit for childless adults is fully phased out at $16,480 for single filers in 2022, far lower than for those with children. Indeed, childless adults are often used as a control group to measure the impacts of the EITC (Meyer and Rosenbaum 2001; Hoynes and Patel 2018; Neumark and Williams 2020), with the justification that "individuals with no children are essentially ineligible for the EITC" (Chetty, Friedman, and Saez 2013) and that "the small credit offered is unlikely to induce a significant behavioral labor supply response" (Neumark and Williams 2020).

However, childless adults do account for a quarter of EITC recipients—nearly 7 million taxpayers—even as they only receive 3% of EITC payments, with an average claimed credit of $302 (Crandall-Hollick 2021). Recent policy efforts have emphasized expanding the EITC for childless adults: as part of the response to the coronavirus pandemic, the American Rescue Plan Act reduced the minimum age of eligibility from 25 to 19 for the 2021 tax year, increased the phase-in (and phase-out) rate, nearly tripled the size of the credit, and expanded the income range (Crandall-Hollick, Falk, and Boyle 2021). The proposed Build Back Better Act would make this change permanent.[1]

States play a large role in the EITC program. More than 30 states have their own EITC program, structured as a percentage of the federal credit. In 2022, all but six of those are fully refundable. Generosity ranges widely, from 3% to 100% of the federal credit (Tax Policy Center 2022). Combined, the maximum refundable EITC a childless adult could claim for the 2022 tax year ranges from $560 to $1,120, depending on the state. Witter (2020) finds that state EITC expansions between 1994 and 2017 led to small but significant increases in employment and labor force participation for younger childless women. Miller et al. (2018) similarly find small increases in employment, tax filing, and child support payments among noncustodial parents in response to the New York City Paycheck Plus program (an EITC-like program). These two studies looking at state expansions of the EITC offer promising but incomplete evidence that expanding the federal EITC can lead to increases in employment and labor force participation, as well as positive impacts on tax revenue and children with low-income noncustodial parents.

Rather than exploit variation in state or local EITC eligibility, we use the federal EITC's age-25 eligibility criterion as a source of identifying variation for the impacts on both laborforce participation and employment. Childless adults become eligible for the EITC in the year in which they turn 25, meaning that observationally similar people born just a few days apart are eligible to receive the credit a full year apart.[2] Recipients cannot manipulate the running variable, birth date, given that individuals in our sample were born before the EITC was introduced for childless adults in 1994. We use the 2001, 2004, 2008, and 2014 waves of the Survey of Income and Program Participation (SIPP) to examine outcomes on either side of this cutoff. That is, we compare outcomes for those turning 25 at the very end of the calendar year—who are eligible for EITC payments based on their labor income in that year—to those who are born shortly afterward, in the next year, and are thus ineligible until the following year.[3]

We find no effects on labor force participation or employment around this cutoff, either in the first year of eligibility or the following year. This effect may be driven by several mechanisms. It may be that the amount of the credit is too low to induce entry into the labor force, as hypothesized in Neumark and Williams (2020). It is also possible that the complexity of the eligibility requirements in particular, and of tax filing in general, reduces participation (Miller and Mumford 2015; Benzarti 2020, 2021). Although about four-fifths of eligible households take up the EITC, participation is lowest for the group we examine.[4] But Kopczuk and Pop-Eleches (2007) document an increase of nearly 4 million EITC recipients in 1994 "mostly due to extending eligibility to childless individuals." E-filing and assisted preparation also reduces complexity and increases participation (Kopczuk and Pop-Eleches 2007; Goldin 2018). Although knowledge of the structure of the EITC affects how individuals report their earnings (Chetty et al. 2013), most evidence indicates that providing information to potentially eligible households has little effect on EITC participation (Cranor, Kotb, and Goldin 2019; Linos et al. forthcoming).[5] Furthermore, labor force participation is very high among this group of young adults. Many of those who are never in the labor force during the sample period report a work-limiting disability. As such, this may simply be a margin of potential workers who are unlikely to enter the labor force, especially in response to such a small incentive.

A short-run analysis indicates that the incidence of such a subsidy will be shared between employers and employees if supply increases meaningfully, muting the impact of the transfer. Because we find no such effects, the incidence of the transfer accrues to employees to the extent that they take up the credit.[6] And because there is no change in the eligibility of those with children at this age cutoff, there should be little concern about general equilibrium effects that lead to spillovers in this context.

Our findings cannot be extrapolated to measure the impact or incidence of proposals that triple the maximum EITC for childless adults.[7] But they do shed light on the degree to which the current incarnation of the EITC has affected behavior. In Section II, we discuss the creation of the data set and our empirical approach. Section III presents the results of the regression discontinuity analysis, and Section IV concludes.

II. Data and Empirical Approach

A. Data

The EITC was introduced in 1975 for households with at least one dependent, with a modest increase in benefits introduced in 1986. In 1990, the federal EITC became more generous for families with two or more children relative to one-child families, phased in over several years. A significant increase was introduced in 1993, and in 2009, the EITC expanded for families with three or more children. The federal EITC for childless adults was introduced in 1994, and its generosity has not been expanded since, except for inflation adjustments and the temporary increase during the 2021 tax year.

To qualify for the EITC without a child, tax filers must be between the ages of 25 and 64, have earned income from wages, self-employment, or business, and live in the United States for at least half the year. They cannot be claimed as a dependent on another household's tax return or have investment income above a threshold ($3,650 in 2020; temporarily increased to $10,000 for 2021). Filers with children can still be considered "childless" when filing their taxes if the child lives with them for less than 6 months or is claimed as a dependent on another return.[8] Indeed, childless adults are diverse in terms of their household structure and family histories. Many are parents without custody of their children or have children who are grown and moved away from home.

In 2022, EITC credit amounts for childless adults are determined as follows. The phase-in rate for the EITC for single childless adults was 7.65% and extends over a range of $0–$7,320 in annual earnings. Single childless adults with annual earnings between $7,320 and $9,160 are eligible for the maximum EITC of $560. The phase-out rate is the same as the phase-in rate of 7.65% and extends from $9,160 to $16,480, where the EITC becomes $0. In other words, EITC amounts are equal to (0.0765 × Annual Earnings) for those with incomes in the phase-in range, $560 for those eligible for the maximum EITC, and ($560 − [0.0765 × Annual Earnings]) for those with incomes in the phase-out range. The credit is structured the same for jointly filing married couples except that it begins phasing out at a higher income threshold.[9]

Our sample is drawn from the 2001, 2004, 2008, and 2014 panels of the SIPP, covering 2000–16. Each SIPP panel surveys a set of households for several years, conducting interviews every 4 months and covering activities since the previous interview, including labor force participation and employment status in each week.[10]

We construct our eligibility measure using respondents' ages on the last day of the calendar year. Eligibility for married couples is determined by the age of the older spouse. We therefore use that age for married respondents; the qualitative conclusions are unaffected by using actual age.[11] Because taxes are filed annually, we aggregate the panel to the individual-year level. Our primary outcome measures are the proportion of weeks in the labor force or employed. Our results are similar when we use month-based observations instead. Because the entry and exit of survey participants into the SIPP panels do not line up perfectly with calendar years, many annualized observations are based on less than a full year's worth of reporting. Our results are unaffected when limiting the sample to observations based on 3, 6, or 9 months of individual data in a given year.

Full-time students under the age of 24 are eligible to be claimed as a dependent by others, so we exclude those with more education than a high school degree. We also exclude all SIPP respondents who had children at any point during the sample, as well as those under 18 or over 65. Otherwise, we impose no restrictions on the sample. Altogether, our data consist of 106,700 annual observations on 35,321 individuals, of whom 6,942 were, at their oldest, between the ages of 20 and 30 (inclusive) during the sample period. These individuals represent 16,641 person-year observations and form the core of our sample; bandwidth selection reduces the size of the sample, depending on the specification.

Of this sample, 67.0% report being in the labor force in every week about which they were asked in a given year, and 14.5% report not being in the labor force in any week about which they were asked; the percentages for employment status are 57.2% and 21.2%, respectively. The overall proportion of weeks in the labor force is 78.4%, and the percentage is 70.0% for employment. Some 82.8% were employed at any point during the sample. See table 1 for summary statistics.

Table 1
Summary Statistics

	Mean	Standard Error
Observations for persons:		
Female	.333	.471
Ever married	.166	.372
Ever in the labor force	.896	.306
Ever employed	.829	.376
Observations for person-years:		
Share of weeks in the labor force	.785	.373
Share of weeks employed	.700	.417
Married	.124	.330
Age on December 31	24.773	2.917
Hours worked	1,357	1,068
25th percentile	0	
Median	1,620	
75th percentile	2,085	
Total earned income (2019$)	23,718	30,597
25th percentile	3,128	
Median	19,147	
75th percentile	32,354	

Note: The first set of summary statistics uses 6,942 observations at the individual level, limited to those whose own maximum age or spouse's age in December was between 20 and 30 years during the entire sample. The second set of summary statistics uses 16,641 observations at the individual-year level, limited to those whose age in December was between 20 and 30 years. The analytical sample used for each specification is a subset of these person-year observations that depend on the optimal bandwidth.

B. *Empirical Approach*

We rely on the assumption that childless adults who turn 25 just before the end of the tax year are similar to those who turn 25 just after the end of the tax year, with the exception that those born before are eligible to claim the EITC in the following year. Our estimating equation is a simple regression discontinuity around the eligibility cutoff:

$$Y_{i,t} = \beta_0 + \beta_1 T_{i,t} + \beta_2 \text{Age}_{i,t} + \beta_3 T_{i,t} \times \text{Age}_{i,t} + \varepsilon_{i,t}.$$

$T_{i,t}$ is an indicator for being under 25 years of age prior to the end of the of the tax year, and β_1 measures the discontinuity in the outcome $Y_{i,t}$ for those who were 25 before the first day of the sample year. Age has a linear effect on the outcome on either side of the discontinuity; results are unchanged when using a quadratic. The bandwidth around the cutoff is selected using mean squared error optimal bandwidths and a triangular kernel (Calonico et al. 2017). Because there are generally multiple observations per individual, we cluster the standard errors at the individual level (Calonico et al. 2017). We use sample weights from the SIPP, though the results are unchanged when not using weights. We also estimate the effects after residualizing the outcome variable for state-year effects and individual effects (Lee and Lemieux 2010); the results are very similar.

Figure 1 shows the distribution of observations by age on December 31. There does not appear to be any manipulation of the running variable based on this figure. We also examine whether there are discontinuities across the cutoff in gender or whether the respondent has ever been married; there are no discontinuities present. Taken together, this suggests that our approach of examining outcomes for those who are just below the age-25 eligibility cutoff at the end of the year to those who are just over it will yield causal estimates of the impacts of the EITC on the labor market outcomes of childless adults.

III.   Results

We begin with the predicted EITC eligibility and amount, in figures 2 and 3. These are calculated using detailed information on family size, geography, and income information from the SIPP panels using the NBER TAXSIM v35 Stata Interface.[12] These estimates include state EITC amounts, for which a small number of childless adults under 25 are eligible. The discontinuity in this intent-to-treat first stage is clear, with those who are just

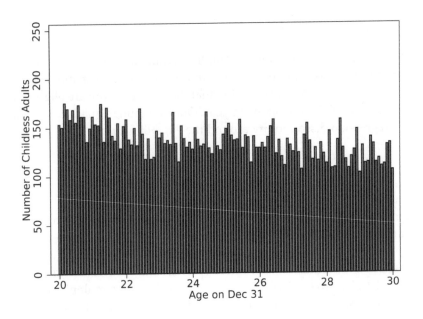

Fig. 1. Frequency of observations by age on December 31.

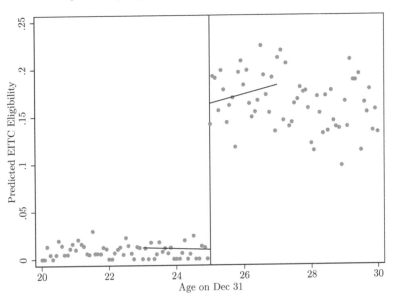

Fig. 2. Predicted earned income tax credit (EITC) eligibility. This figure shows results for predicted EITC eligibility (calculated using NBER TAXSIM), weighted using Survey of Income and Program Participation weights and estimated using a triangular kernel. The running variable is the individual's age on December 31 of that year. The symmetric bandwidth is MSE-optimal and is 1.99 years, using 7,654 observations.

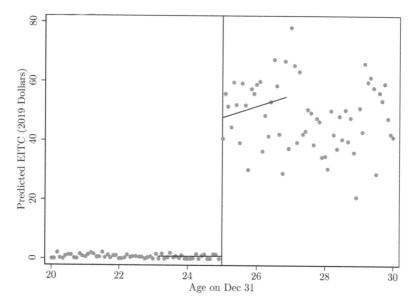

Fig. 3. Predicted earned income tax credit (EITC) amount. This figure shows results for predicted EITC amount received (including zeroes and calculated using NBER TAXSIM), weighted using Survey of Income and Program Participation weights and estimated using a triangular kernel. The running variable is the individual's age on December 31 of that year. The symmetric bandwidth is MSE-optimal and is 1.86 years, using 7,326 observations.

above age 25 being about 15.4 percentage points ($SE = 1.5$ percentage points) more likely to be eligible for the EITC. Including zero-dollar recipients, the predicted real amount received has a discontinuity of $46.88 ($SE = \$5.00$).

Figure 4 shows a simple examination of the effect of age-25 eligibility on the share of the year spent in the labor force by childless adults. There is no discontinuity for those who are just barely eligible for the EITC in a given year, based on their age, as compared with those who are just barely ineligible. The estimated discontinuity is -0.0076 ($SE = 0.020$). Similar results are seen in figure 5, which measures the discontinuity for employment. The measured effect for that outcome is -0.0006 ($SE = 0.020$). Table 2 shows results for labor force participation, and table 3 shows those for employment.[13]

The discontinuity across the age-25 cutoff is fuzzy. We can scale up the results in figures 4 and 5 by a factor of about 6.5, assuming that any estimate is driven entirely by those who are (intended to be) eligible for the EITC. The effect becomes much larger, of course, about -5 percentage points for labor force participation but only -0.4 percentage

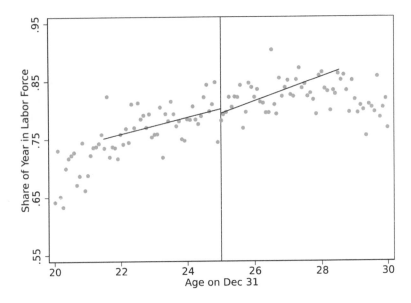

Fig. 4. Labor force participation. This figure shows results for the share of weeks in the labor force, weighted using Survey of Income and Program Participation weights and estimated using a triangular kernel. The running variable is the individual's age on December 31 of that year. The symmetric bandwidth is MSE-optimal and is 3.53 years, using 11,582 observations.

points for employment. The predicted effect is expected to be positive: the EITC is encourages participation and employment. These estimates are not only noisy (and, in the case of employment, still very small) but negative.

As discussed above, it is possible that the population around this cutoff is unaware of the EITC and, as such, we would not expect to see any differences in labor market participation in the year in which they turn 25. Those to the right of the cutoff—that is, those who are old enough to qualify—may discover that they had been eligible and adjust their behavior in the following year. If so, we would expect labor force participation to increase, as has generally been seen in the EITC literature on single mothers. Figures 6 and 7 show the results for labor force participation and employment, respectively, in the following year. The discontinuities are small, statistically insignificant, and negative, running in the opposite direction of what would be expected. As such, we conclude that there is no evidence for dynamic effects of eligibility; again, these may be driven by lack of information or simply lack of response to the relatively small credit.[14]

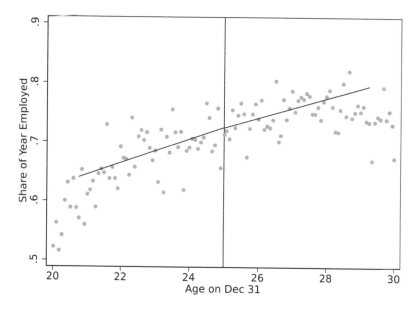

Fig. 5. Employment. This figure shows results for the share of weeks employed, weighted using Survey of Income and Program Participation weights and estimated using a triangular kernel. The running variable is the individual's age on December 31 of that year. The symmetric bandwidth is MSE-optimal and is 4.25 years, using 14,059 observations.

We also estimate effects for those who are more likely be aware of the EITC. People who had a positive tax liability in the previous year are more likely to have filed taxes and become aware of the EITC. The estimated discontinuity for this group continues to be small and statistically insignificant, at −0.015 ($SE = 0.020$) for labor force participation. Another proxy for federal EITC awareness is the existence of a state-level EITC. Neumark and Williams (2020) find that state EITC expansions lead to increases in federal tax filing. However, when we look at discontinuities separately for childless adults in states with EITCs versus those without

Table 2
Labor Force Participation

	(1) Linear	(2) Quadratic	(3) Following Year (Linear)
Estimated discontinuity at age 25	−.008	−.014	−.006
	(.020)	(.024)	(.024)
Number of observations used	11,582	15,775	6,549

Note: Each column reports the estimated discontinuity in the share of weeks reporting being in the labor force around the age-25 earned income tax credit eligibility. Estimates are weighted using Survey of Income and Program Participation weights and use a triangular kernel and MSE-optimal bandwidth.

Table 3
Employment

	(1) Linear	(2) Quadratic	(3) Following Year (Linear)
Estimated discontinuity at age 25	−.001	.004	−.011
	(.0204)	(.025)	(.026)
Number of observations used	14,059	17,159	6,708

Note: Each column reports the estimated discontinuity in the share of weeks reporting being in the labor force around the age-25 earned income tax credit eligibility. Estimates are weighted using Survey of Income and Program Participation weights and use a triangular kernel and MSE-optimal bandwidth.

EITCs, the differences in labor force participation and employment are negligible in both significance and magnitude.

Because many people in the sample are never in the workforce, it may be that we are unable to measure a labor force participation response for the margin of those who might actually join the workforce. Figure 8 shows the discontinuity in labor force participation for those who were in the labor force at any point during the sample period. The discontinuity is, again, small and statistically insignificant. In the same vein, we limit the

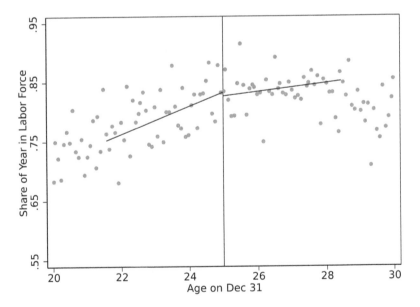

Fig. 6. Following-year labor force participation. This figure shows results for the share of weeks in the labor force in the year following the age used as the running variable, weighted using Survey of Income and Program Participation weights and estimated using a triangular kernel. The symmetric bandwidth is MSE-optimal and is 3.43 years, using 6,549 observations.

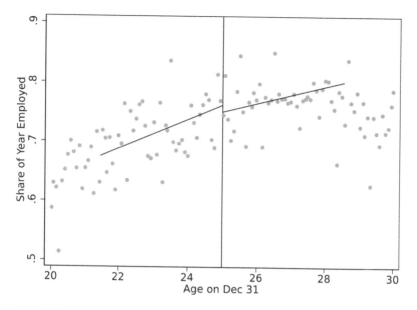

Fig. 7. Following-year employment. This figure shows results for the share of weeks employed in the year following the age used as the running variable, weighted using Survey of Income and Program Participation weights and estimated using a triangular kernel. The symmetric bandwidth is MSE-optimal and is 3.55 years, using 6,708 observations.

sample to those whose lowest level of annual earned income (both individual and spouse, if applicable) in the sample was less than $30,000. Based on the income eligibility criteria, these households were far more likely to be exposed to the EITC. The results are unaffected, with the discontinuity for labor force participation estimated at –0.0028 ($SE = 0.021$).

We can look at labor force participation and employment in a slightly different way to ensure we are fully capturing the potential extensive margin effects of the EITC on labor force participation and employment. We do this by running our regression discontinuity specification on binary indicators of whether childless adults were in the labor force or were employed at any time during the year. The first thing of note here is that labor force participation among both eligible and ineligible groups of childless adults is already pretty high. In fact, only about 10% of individuals ages 20–30 are never in the labor force during the sample period. We estimate insignificant discontinuities in labor force participation of about 0.71 percentage points ($SE = 1.35$ percentage points) and 1.03 percentage points ($SE = 1.63$ percentage points) in employment. Of those 10% of young childless adults who are never in the labor force, 39.7% report having a disability that limits their ability to work or prevents them from

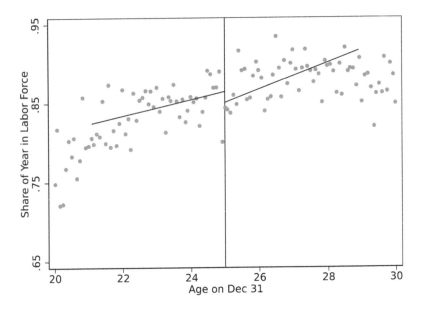

Fig. 8. Labor force participation (for those ever in the labor force). This figure shows results for the share of weeks in the labor force for individuals who were ever in the labor force during the sample period, weighted using Survey of Income and Program Participation weights and estimated using a triangular kernel. The running variable is the individual's age on December 31 of that year. The symmetric bandwidth is MSE-optimal and is 3.90 years, using 11,762 observations.

working entirely. There may be little scope to induce entry into the labor force in this group, providing an additional explanation for the miniscule effects that we find across this young childless adult population.

We also examine results after residualizing the outcome variable, taking out individual fixed effects as well as state-by-year fixed effects.[15] We are therefore looking at within-individual responses to EITC eligibility based on age at the end of the year. The results, in figure 9, show a statistically insignificant discontinuity of −0.014 (SE = 0.014) in labor force participation.

Figure 10 shows the discontinuity for annualized hours of work, and figure 11 shows it for earned income (including spousal income, if applicable). The discontinuities are negligible in magnitude. We also examine results by gender and marital status. Figures 12A and 12B estimate the discontinuity in labor force participation for unmarried and married women, respectively, and figures 13A and 13B show those for men. There are no meaningful patterns or significant differences in effect sizes. Effects for married childless adults are noisy and sensitive to bandwidth selection.

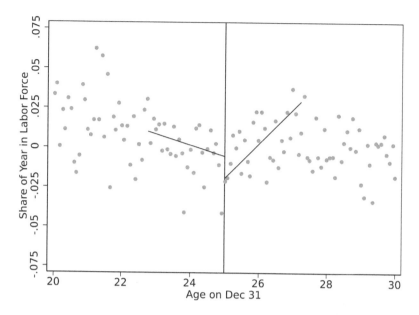

Fig. 9. Labor force participation (residualized). This figure shows results for the share of weeks in the labor force, residualized to remove individual fixed effects as well as state-year fixed effects. The estimation is weighted using Survey of Income and Program Participation weights and estimated using a triangular kernel. The running variable is the individual's age on December 31 of that year. The symmetric bandwidth is MSE-optimal and is 2.24 years, using 6,369 observations.

There are far fewer young married childless adults than young single childless adults. Those results should be interpreted with caution.

Last, we look at labor force participation and employment results separately for those with earnings above and below the earnings threshold where the EITC eligibility amount is maximized. Labor theory predicts that workers will work fewer hours or weeks when their earnings levels are positioned on the plateau or phase-out region of the EITC schedule, because both the income and substitution effects push toward leisure (Meyer 2002). To investigate this further, we plot the frequency distribution of single and married earners overlaid with their predicted EITC. Figures 14A and 14B show that there are more earners with earnings above the phase-in portion of the EITC schedule (about $7,000). Next, we estimate the discontinuities in labor force participation and employment for those earning above or below that threshold separately. We find similar insignificant effect sizes as reported above. This suggests that the insignificant negligible effect sizes we find in our main specifications are not the result of an averaging of coefficients from childless adults populations with opposite labor supply incentives.

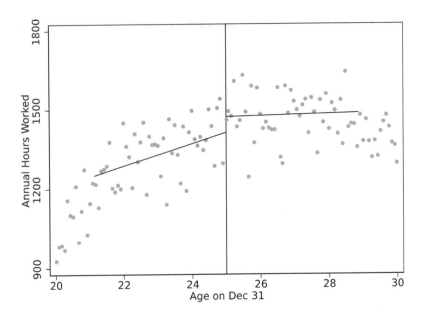

Fig. 10. Hours. This figure shows results for annual hours worked. The estimation is weighted using Survey of Income and Program Participation weights and estimated using a triangular kernel. The running variable is the individual's age on December 31 of that year. The symmetric bandwidth is MSE-optimal and is 3.87 years, using 12,688 observations.

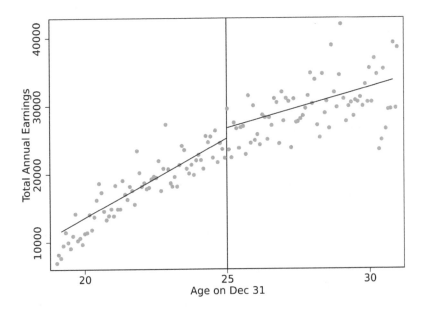

Fig. 11. Earned income. This figure shows results for total earned income in US dollars (includes spousal income, if relevant). The estimation is weighted using Survey of Income and Program Participation weights and estimated using a triangular kernel. The running variable is the individual's age on December 31 of that year. The symmetric bandwidth is MSE-optimal and is 5.84 years, using 19,500 observations.

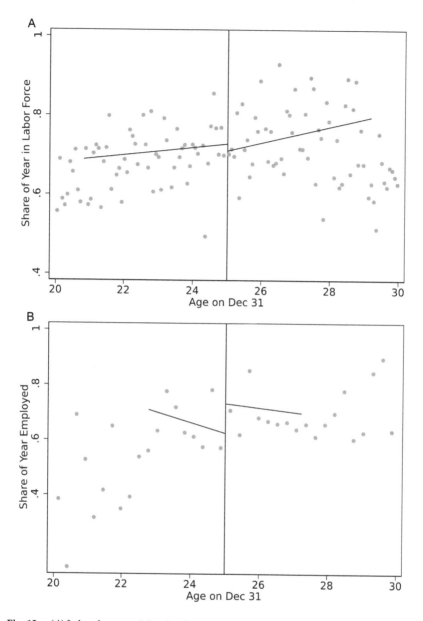

Fig. 12. (*A*) Labor force participation (unmarried females). This figure shows results for the share of weeks in the labor force for unmarried females, weighted using Survey of Income and Program Participation weights and estimated using a triangular kernel. The running variable is the individual's age on December 31 of that year. The symmetric bandwidth is MSE-optimal and is 4.19 years, using 3,654 observations. (*B*) Labor force participation (married females). This figure shows results for the share of weeks in the labor force for married females, weighted using Survey of Income and Program Participation weights and estimated using a triangular kernel. The running variable is the individual's age on December 31 of that year. The symmetric bandwidth is MSE-optimal and is 2.06 years, using 360 observations.

191

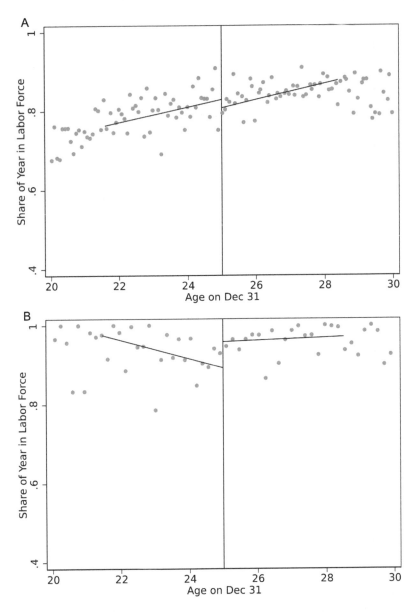

Fig. 13. (*A*) Labor force participation (unmarried males). This figure shows results for the share of weeks in the labor force for unmarried males, weighted using Survey of Income and Program Participation weights and estimated using a triangular kernel. The running variable is the individual's age on December 31 of that year. The symmetric bandwidth is MSE-optimal and is 3.40 years, using 6,681 observations. (*B*) Labor force participation (married males). This figure shows results for the share of weeks in the labor force for males, weighted using Survey of Income and Program Participation weights and estimated using a triangular kernel. The running variable is the individual's age on December 31 of that year. The symmetric bandwidth is MSE-optimal and is 3.53 years, using 958 observations.

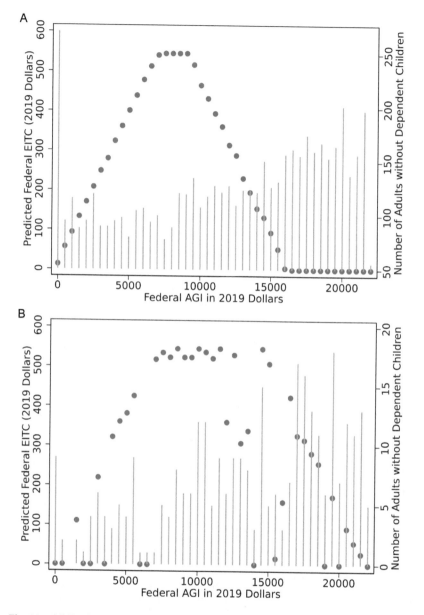

Fig. 14. (*A*) Predicted earned income tax credit (EITC) and income distribution (unmarried). AGI = adjusted gross income. (*B*) Predicted earned income tax credit (EITC) and income distribution (married). AGI = adjusted gross income.

IV. Conclusions

We examine the impact of the age-25 EITC eligibility cutoff for childless adults, a group whose economic well-being has been the subject of an increased focus for policy makers. Comparing the labor market behavior of those who became eligible in a given year with those who were just outside the eligibility range, we find no impacts on labor force participation, employment, or hours worked either in the year in which people become eligible or in the following year. These findings could be driven by a lack of information about the credit, a lack of response to it due to its small size, or the fact that only 6% of young childless adults are both out of the labor force and do not have a work-limiting disability. The lack of employment effects contrasts with previous studies looking at the impact of state and local EITC expansions on employment among the childless adult population. These differences likely arise from the fact that this study looks at effects around the age-25 cutoff specifically, whereas the other studies look at wider ranges of childless adults. Differences could also stem from differential baseline employment or labor force participation rates between expansion and nonexpansion states, awareness of own EITC eligibility, EITC generosity, or all of the above. A large expansion of the federal EITC may have very different effects.

Endnotes

Author email addresses: Meer (jmeer@econmail.tamu.edu), Witter (witter.joshua@gmail .com). We are grateful for comments from Bill Gale, Jeffrey Clemens, Wojtek Kopczuk, Robert Moffitt, David Neumark, Michael Strain, Riley Wilson, and attendees at the 2022 Tax Policy and the Economy workshop. Margaret Jones and Julian Bernando provided insight on EITC take-up rates. For acknowledgments, sources of research support, and disclosure of the authors' material financial relationships, if any, please see https://www.nber.org/books -and-chapters/tax-policy-and-economy-volume-37/effects-earned-income-tax-credit-child less-adults-regression-discontinuity-approach.

1. In 2016, Speaker Paul Ryan and President Barack Obama proposed nearly identical plans to lower the eligibility age for that group, expand the eligible income range, and increase the maximum credit amount. No legislative action resulted due to disagreements about paying for the expansion.

2. Shirley (2020) uses a similar approach around the timing of a first birth (and thus EITC eligibility) to examine mothers' labor-supply responses. Barr, Eggleston, and Smith (2022) do so to investigate long-run outcomes for those children.

3. There is a robust literature on the relationship between the season of birth and attributes such as family socioeconomic status (Buckles and Hungerman 2013), but these seasonal differences do not show up between December and January births, the discontinuity we exploit in our study (Wingender and LaLumia 2017).

4. US Census documents show that the take-up rate among eligible taxpayers without qualifying children was 64% in tax year 2017 (Jones 2020), a rate that has been fairly consistent over time (Plueger 2009). Guyton et al. (2016) show that about three-quarters of potentially eligible nonfilers have qualifying children.

5. Bhargava and Manoli (2015) find that additional information can increase EITC participation among those who had already been notified that they failed to claim benefits; about 15% of unclaimed credits were taken up due to that intervention. Clemens and Wither (2021) find complementary evidence that low-wage individuals face frictions to adjusting their labor supply in response to moderate changes to their budget constraints.

6. Leigh (2010) analyzes employment and wage changes using staggered state EITC expansions and differences in demographics during the federal EITC expansion and finds wage losses of 2%–5% for both eligible and noneligible workers.

7. Moreover, if the EITC causes wages to fall, workers may choose to use the additional posttax income to consume nonwage job attributes such as schedule flexibility. See Clemens (2021), who shows that models incorporating nonwage attributes of jobs can substantially alter the conclusions of incidence analyses of minimum wages, with similar implications for analyses of a wage subsidy like the EITC.

8. See https://www.irs.gov/credits-deductions/individuals/earned-income-tax-credit/qualifying-child-rules for a full explanation of the rules regarding "qualifying children."

9. The EITC for adults with no dependents and a tax filing status of married filing jointly begins its phase-out at a higher level of earnings, $15,920. The EITC phases out completely for married filers earning more than $22,610.

10. The SIPP was redesigned in 2014 as an annual survey.

11. About 4% of the sample has different birth dates listed at different points in the sample. Our results are unaffected by using the youngest or oldest listed ages or dropping those individuals from the data.

12. More information on the TAXSIM can be found at http://taxsim.nber.org.

13. Carr, Moffitt, and Wiemers (2020) show that imputed values in the SIPP can lead to problems with inference. We also estimate our specifications excluding those with imputed labor force participation values; the conclusions are unchanged.

14. An alternate approach is to use age 26 as a cutoff rather than following-year outcomes for those who are age 25. The conceptual approach is the same and the samples have a good deal of overlap. Figures 4 and 5 show no obvious discontinuity at age 26. The estimated discontinuity is very small: -0.0027 ($SE = 0.020$) and 0.0022 ($SE = 0.022$) for labor force participation and employment, respectively.

15. To examine whether there are different effects of labor-supply incentives when labor demand changes with the business cycle, we also estimate the discontinuity for the three panels separately. None are statistically significant.

References

Agan, A., and M. Makowsky. 2018. "The Minimum Wage, EITC, and Criminal Recidivism." Working Paper no. 25116, NBER, Cambridge, MA.

Barr, A., J. Eggleston, and A. Smith. 2022. "Investing in Infants: The Lasting Effects of Cash Transfers to New Families." *Quarterly Journal of Economics* 137 (4): 2539–83.

Bastian, J. 2017. "Unintended Consequences? More Marriage, More Children, and the EITC." *Proceedings. Annual Conference on Taxation and Minutes of the Annual Meeting of the National Tax Association* 110:1–56.

Bastian, J., and K. Michelmore. 2018. "The Long-Term Impact of the Earned Income Tax Credit on Children's Education and Employment Outcomes." *Journal of Labor Economics* 36 (4): 1127–63.

Baughman, R., and S. Dickert-Conlin. 2009. "The Earned Income Tax Credit and Fertility." *Journal of Population Economics* 22 (3): 537–63.

Benzarti, Y. 2020. "How Taxing Is Tax Filing? Using Revealed Preferences to Estimate Compliance Costs." *American Economic Journal: Economic Policy* 12 (4): 38–57.

———. 2021. "Estimating the Costs of Filing Tax Returns and the Potential Savings from Policies Aimed at Reducing These Costs." *Tax Policy and the Economy* 35 (1): 55–85.

Bhargava, S., and D. Manoli. 2015. "Psychological Frictions and the Incomplete Take-Up of Social Benefits: Evidence from an IRS Field Experiment." *American Economic Review* 105 (11): 3489–529.

Buckles, K. S., and D. M. Hungerman. 2013. "Season of Birth and Later Outcomes: Old Questions, New Answers." *Review of Economics and Statistics* 95 (3): 711–24.

Calonico, S., M. Cattaneo, M. Farrell, and R. Titiunik. 2017. "rdrobust: Software for Regression-Discontinuity Designs." *Stata Journal* 17 (2): 372–404.

Carr, M., R. Moffitt, and E. Wiemers. 2020. "Reconciling Trends in Volatility: Evidence from the SIPP Survey and Administrative Data." Working Paper no. 27672, NBER, Cambridge, MA.

Chetty, R., J. Friedman, and E. Saez. 2013. "Using Differences in Knowledge across Neighborhoods to Uncover the Impacts of the EITC on Earnings." *American Economic Review* 103 (7): 2683–721.

Clemens, J. 2021. "How Do Firms Respond to Minimum Wage Increases? Understanding the Relevance of Non-Employment Margins." *Journal of Economic Perspectives* 35 (1): 51–72.

Clemens, J., and M. Wither. 2021. "When Is Tinkering with Safety Net Programs Harmful to Beneficiaries?" *Southern Economic Journal* 2021:1–44.

Crandall-Hollick, M. 2021. "The 'Childless' EITC: Temporary Expansion for 2021 under the American Rescue Plan Act of 2021." Document IN11610, Congressional Research Service. https://crsreports.congress.gov/product/pdf/IN/IN11610.

Crandall-Hollick, M., G. Falk, and C. Boyle. 2021. "The Earned Income Tax Credit (EITC): How It Works and Who Gets It." Document R43805, Congressional Research Service. https://crsreports.congress.gov/product/pdf/R/R43805.

Cranor, T., S. Kotb, and J. Goldin. 2019. "Does Informing Employees about Tax Benefits Increase Take-Up? Evidence from EITC Notification Laws." *National Tax Journal* 72 (2): 1–8.

Eissa, N., and H. W. Hoynes. 2000. "Explaining the Fall and Rise in the Tax Cost of Marriage: The Effect of Tax Laws and Demographic Trends, 1984–97." *National Tax Journal* 53 (3): 683–711.

———. 2004. "Taxes and the Labor Market Participation of Married Couples: The Earned Income Tax Credit." *Journal of Public Economics* 88 (9–10): 1931–58.

Evans, W., and C. Garthwaite. 2014. "Giving Mom a Break: The Impact of Higher EITC Payments on Maternal Health." *American Economic Journal: Economic Policy* 6 (2): 258–90.

Goldin, J. 2018. "Tax Benefit Complexity and Take-up: Lessons from the Earned Income Tax Credit." *Tax Law Review* 72:59–108.

Guyton, J., D. Manoli, B. Schafer, and M. Sebastiani. 2016. "Reminders and Recidivism: Evidence from Tax Filing and EITC Participation among Low-Income Nonfilers." Working Paper no. 21904, NBER, Cambridge, MA.

Holtzblatt, J., and R. Rebelein. 2000. "Measuring the Effect of the EITC on Marriage Penalties and Bonuses." *National Tax Journal* 53 (4): 1107–33.

Hoynes, H., D. Miller, and D. Simon. 2015. "Income, the Earned Income Tax Credit, and Infant Health." *American Economic Journal: Economic Policy* 7 (1): 172–211.

Hoynes, H., and A. Patel. 2018. "Effective Policy for Reducing Poverty and Inequality? The Earned Income Tax Credit and the Distribution of Income." *Journal of Human Resources* 53 (4): 859–90.

Hoynes, H., and J. Rothstein. 2016. "Tax Policy toward Low-Income Families." Working Paper no. 22080, NBER, Cambridge, MA.

Internal Revenue Service. 2019. "Earned Income Tax Credit and Other Refund-
able Credits." https://www.eitc.irs.gov/eitc-central/about-eitc/about-eitc.
Jones, M. 2020. "American Community Survey Earning Income Tax Credit Par-
ticipation Rate for TY2017." Center for Economic Studies, Washington, DC.
Jones, M., E. Simeonova, and R. Akee. 2020. "The EITC and Intergenerational
Mobility." Working Paper no. CED-20-35, Center for Economic Studies, Wash-
ington, DC.
Kleven, H. 2019. "The EITC and the Extensive Margin: A Reappraisal." Working
Paper no. 26405, NBER, Cambridge, MA.
Kopczuk, W., and C. Pop-Eleches. 2007. "Electronic Filing, Tax Preparers and
Participation in the Earned Income Tax Credit." *Journal of Public Economics*
91 (7–8): 1351–67.
Kuka, E., and N. Shenhav. 2020. "Long Run Effects of Incentivizing Work after
Childbirth." Working Paper no. 27444, NBER, Cambridge, MA.
Lee, D., and T. Lemieux. 2010. "Regression Discontinuity Designs in Economics."
Journal of Economic Literature 48:281–355.
Leigh, A. 2010. "Who Benefits from the Earned Income Tax Credit? Incidence
among Recipients, Coworkers and Firms." *BE Journal of Economic Analysis and
Policy* 10 (1): Article 45.
Linos, E., A. Prohofsky, A. Ramesh, J. Rothstein, and M. Unrath. Forthcoming.
"Can Nudges Increase Take-Up of the EITC? Evidence from Multiple Field
Experiments." *American Economic Journal: Economic Policy* 14 (4):432–52.
Maag, E., and G. Acs. 2015. "The Financial Consequences of Marriage for Cohab-
iting Couples with Children." Urban Institute, Washington, DC.
Markowitz, S., K. Komro, M. Livingston, O. Lenhart, and A. Wagenaar. 2017.
"Effects of State-Level Earned Income Tax Credit Laws in the US on Maternal
Health Behaviors and Infant Health Outcomes." *Social Science & Medicine*
194:67–75.
Meyer, B. D. 2002. "Labor Supply at the Extensive and Intensive Margins: The
EITC, Welfare, and Hours Worked." *American Economic Review* 92 (2): 373–79.
Meyer, B. D., and D. T. Rosenbaum. 2001. "Welfare, the Earned Income Tax
Credit, and the Labor Supply of Single Mothers." *Quarterly Journal of Econom-
ics* 116 (3): 1063–114.
Michelmore, K. 2013. *The Effect of Income on Educational Attainment: Evidence from
State Earned Income Tax Credit Expansions*. Ithaca, NY: Cornell University.
Miller, B. M., and K. J. Mumford. 2015. "The Salience of Complex Tax Changes:
Evidence from the Child and Dependent Care Credit Expansion." *National
Tax Journal* 68 (3): 477–510.
Miller, C., L. F. Katz, G. Azurdia, A. Isen, C. B. Schultz, and K. Aloisi. 2018. *Boost-
ing the Earned Income Tax Credit for Singles: Final Impact Findings from the Pay-
check Plus Demonstration in New York City*. New York: MDRC.
Neumark, D., and P. Shirley. 2017. "The Long-Run Effects of the Earned Income
Tax Credit on Women's Earnings." Working Paper no. 24114, NBER, Cam-
bridge, MA.
Neumark, D., and K. Williams. 2020. "Do State Earned Income Tax Credits In-
crease Participation in the Federal EITC?" Working Paper no. 27626, NBER,
Cambridge, MA.
Plueger, Dean. 2009. "Earned Income Tax Credit Participation Rate for Tax Year
2005." Working paper, Internal Revenue Service, Washington, DC.
Schanzenbach, D., and M. Strain. 2021. "Employment Effects of the Earned Income Tax Credit: Taking the Long View." *Tax Policy and the Economy* 35 (1):
87–129.

Shirley, P. 2020. "First-Time Mothers and the Labor Market Effects of the Earned
    Income Tax Credit." *IZA Journal of Labor Policy* 10 (7): Article 7.
Tax Policy Center. 2022. "State EITC as Percentage of the Federal EITC." https://
    www.taxpolicycenter.org/statistics/state-eitc-percentage-federal-eitc (Accessed
    August 2022).
Wilson, R. 2020. "The EITC and Employment Transitions: Labor Force Attach-
    ment and Annual Exit." *National Tax Journal* 73 (1): 11–46.
Wingender, P., and S. LaLumia. 2017. "Income Effects on Maternal Labor Supply:
    Evidence from Child-Related Tax Benefits." *National Tax Journal* 70 (1): 11–52.
Witter, J. 2020. "The Earned Income Tax Credit and Employment for Childless
    Adults." Unpublished Manuscript, Texas A&M University, College Station,
    TX.